INSUBORDINATE SPIRIT

A True Story of Life and Loss in Earliest America

1610–1665

MISSY WOLFE

Guilford, Connecticut

Copyright © 2012 by Missy Wolfe

Layout: Joanna Beyer
Project editor: Ellen Urban

Maps by Melissa Baker © Morris Book Publishing, LLC

Library of Congress Cataloging-in-Publication Data is available on file.

ISBN 978-0-7627-8040-2

Printed in the United States of America

10 9 8 7 6 5 4 3 2 1

Contents

The eating teeth of time devour all things.

A hogshead of ancient papers of value to our family, lost at Ipswich in New England.

A barrellful of papers &c. burnt in a warehouse in Boston.

—A NOTE FOUND AMONG WINTHROP FAMILY PAPERS

Acknowledgments

The academic expertise of some remarkable scholars greatly enhanced my understanding of Massachusetts, Connecticut, and New York in America's earliest colonial time. Dr. Charles Gehring, Director of the New Netherland Research Center, continues to translate Dutch New York's four-hundred-year-old documents to this day to reveal the world that was New Netherland. His comprehensive and careful work has revealed a host of significant new insights that would never have been known without his devoted scholarship for so many years. Professor Steven Grumet from the University of Pennsylvania has recently published *The Munsee Indians: A History*. This outstanding and insightful research on Manhattan-area Indians also provides a wealth of information about the Indians who lived in the tri-state area and clarifies many demographic issues left unresolved for decades. I am deeply grateful for his research and analysis.

Evan Haefeli, Columbia University associate professor of history and scholar of the roots of radical religious development in the Dutch period, provided invaluable feedback and commentary on my manuscript and I thank him deeply for his expert perspectives. The many studies of America's earliest colonial women by Harvard University professor Laurel Thatcher Ulrich and University of Edinburgh's Susan Hardman Moore are also wonderful works of academic investigation. Their research allowed me to more accurately understand, develop, and describe the life of Elizabeth Fones Winthrop Feake Hallett as woman of her time, culture, and conviction and to understand how and why she changed as a person in reaction to the political, cultural, and social pressures at work all around her. I am also indebted to Anya Seton, 1950s author of the beloved historical novel *The Winthrop Woman*, which first alerted me to Elizabeth's life and sparked my lifelong interest in her story, which I hope is now more fully told.

Nothing would be in print without Beth Bruno, a most knowledgeable editor who has a lifetime of experience in the publishing world and who guided me through a complex process with skill, humor, encouragement, and loads of good advice. Rita Rosenkranz also sagely steered me to Erin Turner, Courtney Oppel, Ellen Urban, and Joshua Rosenberg of Globe Pequot Press. This professional team took a wide-ranging story and brought it into finer focus.

One of my greatest pleasures in researching this work was finding and meeting the eleventh-generation William Hallett, who is descended from Elizabeth and William Hallett's last child, Samuel. Still living quite near his original family holdings on Long Island, Dr. Hallett continues to protect and care for his family's many original seventeenth-century documents, including the original William Hallett's will. His excitement and interest in his family's unique heritage surely makes his ancestors very proud.

Walter Woodward, the Connecticut state historian and John Winthrop Jr. expert, encouraged my research and writing, as did Nicholas Bellantoni, Connecticut state archaeologist, who pointed me toward many useful resources. Ron Marcus of Stamford Historical Society patiently verified Stamford's earliest names, dates, and locations. In Greenwich, historian Joe Zeranski was an insightful critic and sounding board, providing his invaluable and thirty-year knowledge of Greenwich's many names, nooks, and crannies. He rightfully notes that Nassau Place's pedigree may be more romantic than real. Debra Mecky and Davidde Strackbein of the Greenwich Historical Society and John Stockbridge, director of the Bedford, New York Historical Society, proposed thought-provoking questions and provided helpful commentary, as did the Reverend William Evertsberg of the First Presbyterian Church in Greenwich, who helped me understand the finer points of Christian theology. As this story progressed to Long Island, Bob Singleton, director of the Greater Astoria Historical Society, and Richard Hourahan of the Queens Historical Society, Rosemary Vietor, a Bowne family descendant, and Ann Paul of the Bowne

House in Flushing were additional helpful resources as was David Gigler, superintendent of the Mt. Olivet Cemetery in Maspeth, New York, where many of the first generations of the Hallett family are interred.

My work would not have been possible without the resources and staffs of the New York, Massachusetts, and New London Historical Societies, as well as that of the New York Public Library's Rare Book and Manuscript Room and Google's Book Search, which let me access sources that would have been impossible to view otherwise. In speculating on locations for the great Munsee massacre, I thank Connecticut State Archaeologist Nick Bellatoni, and Tony Godino and his friends in the Westchester Archaeology Society.

My dear friend Sharon Klammer devoted her valuable time and talents to reading early manuscripts and cheering me on. I end with huge thanks to my three children, William, Elizabeth, and Christian, and to my husband Scott, whose cheerful optimism, technical know-how, awesome kindness, intelligence, and energy set an example I emulate, but can never duplicate.

NOTES:

The author has modernized spelling, grammar, and punctuation in period correspondence.

DATE FORMATS:

Dates will sometimes appear written in antique letters as "1 January 1630/1." This was a way people in the 1600s recalibrated the difference between conflicting Julian and Gregorian calendars. Before 1752, following the conventions of the Julian calendar, the year began on 25 March. Documents between 1 January and 24 March are cited in the year form 1630/1 to reflect both the old and the new style. Often writers would further clarify a date by additionally writing "old style" or "new style" next to the date.

HALLETT FAMILY TREE

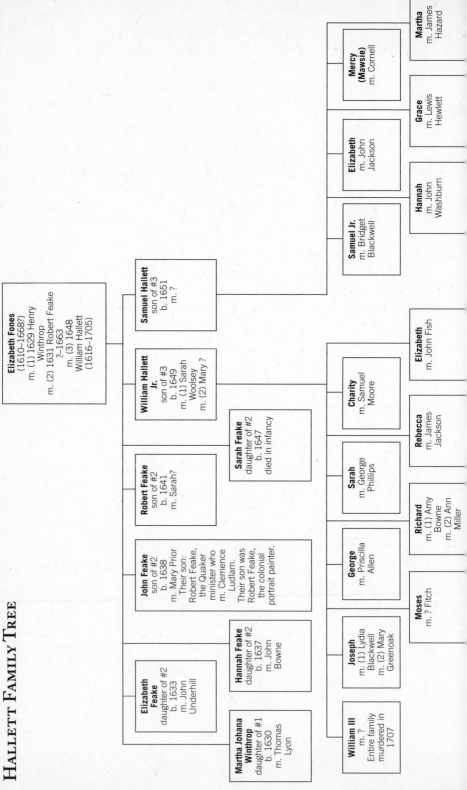

Elizabeth Fones
(1610–1668?)
m. (1) 1629 Henry
Winthrop
m. (2) 1631 Robert Feake
?–1663
m. (3) 1648
William Hallett
(1616–1705)

Martha Johana Winthrop
daughter of #1
b. 1630
m. Thomas Lyon

Elizabeth Feake
daughter of #2
b. 1633
m. John Underhill

Hannah Feake
daughter of #2
b. 1637
m. John Bowne

John Feake
son of #2
b. 1638
m. Mary Prior
Their son:
Robert Feake,
the Quaker
minister who
m. Clemence
Ludlam.
Their son was
Robert Feake,
the colonial
portrait painter.

Robert Feake
son of #2
b. 1641
m. Sarah?

Sarah Feake
daughter of #2
b. 1647
died in infancy

William Hallett Jr.
son of #3
b. 1649
m. (1) Sarah Woolsey
m. (2) Mary ?

Samuel Hallett
son of #3
b. 1651
m. ?

William III
m. ?
Entire family
murdered in
1707

Joseph
m. (1) Lydia Blackwell
m. (2) Mary Greenoak

Moses
m. ? Fitch

George
m. Priscilla Allen

Richard
m. (1) Amy Bowne
m. (2) Ann Miller

Sarah
m. George Phillips

Rebecca
m. James Jackson

Charity
m. Samuel Moore

Elizabeth
m. John Fish

Samuel Jr.
m. Bridget Blackwell

Hannah
m. John Washburn

Elizabeth
m. John Jackson

Grace
m. Lewis Hewlett

Mercy (Mawsie)
m. Cornell

Martha
m. James Hazard

Patrick/Feake Family Tree

Anna Van Beyeren
1610–1656
m. (1) 3/3/1630
Daniel (Kirk) Patrick
1605–1643
m. (2) 1645?
Tobias Feake
1622–1672

Annetje Patrick
b. 1634?
in Watertown, MA
daughter of #1
m. Bartholomew
Applegate 1650 in
Gravesend, NY
Onetime maid to
Cornelius Tienhoven
family. In 1671 held as
an Indian hostage w/her
child. £10 ransom paid in
coin and red cloth. Moved
to Monmouth, NJ[1]

**Patientia (Patience)
Patrick**
b. 1636? in Watertown,
MA
daughter of #1
m. Cornelius Arent
Lived in Flushing, NY.
Their son, John Cornelius,
married Mary Yates in
Flushing, NY 1682.

Beatrice Patrick
b. 1640
in Greenwich, CT
daughter of #1
Baptized in the New
Amsterdam Reformed
Dutch Church October
21, 1640
Died in infancy

Daniel Patrick
b. 1642
in Greenwich, CT
son of #1
d. before 1671
m. (1) Dorcas Erwine b.
1643
m. (2) Dinah Yates
They had four children.
Stepbrother James
Feake lived with them
in Flushing. After 1704
Patrick family and
James Feake moved to
Westchester, NY. Daniel II
registered his earmark as
Kirk Patrick.[2]

Samuel Patrick
b. 1642
in Greenwich, CT
son of #1
Baptized in the Dutch
Reform Church July 17,
1642
d. before 1700
Noted living with both
Tobias Feake and Mary
Patrick Feake and
Annetje Patrick and
Barholomew Applegate in
Gravesend, NY

James Feake
b. 1649
in Greenwich, CT or
Flushing, NY
son of #2
Bought land with Daniel
Patrick Jr. in Castle Hill
Neck, Westchester, NY
d. 1727

Prologue

THERE IS A SHORT LITTLE STREET IN THE WELL-KEPT TOWN OF Greenwich, Connecticut, that hundreds of motorists pass daily when they drive through the village of Cos Cob on the Boston Post Road. It is called Nassau Place and it is a silent sentinel of sorts, the town's one link to an uncomfortable, cruel, and uncompromising past: one in which the largest massacre of Native Americans in the Northeast occurred, the town's first English woman was threatened with death for her insolent strategy to survive here, and New England and New Netherland battled for jurisdiction over the very property this small green street sign surveys.

It is such a grand name for such an insignificant street, a name that refers to the royal Dutch household of Orange-Nassau, the rulers who sanctioned all West India Company operations in America. No grand boulevard, this street might once have been a winding Indian footpath that reached up from the banks of the Mianus River to clamber over a high and rocky hillside to reach the interior, and today it functions in much the same way. Nassau Place keeps a lasting vigil over the aspirations of the area's first West India Company owners, and it ridicules their pretenses.

When the English Puritans spread south from their beachhead in Boston and the merchant Dutch spread north from Manhattan to further their colonial ambitions, the grandiose dreams of unlimited sovereignty by both ran into a stubborn reality in the area of southwestern Connecticut just south of Stamford. In the determined fight for dominance by these hostile governments, the native Munsees and the town's first Europeans got caught in the crossfire. The ultimate English victors wiped out most traces of a Dutch and Munsee past in Greenwich, but they forgot about Nassau Place, which beckons to us to understand what really happened here.

CHAPTER ONE

"Such braving oppositions"

JOHN WINTHROP WAS FED UP WITH HIS SON HENRY, AN INDOLENT and insolent seventeen-year-old who hated listening to his father. After countless lectures to a boy who was far more interested in parties, pranks, and poker than his father's earnest instructions, an exasperated John almost gave up on trying to change his son's impulsive nature into one of sober responsibility, and the two parted ways for a while. This was Winthrop's first taste of trying to impress his deeply considered opinions on others and losing, for some of his own followers would come to reject his finely designed points of view when he governed the Puritans' first settlement in Boston. There, when disagreements surfaced about how to best manage the Massachusetts Bay Colony, some also separated from Winthrop in anger and on principle to found new colonies throughout Massachusetts, Rhode Island, and Connecticut. In fact, this resistance to, and separation from authority was nothing more than what John Winthrop himself had done when he resisted his own king's demands and participated in a political and religious revolt that split his followers apart from the English government and its mandated state religion. "If you don't like it, leave," was the cleaving premise that motivated John Winthrop to leave England, his son to leave him, and John's followers to leave the Bay Colony to settle throughout New England. Similarly, the first European settlers of southwestern Connecticut left newly built Boston homesteads when their leaders' iron-clad instructions became incompatible with the rigors and realities of living frontier lives. Like branches from a tree, southwestern Connecticut's first settlements were born of an attempt to create a more ideal society that soothed the hardships of life in the 1600s and resolved an abundance of intellectual conflicts that settlers found residing deep within their souls.

Henry was a handful to John Winthrop, who, to his credit, tried everything most parents would do today to raise an uncooperative teen who too often takes wrong turns. Luckily, the widowed John had a large and supportive family of three sisters to turn to who had helped him raise his family in England long before he moved to America to manage the country. His sisters, Lucy, Anne, and Jane, respected their intellectual and affectionate older brother and they relied heavily upon his advice. The family bonds between these Winthrops lasted throughout their lifetimes, and earliest America was counseled behind the scenes by their helpful family suggestions.

When his sister Lucy married an attorney named Emmanuel Downing, Anne married a London apothecarist named Thomas Fones, and Jane married Thomas Gostlin, John became best friends with his caring and educated in-laws. They discussed their many business partnerships, family considerations, and political views together, undaunted by vast distances even after John had emigrated to America. They formed a tight-knit group of confidantes who counseled each other as well as they could as their lives took dramatic new turns, and their children outgrew their control.

HENRY WINTHROP

Henry was not the first Winthrop to cause his father frustration, for John had to straighten out a tangle of inheritance issues created by his illegally married uncle in Ireland; but Henry was the one who caused him his deepest aggravations. Largely unconcerned over whether he caused his father fits, Henry was quite unlike his brothers, John Jr. and Forth, and his

John Winthrop (1588–1649) 1834 (oil on canvas) by Charles Osgood (1809–1890) © MASSACHUSETTS HISTORICAL SOCIETY, BOSTON, MA, USA / THE BRIDGEMAN ART LIBRARY

little sister, Mary, who respected and accepted the teachings of their father. Managing a law practice, several real estate partnerships, and his family's farm while acting as the local justice of the peace and participating in a large and growing religious revolution meant John Winthrop may have been a distracted single parent who was absent too often from his one rebellious son. His first wife, Mary Forth, died when the children were small, and his second wife lived for only one year after their wedding.

Henry's badly planned and roughly phrased letters show that he was a poor student with few academic interests to sustain a long-term education and that he had chosen instead to lead a cavalier life that defied his father's faith for sport. Such a lack of respect and indifference to authority within his own family caused John to consider Henry's failings with a wider perspective, as a cosmic trial of his ability to lead the many who would soon move with him from England to settle somewhere within northeastern America. John worried his son's dissolute and self-destructive ways would inspire God's anger toward the boy, which had the potential of dangerously expanding to include himself and the greater Winthrop family. A pattern of events that pointed to God's displeasure with the Winthrops would be deeply embarrassing in front of his followers, who were the religiously intellectual and increasingly influential minor gentry of Puritan society on the Essex-Suffolk border in England's Stour Valley. John believed that his success in parenting Henry would tangibly demonstrate his leadership skill to his many peers and inspirationally allow them to witness firsthand the benefits that followed when Henry had his epiphany and embraced the Puritan way.

John Winthrop was recognized for his dedication to the Puritan movement and for being one of their most insightful, energetic, and articulate advocates who was not a clergyman. When John continued to implore Henry to lead the highly principled and disciplined life that he found so natural, Henry found it impossible to achieve and lacking in any kind of personal distinction that he wanted for himself. In revolt, he surrounded himself with a circle of fast-living and flamboyant friends who set him apart from his family. His cocky crowd of cronies gambled frequently, drank heartily, and caroused far too often, to the Winthrops' increasing distress.

To discipline his son in this late Elizabethan age of England, John removed Henry from his delinquent social circle and had him join an expedition that was establishing a Puritan plantation in Barbados in 1626. John knew Henry could earn a decent living there if he worked hard enough, and he would be paid £100 a year for a three-year term of service. This arrangement would be an educational use of Henry's time that came with the added bonus of forcing him to manage money better, hopefully ending the boy's constant requests for more cash. Smitten with the idea of an adventure that would allow him to escape from his father, Henry bragged that he would not only succeed in Barbados but also export five hundred to a thousand pounds of tobacco from the new plantation almost as soon as he set foot there.[3]

Henry quickly decamped for the cane fields of Barbados without taking the basic necessities of tools, clothing, footwear, or committed determination with him. By his second less-than-stellar year there, Henry disappointed with his poor financial planning and almost nonexistent interest in Caribbean agriculture. At the end of January 1628, John complained to his son that he could not sell the first shipment of tobacco Henry sent him from the Caribbean because it had arrived in England "very ill conditioned, foul, full of stalks and evil colored."

Henry's experience, two years before the Puritans' planned departure for America, was, inadvertently, a critical lesson for John, now the expressly appointed governor of the Puritans' effort to establish a settlement in America. Henry's experience clearly demonstrated the kinds of promises he could and could not make when he solicited people to join him in creating an entirely new kind of existence overseas. He saw that his message had to be aspirational enough to lure people away from their familiar English homes to sail for ten trying weeks in very uncomfortable ships for the opportunity to live, think, and pray in a way that would make God smile down upon their society more than anywhere else on earth. He also realized that his promises could not raise his followers' expectations unrealistically. He had to prepare his people, who were primarily middle class city and suburban dwellers of their day, to arrive in an entirely untamed wilderness that lacked any sort of infrastructure. His son Henry's boastful arrogance and swift disillusionment showed John the need to build just the right balance between his group's intention to live an intellectually purer, more biblical way of life and the bone-shattering work that would be required to construct every bit of their community's future physical fabric.

A great many people who lived with the deprivations of life in England in the early 1600s were excited about worshipping God in the Puritan Way. They believed this particular outlook on life held the promise of making God like them better, which would be manifested by an improvement in the overall quality of their everyday lives on earth now, as well as later in their afterlives. These Puritans had only the highest goals in mind when they sought nothing less than to perfect a mechanism that would create an endlessly escalating feedback loop of reciprocal, positive stroking between mankind and God. The trick was to find just the right way to think, act, and pray that would please God better. No one, believed the Puritans, had executed just the right strategy yet in England, save themselves, and even they couldn't perfect it there because their king, who had Catholic leanings, kept trying to outlaw their way of thinking and throw their clergy into prison because it challenged his authority. Their excitement in leaving England was because they believed that going to the New World was like conducting an experiment in a pristine and sterile new laboratory where they could practice a new version of faith in a land that was unsullied by other peoples' spiritual communication strategies. Here they would see if they really had found the way to contact

God more clearly and more often—a revolutionary and entirely exciting new prospect! If they had found just the right way to open the door to the spiritual world more widely—and they were convinced that they had—it would be a breakthrough for all of humanity and for England, at the very least.

As to the logistical side of this experiment, Henry's experience underscored the need to bring enough food, livestock, seed, and construction material to the New World for the feeding, housing, farming, and governing of a brand new colony located across the wide ocean from England. The very shaky start to the Plymouth colony on Cape Cod a decade earlier, which had caused its settlers to starve and steal Indian food, and the Jamestown, Virginia, disaster two decades prior, which resulted in its colonists cannibalizing each other, were debacles that couldn't possibly be repeated.

Such enlightenment did not, however, let Henry off his father's disciplinary hook. As the Barbados boondoggle continued, Henry carried on with his gambling and dug himself even deeper in debt until it really annoyed his two uncles, Thomas Fones and Emmanuel Downing, who finally tired of covering his many losses.[4] At wit's end with Henry in 1628, John Winthrop blasted him in one letter[5] in which he declared in no uncertain terms that he was ending all financial support and that Henry's farming farce was over. John thundered:

> *Son Henry, It is my daily care to commend you to the Lord so that he would please to put his true fear into your heart . . . in truth I have no money, and I am so far in debt already to both your Uncles, as I am ashamed to borrow any more. I have disbursed a great deal of money for you than my estate will bear. I paid for your debts . . . and I can supply you no further. I have many other children that are unprovided, and I see my life is uncertain. I marvel at your great undertakings, having no means, and knowing how much I am in debt already . . .*

7

It [would be] more becoming to your youth to have contented yourself in a more moderate course for your three years and by that time, by your own gettings and my help, you might have been able to have done something, but this has always been the fruit of your vain over-reaching mind, which will be your overthrow, if you attain not more discretion and moderation of your years.

I do wonder upon what ground you should be led into so gross an error to think I could provide 10 men as you write for and disburse a matter of £200 (when I owe more already, than I am able to pay, without sale of my land) and to do this at some two or three months warning . . . I pray God make you more wise and sober and bring you home in peace in his due time.

In his anger, John assumed that God was angry with Henry too, and John obsessed over discerning God's opinions correctly. He agonized over how he could better conduct himself to win God's favor more consistently, with far greater certainty and with far more tangible proof. He anguished over the unrepentant nature of his son, writing, "The dislike of his ill course . . . made me estrange myself towards him. He promises to amend his life and I beseech him to do so, otherwise he will soon be undone," for he also believed that the anger and estrangement that existed between the two was an analogy to the problem that he perceived existed at the time between God and the religiously adolescent England.

On Henry's premature return from his failed Barbados experiment, and in hope that he would live more conscientiously with someone else, John asked his brother-in-law Thomas Fones, who had married the widow Priscilla Paynter Sherman after Anne Winthrop's early death, to house his wayward son. Agreeing to take his nephew in was a big mistake for Thomas Fones, but great fun for his children. Henry's entry into their home, located by a tavern called The Three Fawns on the west side of London, let in a flood of chaos, color, and confusion that entirely upset the

8

Fones family's heretofore sober and serious lives. Henry's dashing fashions, suave new slang, and irreverent jokes delighted his cousins, Martha, Elizabeth, and Sam Fones, and their stepsister Ursula Sherman. The family's new baby, Mary, probably added her infant squalling to the overall uproar as well. He teased his cousins outrageously, and lounged about on the Fones's stiffly spindled furniture in their half-timbered house at 28 Ridley. His rowdy friends and brothers joined the crowd too in card games and drinking contests that lasted late into each evening, until the Fones's home came to resemble a tavern more than the symbol of Puritan respectability it was intended to portray. Thomas grew frustrated, ill, and angry with his nephew for bringing over gangs of loud friends and buying extravagant new clothes for which he knew Henry couldn't possibly pay.

The Fones girls and Ursula Sherman, on the other hand, loved this exciting new change in their lives. Capable and responsible, Martha and Elizabeth Fones had grown up quickly since their mother had died eight years earlier. As was expected of these young English teens, Martha and Elizabeth assumed their mother's position in running the Fones household and in raising little Sam, and they had matured with an independence and self-reliance that set them apart from their friends.

Slowed by a serious illness, their father also had trained them to help him manage his apothecary shop, which was likely on the street level of their home in the city. Martha and Elizabeth dealt with the apothecary's many supplies and suppliers, recorded many recipes, concocted their father's potions and lotions for him, made deliveries all over London, kept the accounting, and generally became educated in the medical arts of their era. Their cousin, John Winthrop Jr., was first exposed to the apothecary arts in the Fones home, which ignited his lifelong interest in medicine and alchemy that he would pursue in America.

Henry's familiarity with Elizabeth Fones, whose nickname was Bess or Bessie, quickly turned romantic through their close and daily proximity. Their families were shocked and dismayed when they learned that the couple planned to marry, and marry without much notice. When Henry appeared in her highly structured world, Elizabeth was attracted to the cavalier cut-up, and he offered her an exciting escape from the routines and predictability of her family's daily life.

She accepted his improper friends, his boasts without basis, and his habit of gambling most evenings away. Against the advice of her father, she borrowed money herself to pay off his debts and planned, perhaps, that she could change him. A sad and tired Thomas Fones morosely described the situation between their children to John Winthrop, on April 2, 1629. He complained of Henry's friends who included a "Papist" or "Pope-ist" (meaning a Catholic fellow), his late hours, and his particularly upsetting new set of red clothes. Elizabeth's father found the smallest glimmer of respectability in the couple's future arrangements in that they planned to have a wedding instead of an elopement.[6]

My good Brother, I did not write last week being so lame I could not feed myself with any hand nor stir out of my chamber and am still very weak so that though I have much to write I have little ability of body or mind being overwhelmed with troubles and afflictions on all sides and increased exceedingly by those from whom I have deserved better . . . but yet thus far my desire to keep my nephew, your son, from much expense and riotous company made me . . . give him entertainment to lodge and diet in my house when I had no small trouble with him. . . . My house was like an Inn, and . . . he entertained, a Papist . . . I durst give him no longer entertainment. Your son hath wooed and won my daughter Besse for a wife and they both pretend to have proceeded so far that there is no recalling of it. [There is] at least promise of marriage and all without my knowledge or consent. What grief this is to me. I leave it to your consideration, [it] being no fit match for either of them. I will not multiply arguments against my nephew being your son, but his heart is much too big for his estates: he hath now made himself a scarlet suit and cloak which is lined through with plush, which I believe he owes for . . . my daughter borrowed for him when I could come by no money . . .

I cannot write you the many troubles of my mind what to do for my nephew says plainly if he cannot have my goodwill to have my daughter he will have her without it:

He comes and stays at unfitting hours . . . I am sure he is in debt for his own occasions . . . I fear . . . for others whose company he uses . . . but I am weak and cannot I see now be master in mine own house and tis hard meddling between the bark and the tree for if he were not so near allied to me, and the son of him whom I so respect, I could hardly bear such braving oppositions in mine own house . . . I doubt he will draw her forth . . . and suddenly marry her without any scruples.

The Fones and Winthrop families withheld their consent to this marriage. By ignoring her father's counsel and that of her formidable Uncle John, Elizabeth seriously challenged the paternal structure of Puritan authority and probably would never have done so without Henry's urging and support, and the real possibility she was pregnant. That she and Henry "both pretend to have proceeded so far that there is no recalling of it," goes far to explaining their urgency.

The fact that Elizabeth and Henry were cousins was not what precipitated their parents' objections. Consanguineous marriage, wherein cousins marry each other, was not uncommon then. Rather, it was his irresponsible spending and overall poor planning that upset her family so. While the Winthrops were respectable and could be relied on for small assistance, Henry showed no signs of a personal course correction. He continued to flaunt his family's rules, risk their reputations, and demonstrate complete disregard over collateral consequences that could affect those near and dear to him. So excited about attracting this exotic bon vivant, Elizabeth defended and excused most of his shortcomings while her family mourned the fact that her decision had just significantly reduced her chances of creating a successful and responsible family. They worried that she had also quite possibly just committed herself to a one-way path into poverty. Henry's defiance was just another rejection of his father's way of life, and by co-opting his cousin he had enlisted her in his very high-risk rebellion.

Just three weeks after Thomas Fones wrote his complaints to John Winthrop, Henry and Elizabeth married on April 25, 1629, at the Church of St. Sepulchre at New Gate. Thomas Fones died two weeks later. The best thing Elizabeth's Aunt Lucy Downing could say about their wedding was to describe it quite glumly as "tedious."

(At Lucy's later complaint to her brother John that there was no school in America for her son George, John helped establish Harvard College in Boston and George Downing graduated from its first class of nine students in 1642. He later denied the Puritan cause, became a wealthy baronet in England, and gave the land in London for 10 Downing Street, the current residence of England's prime ministers.)

In his will, Thomas Fones appointed John Winthrop to be the moral guardian over Elizabeth and seventeen-year-old Martha, and to have actual wardship over thirteen-year-old Samuel Fones. John Winthrop thus became a surrogate father to the Fones children, as well as actual father-in-law and uncle to Elizabeth.

Henry and Elizabeth's wedding, however unsuitable, provoked further envy, excitement, and consanguinity among the remaining Fones, Winthrop, and Sherman children. John Winthrop Jr. soon proposed to Elizabeth's sister, Martha Fones, and they married on February 8, 1631. This wedding too was not without hassle as the London Court of Aldermen fined John Jr. five marks for marrying a minor without their consent. John Winthrop's third son, named Forth, who may have not wanted to be left out of all the excitement and was perhaps planning to move to America with a wife in hand as well, asked the Fones's stepsister, Ursula Sherman, to marry him as soon as he finished his schooling.

Henry was twenty-one and Elizabeth was nineteen when they married, which was the average age of marriage in England at this time,[7] and they moved from the Fones home in London to the Winthrop farm in the country called Groton Manor. John Winthrop warned his own new third wife, Margaret Tyndal, who was not much older than Henry and Elizabeth herself, to watch carefully over Henry there lest he visit the town closest to their home and "continue his riotous ways."[8]

If Elizabeth was pregnant at her spring wedding, she never carried the baby to term, but she successfully became pregnant later that fall. Margaret Tyndal also became pregnant near this same time by John Winthrop Senior, and he hired a midwife to care for both women. The timing of their due dates conflicted with John's planned departure to America, which would take Henry, John Jr., and Martha along with him, so the family agreed that Margaret and Elizabeth should remain behind together in England until after the birth of their children.

Chapter Two

The Move to America

John Winthrop's Puritans were never as radical as the Pilgrims, who had arrived in America a full ten years earlier. The Pilgrims, sailing in 1620, came to enforce a far more ambitious agenda, for they felt that the Church of England worshipped God in a manner so far removed from their own beliefs that it had to be scrapped altogether.

The Church of England, which offended them so, sprang from a dispute created when the leader of the Catholic Church, the pope, prevented the king of England from divorcing his wife Catherine, the queen, to marry another woman, Anne Boleyn. The pope's refusal to approve of this divorce and remarriage, which was fraught with complexity, maddened King Henry VIII, who had in the past submitted to the pope, and he began to consider how it came to be that a religious man in a faraway country could rule over kings that lived elsewhere. His anger grew deeper when he dwelled on the fact that the pope controlled the religious affairs of many other countries and interfered on occasion with some of their civil or secular affairs as well. Seeing the pope in this worrisome new light, Henry VIII perceived that the pope actually acted as a King of Kings on earth, enforced by a previously powerful papal army and the perception by many that he was "divine," a unique human being endowed with special metaphysical abilities who communicated most closely with God. His anger further deepened when he realized that the pope's authority over him reached far beyond his marriage and, in fact, had the potential to usurp most of his sovereign authority. Utterly incensed, Henry became absolutely committed to stopping the pope, whose divinity he now thoroughly disrespected, from having any further say over the personal, civil, and religious affairs of England. In a cataclysmic action that rocked all of Europe for many generations, the king completely rejected the pope's authority over himself, his country, and all of its churches and created a new religion that outlawed or "protested" Catholicism in England. Its adherents accordingly became known as "protest-ants" or Protestants.

Henry named his new church "The Church of England," and made the Protestant religion England's new state religion and the spiritual law of the land. Everyone had to believe in it and put it into practice or their assets were confiscated, and those who resisted were killed. This prompted a titanic upheaval in England's class and social structure; resulted in a violent period of death and torture to priests and devout Catholics, destroying hundreds of gorgeous churches and monasteries; and caused thousands of Catholics to flee from the country.

Religious crises continued after Henry VIII's death when his son Edward died at age fifteen and the line of succession turned toward his two daughters: his Catholic daughter, Mary, by his first royal wife Catherine; and his Protestant daughter, Elizabeth, born by his second wife, Anne Boleyn. Mary ruled first and attempted to reestablish the Catholic faith in England through such devices as roasting hundreds of Protestant dissenters alive; for this she was nicknamed Bloody Mary. After Mary's relatively short rule and death, Elizabeth I took the throne. This queen, who enjoyed watching the cruel sport of bear baiting, wherein large dogs are set upon a bear for a fight to the finish, is credited with leading England more peaceably through its "golden age." She, too, burned a few Catholics alive for their refusal to morph into Protestants, although the number of these deaths was very small compared to the slaughter committed by her half-sister. For sixty years Elizabeth I restored Protestantism to England.

England's new national religion now had a king or queen as its leader instead of a pope, which even more closely bonded the church with the state, but it lacked a comprehensive and well-defined non-Catholic doctrine to which its followers could subscribe. Protestants knew they stood against Catholicism, but what they stood for in substitution was indisputably quite murky. Under Henry VIII, Protestantism was essentially Catholicism without its pope, but for decades afterward, Protestants searched for a more differentiated doctrine that they believed would enable them to reach God's ear more effectively than the Catholics had, and would produce demonstrably superior results.

After Elizabeth I died, succeeding English administrations waffled in the closeness they kept between England's one state church, the Church of England, and the Catholic Church, which still controlled most of Europe. With changes that further affected England's religious direction, such as a marriage of an English king to a foreign Catholic queen, or an imported, new, pro-Catholic ruler, the British public had to recalibrate, accommodate, and conform to the practices of the current ruler, who manipulated England's one religion.

By 1620, the very demanding Pilgrims, who agreed with Henry VIII's actions, perceived that the Church of England had also failed to deliver any significant improvement to their lives after almost one hundred years. Many decided that this was because the Church was still too Catholic in its teachings and trappings and that this was preventing their world from attaining the level of perfection they had been expecting.

Tired of waiting for England's religion to evolve, the Pilgrims sought to completely cut ties with it, becoming "Separatists," both psychologically and physically, and they were the first English to move to America and settle on Cape Cod. By entirely rejecting the Church of England, they were exacting idealists, a minority group in terms of their numbers, and people with whom the Puritans didn't completely agree.

Ten years after the Pilgrims separated themselves and settled at Plymouth, England's turmoil over Protestant-Catholic issues re-escalated and in 1630 a second, larger wave of emigrants, John Winthrop's Puritans, set sail for America. Their primary impetus was the recent marriage of their king, Charles I, to a fervent Roman Catholic, Henrietta Maria of France, who had been instructed by the pope to turn England Catholic once more and she was taking pains to do so. This deeply concerned John Winthrop and many others in his generation, who left in fear that the tables were about to turn and Catholics would now gain the upper hand to persecute the Protestants in England as mercilessly as the Protestants had done to the Catholics.

Those who moved with Winthrop also left in hopes that an American relocation would give them a unique new chance to live in a place that was devoid of any corrupting religious influence. They saw America as a religiously virginal land, most suitable for living life in an elemental spiritual state and for imagining new ideas about how to further "purify" the Church of England's religious doctrine. It was an exciting experiment in their theological quest that potentially had the power to save their souls, their church, and their country. Oliver Cromwell, the militant Puritan leader who stayed in England to further direct its ecclesiastical course, was so disturbed over the renewed influence of the Catholic Church over English affairs that he began his argument for an English civil war, and he eventually succeeded in having his king, Charles I, beheaded as a traitor for failing to stop the renewed advance of Catholicism back into the country.

It was enormously important to Winthrop, Cromwell, and like-minded Puritans that they were seen not as radical separatists but as moderate revisionists who could attract a great many people to their highly palatable and less-extreme ideology in order to create a significant opposition to a Catholic resurgence. They also worked very hard to maintain the many legislative roles they already held within the English Parliament in order to reform the English church from within, rather than abandon it altogether. By gaining large numbers of sympathizers and maintaining their legislative footholds, the Puritans not only posed a real threat to the

Henrietta Maria, 1638 (oil on canvas) by Sir Anthony Van Dyck (1599–1641), The Royal Collection © 2011 HER MAJESTY QUEEN ELIZABETH II / THE BRIDGEMAN ART LIBRARY

king's authority, but also were effective in changing the course of English history. Because of this deep integration into Charles I's government, the Puritans were able to push through Parliament many of the political and religious changes they demanded.

In response to the Puritans' charges of an escalating Catholicism within the Church of England, and greater affronts to his civil authority, Charles I became determined to suppress their movement, which began their "great migration" to America in 1630. While just a few had left by 1633, including the Winthrop family, the largest influx arrived between 1634 and 1638, as Catholic influences gained strength throughout England and many Protestant families experienced real fear for their lives. Those loyal to Charles I denounced the Puritans and the word "Puritan" was, in fact, a derogatory taunt referring to the movement's conceit in attempting to create a purified and superior society. Detractors derided those who left for America at this time as "the poorest of the poor," and "the scum of the earth."

While John Winthrop's followers demonstrated the most zeal to reform the Church of England outside of England, others who left spanned a spectrum of dedication to his reformist intentions. Some came out of fear that God was about to retaliate on England for its failure not to have perfected its church in time, while others saw America as just a safe haven until religious persecutions cooled down at home. Many of the seamen, tradesmen, craftsmen, and shopkeepers who came were motivated for purely economic reasons: the possibility of a more profitable existence in America, where greater natural resources lay unclaimed, and the chance to own vast tracts of land, the likes of which one could never have had at home. Social pressures also existed, as people like Elizabeth and Henry saw significant portions of entire communities leave, taking their dearly loved friends and family with them.

Taking all of these reasons for leaving England into consideration, it is estimated that between thirteen thousand and twenty-one thousand

Charles the First by English School (20th century), Private Collection © LOOK AND
LEARN / THE BRIDGEMAN ART LIBRARY

people emigrated to America from England throughout the 1630s and almost every one of them believed in the presence of God and that he played an active and daily role in their existence. That groups of entire Puritan families migrated to New England was one of its unique characteristics; yet for those individuals whose reasons were primarily economic or social, they all became subject to the dominant culture of the Puritan faith once they had arrived on the shores of northeastern America.[9]

Like most of these 1630s emigrants, John Winthrop was not of England's upper class, a titled or entitled royal, or a holder of vast estates by inheritance. He was of England's "thinking class," a politically educated, informed, and aware individual of adequate but not affluent income. In this he was like most other Puritans, who were quite educated due to their group's focus on literacy in order to understand the Bible as a spiritual, social, and educational tool. Well acquainted with England's civil and religious dynamics, John Winthrop was sincerely worried that England's latest upheaval would ruin his mind, his body, and most important, his soul as he sought to discern God's unique plan for his country. Through such meditations he came to the conclusion that he was meant to become a "godly magistrate" in the building and governing of a more godly community on earth that would function as a prototype or model community for all of England to imitate.

In their desired version of the Church of England, the Puritans, like the Pilgrims, rejected anything reminiscent of the Catholic Church, such as its elaborate liturgy, its stained glass windows, its "idolatrous" Christ figures on crosses, and the recognition of saints as a specialized class of deceased human beings who were uniquely endowed with metaphysical abilities. The Puritans saw these as another layer of unnecessary heavenly bureaucracy with whom one had to negotiate before one could communicate with God directly. They also worked toward disabusing their current king that he had any sort of divine right over them, driving the first wedge between the bonding of the church and state in their worldview. They believed that instead of having a king, queen, or pope who acted as their spiritual thought leader, there should be a wide array of common local people who were chosen and hired by individual communities as their appointed religious leaders.

On the voyage over, John Winthrop Sr. delivered a sermon called "A Model of Christian Charity" to his followers, which framed up the new Massachusetts community as a new covenant with God that required its members to "practice a conformity stricter and stronger than the external unity of the Church of England," and he analogized New England to be "as a city on a hill." While most interpret his message to have been about establishing a beacon of enlightenment for the rest of the world to witness, it was also a warning to his followers that their success was imperative, for the failure of their social experiment would be deeply ridiculed, just as a city on a hill is exposed more greatly to view and more vulnerable to bad weather. This speech is still referenced by modern politicians and given many interpretations. Often it's presented to mean that the Puritans began the tradition of allowing multiple religions to flourish in America, but they certainly did not. Allowing a variety of faiths to exist was the furthest thing from John Winthrop's mind, for he needed his particular version of the "Puritan Way" to be America's only way. The Puritans believed that having just one religion in England wasn't England's problem, but that England's one religion had just been too poorly designed.

The tenets of being a Puritan that so drove Winthrop involved the idea of a mediation between two extremes; that God had ultimate authority over all of mankind and that man was universally sinful. To achieve some measure of reconciliation between these two disparate entities, God reached across this great chasm and chose some special people upon whom he bestowed his grace. When it was believed that such a thing had occurred to some people, those so chosen had a superior closeness to God, much like some people have better vision, faster minds, or can sing with perfect pitch. Those few selected individuals who had this "inner light," or these more "godly souls," were assured of salvation, or a sin-less afterlife, and were entirely reconciled with God, which was the ulti-mate goal that Puritans sought to achieve. Whether one became aware that they embodied this special state through a spontaneous revelation or gained it through good works, which leaned toward Catholic thought, was hotly debated and created schisms within Puritan society at this time, much like our modern arguments about when life begins. These cosmi-cally gifted common people were called the "Saints," "the Saved," or "The Elect," and they had the right to govern and preach to others.

In attempting to balance God's will with man's laws, the Puritans held that everyone should follow both as closely as possible to create a logistically functional and morally cohesive society. Anyone whom God selected as a chosen one was assured of salvation, but not absolved of fol-lowing man's laws. If one failed to follow man's laws, the embarrassing results were that a person's inherently sinful nature was put on display and one was prevented from ever experiencing God's love and grace.

The concept of God bestowing grace upon common people was a feared and dangerous concept to Charles I, for it implied that a com-moner could be elevated above a king; having the special spiritual status of "grace" was all in the luck of the celestial draw. "Elect" status born in a common man challenged the authority of kings and, the Puritans believed, particularly those kings who answered to the pope. They consid-ered the pope and his administrative hierarchy of cardinals, bishops, and priests to be middlemen, filters, and obstacles between men and God that blocked man's ability to communicate directly.

The crafty and intellectual Puritans had a real problem with the authorities of their day, and they went well beyond just complaining to constructively circumventing the stranglehold they felt authorities exerted over their lives. Importantly, the innovations they deployed did begin to shift power effectively away from the English government and toward the common people. They promoted literacy, which meant the simultaneous teaching of both reading and writing so that common individuals could understand the world on their own, rather than depend on authorities to interpret it for them. This held the potential for authorities to skew or spin the information a population received and to refashion it to support authority-friendly agendas. Learning to read and write at the same time was an advance over some other European practices of the time that did not teach people to write until they could read the Bible from cover to cover. This resulted in societies with fully grown adults who could read well enough, but couldn't sign their name.

To additionally advance an educated community and clergy, the Puritans pioneered the concept of "free" schooling for those within their social community—paid for with landowners' taxes. This prevented "ignorant zeal," as John Cotton put it, which was "wild-fire without knowledge." Creating a comprehensively educated society also held the promise of allowing common people to make their own decisions rather than having others decide for them. These people reckoned that decisions made by authorities or those enforced through emotional, intimidating, or violent mob rule were considerably less fair and useful than decisions they could personally achieve through reasoning, logic, and structured debate.

Independent-minded Puritans sought to serve God first and satisfy their government second. Not a society of individuals who perceived everyone to be equal, Puritans continually assessed the state of their souls, to see if they belonged to that special class of common people that were God's favorites or "chosen ones" on earth. To determine whether one was of the "Elect," they stressed in-depth Bible study, a lifetime practice of its principles, and the achievement of a verifiable conversion experience that was judged either adequate or insignificant by the community's ministers. Determining one's spiritual status was so important it created a high degree of stress and anxiety in many individuals. It was analogous to working hard throughout your life and anxiously waiting to see if your favorite college would offer you admission, or waiting to find out whether the love-interest of your life loved you in return; acceptance as one of the Elect was the most important form of self-validation. If someone was Elect, the good works they subsequently performed displayed and conveyed their special status to the community. To relieve the stress from worrying about whether they embodied God's grace or not, people were encouraged to increase their familiarity with the Bible and implement its lessons. However, this approach did not fully address all problems for one disturbed woman in Massachusetts; she was so distraught over her position in society that she threw her child down a well to its death to confirm her sinful state once and for all.

"Elect" life came with caveats, for one could still suffer God's abandonment through "backsliding," or falling into Satan's hoary hands, if the Bible's many instructions were abandoned. Puritans policed themselves and others by watching and working to prevent their fellow man's moral remission. The upshot of all this continual care and feeding of one's soul created a Puritan world in New England that denounced many entertainments, employed a minimum of ritual and decoration, and disciplined a spreading population into behaving well through external controls. These most often involved very visible shaming, like wearing a scarlet-colored letter "A" on one's clothing for committing adultery, wearing a horse harness over one's face for practicing bestiality, or being headcuffed in the public stocks for all sorts of civil disturbances. Public shaming was the preferred method for maintaining discipline, and was perhaps more effective in their world than stressing guilt over one's actions, a far more internal control.

THE MOVE BEGINS

John asked Henry and John Jr. to sail with him to the New World, disrupting Henry and Elizabeth's possible pipe dreams of returning to Barbados, and increasing John's ability to more closely supervise his son. When it came time to actually depart, John Winthrop paced up and down his ship's dock, scanning all the wharves for any sign of Henry. The tide was ebbing and a small breeze was blowing as the first shipful of Pilgrims settled themselves, their trunks, their livestock, their babies, and beer kegs on board the *Arbella*, but Henry was nowhere to be found. Again angry and embarrassed, John gave the order for the ship to set sail without him. Henry either had overslept, was hungover, got lost, resented leaving, or deliberately avoided a long sail with his father, but in the end, Henry actually missed his boat to Boston. His brother John Jr., with new wife Martha Fones, did sail, as young John had genuine scientific and geologic interest in exploring America. Forth Winthrop stayed behind in England to finish up his studies.

When their ship landed in the American Northeast after ten weeks at sea, the Winthrop men and their company realized that the Plymouth colony on Cape Cod and another early settlement in Salem were inadequate trading ports, so they sought a superior site. On September 7, 1630, a suitable, protectable peninsula was found and it was "ordered that the trimountain was to be called Boston, Mattapanwas to be called Dorchester and the town upon the Charles River, called Watertown."[10] John Winthrop conducted his 1630 administration out of Boston, natively named "Pigsgusset," and settlers from there quickly branched out west to settle Watertown, which the Indians had known as "Pyquag."

For all of his time in America, Winthrop kept a wary eye on the government he left behind in Europe. He played a coy diplomatic game with Charles I that kept the monarch generally in the dark as to the religious objectives of his Massachusetts Bay Colony, and led the king to believe this was merely an intercontinental extension of his English government. Under Winthrop, the colony actually functioned as a community that mirrored Oliver Cromwell's ideology, which was anathema to the Crown. Winthrop knew that if the king learned of the colony's true nature, there was a real chance that he would prohibit its religious

Oliver Cromwell (oil on canvas) by Sir Peter Lely (1618–1680), Private Collection

practices, wreaking ruin and humiliation on the colony's leaders and all of its community members. Winthrop faced his situation pragmatically; he treated the king pleasantly, and was outwardly obsequious, flattering, and courteous, yet went to great lengths to limit any information that might reach England and trigger a charge of treason.[11] He was so serious about preventing information leaks in the colony's earliest years that when one man objected to the traitorous direction the colony was taking and threatened to report it to the king, Winthrop, whose culture was comfortably acquainted with mutilation as a form of discipline, had one of this man's ears cut off.

In the early 1600s, English society experienced a shift in its fundamental perception of authority such that kings were respected no longer for their divinity but for their popularity in reflecting the will of the people. This enabled Parliament to convene and consider the peoples' will; however, the hierarchy of English authority was still defined as the English believed the Bible instructed them to have it: God over kings, men over women, parents over children, masters over slaves, the English over other Europeans, and Christians over all other cultures. Belief in such a clearly defined society gave comfort, security, and reassurance to these and many other seventeenth-century people who had been roughly buffeted by popes, kings, and wars for decades.

The Puritans attempted to live their lives within this moral and civil framework, and it caused them to judge other societies by the degree to which they differed from their own. They needed such security in their new American colonies to grapple with the utter lack of a comprehensive government and the rise of an entirely new kind of capitalistic economy. By clear definition of social rank, people imposed an order on their thinking that provided a degree of intellectual and moral certainty, and a welcome amount of spiritual consolation.[12] The Puritan ethos had a long-term impact on a juvenile America, and through time it was forced to become less hierarchical and more flexible, responsive, adaptive, and tolerant.

It caused John Winthrop, for example, to see Native American villages abandoned by a smallpox devastation that had struck their communities before his arrival as evidence that God "hath hereby cleared our title to this place." He did not initially feel any need to purchase land with deeds from surviving Indians, in the manner that the Dutch paid them near Manhattan for their land, for Winthrop and his compatriots saw no evidence that the Indians had in any way "subdued," mastered, or added value to the land that merited European payment for it. In fact, there were very few Indians for Winthrop's group to deal with concerning land appropriation, as Indian populations near Boston had been reduced by a series of infectious epidemics before large groups of Europeans had arrived. It is believed that small numbers of European fishermen came to North America in the years before larger-scale European migration and instigated the many epidemics of smallpox and typhoid that spread like wildfire throughout the Indian population. A letter written by an early Bay Colony townsman of the time noted that, "as for the Indians, we have but few amongst us. They are quiet."

A plague had occurred between 1616 and 1618, which is estimated to have killed between 75 and 90 percent of the preexisting native population near Boston. Upon arrival on Cape Cod, the Pilgrims came across many Indian villages with bleached human bones lying neglected and without burial. Near Watertown, Indians of the Pawtucket and Massachusetts group experienced a disease epidemic again in 1630–31, prompting one Englishman to poetically note, "The land was not so much virgin as widowed."[13]

To provide protection for his colony from more remote native populations and other Europeans, John Winthrop depended on a homegrown militia made up of his newly arrived shopkeepers, tradesmen, and farmers. Charles I was preoccupied with the growing civil war that would see Cromwell brought to power, and he was not in a position to send valuable troops to his new American outpost. Perhaps planning that the stiffest challenge in protecting the Puritans would come from the Dutch West India Company on Manhattan and from a few Dutch forts already established in Connecticut, John Winthrop hired two men who were English by birth, but who had trained as professional soldiers in Holland. These men, Captains John Underhill and Daniel Patrick, were the colony's military disciplinarians, or "mustermasters," and their jobs were to train and drill men of all rank who lived within the Bay.

English by birth, they both spoke Dutch and had trained in the Prince's Guard for the Duke of Orange-Nassau in Holland and they were also both married to Dutch women. Watertown historian Henry Bond reports, "It is probable that for the first few years, [1630–1640] Captain John Underhill trained the men on the south side of the Charles River—those of Boston, Roxbury and Dorchester and that Captain Daniel Patrick trained those on the North side—Charlestown, Watertown, Newtown (Cambridge) and Medford, exclusive of those in and about Salem."[14] On March 1636/7 the colony agreed to pay Underhill and Patrick £30 apiece per year for seven years. The fighting prowess and military discipline of these men was a valuable asset to the fledgling colony, and they were perfectly suited in their skill sets and multiculturalism for this time and place. They were common and rough men, and though both could read, write, and speak two languages, it's doubtful that they would have been able to associate with the highest levels of society in Europe as they did in their unusual new world. If John Winthrop could have foreseen the scale of tragedy these two men would come to inflict upon native populations in America's Northeast, perhaps he might have reconsidered his two new hires.

CHAPTER THREE

Elizabeth's Second Wedding

LITTLE DID JOHN WINTHROP REALIZE, NOR DID A PREGNANT ELIZA-BETH when she last kissed Henry goodbye, that neither of them would ever see him alive again. After missing his father's ship, the *Arbella*, Henry caught a ride with the next ship sailing over, the *Talbot*, which docked north of Boston, in Salem, on July 2, 1630, a few weeks after his father had landed in Boston. After ten weeks at sea without exercise and on a meager diet of peas, puddings, and fish, Henry's first impulsive decision off the *Talbot* was to swim across an unknown river in Salem to explore a large Indian village he saw on the opposite bank. A report to John Winthrop from one of the men who had been with Henry detailed the fatal drama of his son's first American adventure:[15]

The very day on which he went on shore in New England, he and the principal officers of the ship, walking out to a place now called, by the Salemites, Northfield, to view the Indian wigwams, they saw on the other side of the river a small canoe. He would have had one of the small company swim over and fetch it, rather than walk several miles on foot, it being very hot weather: but none of the party could swim but himself; and so he plunged in, and as he was swimming over, was taken with the cramp, a few rods from the shore, and drowned.

31

The vivacious and impulsive Henry was twenty-two when he died, fourteen months after he and Elizabeth had married and six weeks after his daughter, whom he never saw, was born in England. His father could not, at first, bear to examine his complex emotions and its cosmic implications, and tersely recorded in his journal, "My son, Henry Winthrop was drowned at Salem." Elizabeth and his extended family were absolutely shattered, for Henry's first day in America had been his last day on earth. John later wailed out in grief in a letter home to his wife Margaret Tyndal in despair over the situation:[16] "We have met with many sad and discomfortable things as thou shall hear after. My son Henry! My son Henry! Ah, poor child!" And after hours spent grieving this loss and chalking it up to God's will, his thoughts then turned toward Elizabeth who was most affected by his death; "Yet, it grieves me much more for my dear daughter. The Lord strengthen and comfort her heart to bear this cross patiently. I know thou will not want her to be in this distress." The year 1630 was a terribly sad one for the Winthrop family with Henry's drowning in July. He was likely buried in Boston near where his father lies in Cambridge today, perhaps even clothed in his "scarlet suit lined throughout with plush." To the family's additional shock and distress, Forth Winthrop died less than three months later that October in England of a sudden illness while preparing for his wedding to Ursula Sherman.

John could not let Forth and Henry's deaths disrupt his greater group's plans, however, and he cast them as sad but not insurmountable setbacks, writing: "Yet for all these things I pray God . . . I am not discouraged, nor do I see cause to repent or despair of those good days here, which will make amends for all. These afflictions we have met with should discourage no one, for the country is exceedingly good, and the climate very like our own . . . here is sweet air, fair rivers and plenty of springs, and the water is better than in England. Here can be no want of anything for those who can raise food out of earth and sea."

Some months later, when the family's immediate sorrow had subsided, the necessity was clear to provide for Elizabeth, now newly widowed and a mother with no family of her own left in London save her little brother Sam. While John Winthrop Sr. and his wife Margaret Tyndal grieved for Henry, they also saw a second chance for Elizabeth to take her rightful place in society with a more responsible man. They arranged for her to meet William Coddington,[17] whom John Senior knew quite well and had worked with in both countries. The two dated for a while in London, for he was a thirty-year-old widower who was also seeking a second marriage. Although friendly and courteous, they did not proceed toward marriage, most likely because Coddington came to disagree with Winthrop on how the Puritans' objectives in America should be achieved and he eventually became the governor of Rhode Island, a region founded through dissent with the Bay Colony's stand on religion and governance. Margaret Winthrop wrote her husband from England to report that Elizabeth was recovering from Henry's loss along with that of her suitor. She was adapting herself to her new situation by "being very much employed in her surgery," inspired by her father Thomas Fones, and "having very good success."[18]

John Winthrop took an active interest in Elizabeth and in his only grandchild, little Martha Johana, because beyond being Elizabeth's de facto guardian, he was the only adult male relative in her life, besides his son, John Winthrop Jr. He urged her to sail to America on the ship *Lyon* with his wife Margaret, and she did, arriving on November 2, 1631—fifteen months after Henry's death—when she was twenty-one. The governor said he would care for her and her child "as if she were his own," which of course she was.[19] Martha Johana was seventeen months old when she arrived but, unfortunately, John and Margaret Winthrop's newborn, Anne, born about the same time as she was at Groton Manor, died one week after setting sail from England. The Winthrops lost yet a third family member when Margaret buried this little baby at sea.

To welcome home the newly widowed Elizabeth and the governor's heartbroken wife, the little Boston community of fewer than two hundred people broke out "fat hogs, kids, venison, poultry, goose, partridges etc, so as the like joy and manifestation of Love had never been seen in New England."[20] Elizabeth realized, however, that she and Martha Johana would quickly wear out their welcome in the newly constructed yet very confined spaces of the new Winthrop household.

In that first winter of 1631, this house, called the "mansion house," was most likely a simple two-story structure consisting of four rooms, with a one-story kitchen spanning its rear width. This was far better lodging than the housing of some of the other first colonists, who spent their first Boston winter in hand-dug pits called cellars. These were lined and roofed with wood planks that had been sawn by hand and inhabited until spring, when the colonists could build a proper wooden structure above these pits and turn them into basements. A sloping roof swept down without a breakpoint from a fully built home's two-story height to cover its one-story rear kitchen extension, giving these houses their iconic and asymmetrical "saltbox" appearance that resembled wooden salt storage boxes.

The two ground-floor rooms in these houses were called the "hall," which was a room and not a passage, and the "parlor," from the French word "parlez," meaning a room meant for speaking or conversation, was in reality used for many purposes. The Winthrop's "hall" was a public room in which most Bay Colony meetings and church services were first held. It also contained some Winthrop family beds that first year, their storage chests, farming hoes, scythes, their kitchen equipment, and foodstuffs, plus a table that served as the governor's desk. In this earliest period of colonization, luxury articles such as pillows, cushions, paintings, pictures, looking glasses, and other decorative objects were rarely seen, as room on the ships sent over from England was devoted to storing poultry, livestock, seed stock, and life's most basic necessities. The homes in the early 1630s appeared entirely utilitarian. Any money generated from farming operations was recycled back into this effort, and money was rarely spent on personal or domestic decoration.

Those crammed into the prestigious Winthrop household were Elizabeth and her child, John Sr. and his wife Martha Tyndal, plus John

Winthrop Jr. and his wife Martha Fones, for a total of five fully grown adults plus one highly active toddler.

Adding to an overall discomfort inside the Winthrop home was the fact that the newly married John Jr. and Martha Fones were experiencing a rocky start to their marriage, though they tried their best to work through it. Martha once apologized to John Jr. after a fight that they'd had by saying, "Be persuaded of my love to thee not withstanding my passions and weaknesses which formerly have caused thee to think to the contrary," with John Jr. responding tensely that, "Thou needs not fear but I am fully persuaded of your love . . . although the clouding of your love sometimes suddenly darkens my mind with grief and sadness." The uncertain young couple took pains to conceal their arguments from their family in the tight physical confines of the house, where privacy for

The rear exterior of the Fairbanks house in Dedham, Massachusetts, with later additions on either side THE FAIRBANKS HOUSE, C. 1637–1641

letter writing was at a premium, by writing in secret code or cipher to each other.[21]

In the fall of 1633 John Jr. was often away from the mansion house exploring the country and supervising the construction of the couple's new home in Agawam, later named Ipswich, which is twenty-five miles north of Boston. Martha fretted that this house would not be finished in time for the birth of their first child, causing John Jr. to advise her to "take heed of being melancholy . . . and to resolve to be cheerful."

To relieve this tension, and perhaps to regain God's favor by marrying someone of whom John Winthrop approved, twenty-two-year-old Elizabeth quickly married an upper-class Englishman she had met within months of her arrival in the Bay. He was Robert Feake, a former London goldsmith from a well-to-do and distinguished multi-generational goldsmithing family and the son of a wealthy draper, or cloth sellers' daughter[22] whose name was variously spelled "Pheex," "Feecxs," "Feeks," "Feex," "Feke," "Pheux," or "Feakes." He was a "gentleman," a rank assigned to those with some financial means that distinguished them from the laboring class. Robert had been a merchant, trained by his father in the family jewelry shop on Lombard Street in London, and he was addressed with the honorific "Mister." John Winthrop Jr. may have enticed Robert to join the Bay community because of their shared interests in mining, mineralogy, and alchemy and for Feake's knowledge of and ability to identify and refine the many new earth minerals that remained to be discovered in their vast and unexplored new world.

When Elizabeth married him she joined yet another crowded household, for Robert Feake was the guardian of his brother's two orphaned teenaged children, Tobias and Judith Feake. Their father had been killed in a brawl with a Shakespearean actor who had dealt him a lethal blow with a candlestick and upon his death his children had been sent to live in Germany with other Feake relatives until Robert retrieved them for his journey.

Elizabeth's identity and status as a woman in the Bay Colony centered on her role as Robert's wife, and her very name changed to reference

John Winthrop Jr. (1606–1676) (oil on canvas) by Sir Peter Lely (1618–1680) (school of) © MASSACHUSETTS HISTORICAL SOCIETY, BOSTON, MA, USA / THE BRIDGEMAN ART LIBRARY

this new partnership. She was not referred to as "Elizabeth Feake" or "Mrs. Feake," but as "Robert Feake, his wife," much like "Mr. Feake, his book," in a very possessive sense. Widows of this time were also called "relicts," as in "relics," in reference to their lost married status, the pinnacle of the English family ideal.

Notwithstanding what in the present might be considered a grammatical slur, in Elizabeth's world, the subjection of a wife to her husband was not the same as a servant to a master or a child to a parent. It was, rather, a consensual relationship that promoted mutual support and respect between couples. Men and women were raised to treat their spouses with compassion, love, and affection to create a harmonious, long-term relationship and a fully functional family. Men's and women's rights and responsibilities were reciprocal and each person's relationship was, of necessity, subject to another.[23] Each person's individuality, equality, or self-reliance was not valued as highly as it is today, for in the hierarchy which sustained their social order, Robert was the titular head of the Feake household, but he incorporated Elizabeth's feelings and views in his decisions. If for some reason he could not continue to manage his household, Elizabeth was expected to stand in his place and act as a "deputy husband" for her family.

She had changed from the exhilarated and rebellious teenager she had been in London, now orphaned and chastened by her father's death, stunned by Henry's drowning, and sobered by being a young mother in the wilderness of an entirely foreign environment. It's possible that she too considered Henry's startling death a sign that God disapproved of her marriage.

Elizabeth, like the other women in the Puritan colony, found guidance in her new role as a mature and responsible woman from the passage of Proverbs 31:10–31, which is the description of Bathsheba, the Puritans' female role model. This biblical woman, queen, wife, and mother embodied their valued dimensions of charity, industry, and curiously that of modesty, since Bathsheba has been considered either a harlot or a rape victim, but for any Bathsheba of 1630s Boston, the characteristic of paramount importance was that of industry. Elizabeth's productivity was celebrated more than her individuality or degree of Winthrop gentility. Bathsheba "looketh well to the ways of her household, and eateth not the bread of idleness." A good wife was productively active, and she was valued by her ability to feed, educate, clothe, care for, supervise, and serve all others in her home and in her community. The degree to which she met the expectations associated with industry, charity, and modesty meant more than her status, wealth, or unique personality in how her community viewed her.

Elizabeth was expected to be a worthy matron, a dutiful wife, a loving mother, and a friendly, charitable neighbor,[24] and the degree to which these roles were satisfied made or broke each woman's reputation. She also was expected to support her husband's reputation in the community by behaving respectably in her speech, manners, and attitude, and raising her children to do likewise. She was to take care in her dress, as well, knowing that it reflected her husband's status, keeping it neither too threadbare nor unkempt to embarrass him or so flashy that she asserted herself over him.

There was one relationship that trumped a married couple's "yokefellow" partnership with each other, and that was each person's relationship with Christ. Individuals were instructed early and often that they were married to Christ well before they were married to each other, and to illustrate this concept, good marriages were often compared to the bond between the Church and Christ, an ideal of oneness with God. This comparison meant that submission to God and submission to one's husband were both the duties of any proper wife. Such a mindset put Elizabeth's obedience to Robert in a fixed and positive framework, for not only was it desirable in a marriage, it was a legal requirement. The idea that one's relationship to Christ was dominant and stronger than one's union with another person was also very practical in a world full of sudden, frequent, and unexpected fatality; for should one's spouse or child die prematurely, one's faith would offer stronger and longer-lasting support than did one's marital or maternal love, and this concept helped individuals work through such emotionally wrenching experiences.

Robert Feake came to the Massachusetts Bay Colony in the fleet that sailed with Governor Winthrop in 1630. Once he had settled in, he explored his new country with the governor and several other men, and they spent days together walking the land around the Shawmut peninsula, the site for the city of Boston, and named many geographic features and waterways after themselves. "They have gone up the Charles River, about eight miles above Watertown, coming to a high pointed rock, having a fair ascent on the west side, which they called Mount Feake, from one Robert Feake, who had married the Governor's daughter-in-law."[25] The group must have been joshing Robert, for Mount Feake is an insignificant one-hundred-foot-high hill, now within Mt. Feake Cemetery next to Brandeis University in Waltham, Massachusetts.

With Elizabeth Winthrop's family connections and Robert Feake's respectable standing in Puritan society, in 1631 Robert was immediately admitted as a "freeman," meaning a church member of the colony, and was part of the inner circle that governed their new home in Watertown, just west of Boston. He became an extensive landowner there, owning a home lot and several farming parcels, as did their next-door neighbors, Captain Daniel Patrick and his Dutch wife, Anna van Beyeren, called "Anneken" as an endearment. Daniel and Anneken had married in 1630, the same year they sailed to America.[26]

Robert's career was on an upward trajectory while they lived in Watertown. He became a member of the local militia and was made a lieutenant under Patrick by December 4, 1632. He held this position until 1636, and also served as selectman for several years. For two years, 1634–1636, he was a representative from Watertown to the General Court in Boston, but ominously, evidence of a serious mental disability that is without a modern diagnosis began to make its appearance.

Robert and Elizabeth had three children during their nine-year residence in Watertown: Elizabeth, born about 1633; Hannah, born five years later in 1637; and John, born one year later in 1638. While pregnancy excused no woman from the work to be done on the home and farm, it did give Elizabeth a special measure of protection and respect. Labor was called a woman's "travail," the French word for work. As many as a dozen women could have been present during Elizabeth's labors, to psychologically encourage, comfort, distract, and support her, even though they included some women—owing to her provincial and isolated existence—whom she probably disliked. Late in her eighth month, Elizabeth brought out the childbed linen, which she had inherited from her mother, Anne Winthrop Fones, and she prepared for her coming company of women by baking "groaning cakes" and "groaning beer" to feed them. This company of assorted female friends, relatives, and neighbors may have spent the night in her home while she labored, packed three or four to a bed or sleeping upright overnight in the few chairs she owned.

The colonial homes of Elizabeth and her neighbors were of varying degrees of cleanliness and they had no screened doors. If they had glass in their windows, it was comprised only of very small diamond-shaped panes that let in little sunshine. They had no running water or electricity, and these homes were sometimes flea-infested. Regardless of the home's condition, neighboring women would come to tend to her as well as to her family, looking after her small children, caring for the family's livestock, and nursing those who may have been ill with a wide variety of diseases, parasites, or worms. (When uncomposted livestock manure was used to fertilize gardens, worm eggs were ingested if vegetables were not thoroughly washed.) As they did for Elizabeth, so she did for them.

In her travail, Elizabeth was attended by a midwife, who may have travelled from another town to provide her specialized services before the larger group of women began assembling. Midwives not only delivered babies, for which they were paid, but also assumed all the roles of a modern hospital staff, acting as an all-purpose nurse, doctor, anesthesi-ologist, nutritionist, pharmacist, and, if need be, mortician.[27] In addition to providing obstetrical care, midwives treated the many disease epidem-ics that regularly ravaged early colonial settlements, including scarlet fever—called "canker rash" or "putrid malignant sore throat"—diphthe-ria, typhus, smallpox, and cholera.

As labor commenced, Elizabeth walked about early on, and ate very lightly. She relieved her pain by drinking an herb tea brewed with honey or sugar and betony or stachys, which she collected from the woods in July and dried.[28] When her labor pains crested in her "hard and sharp travail" she may have bent low upon a midwife's stool to give birth using butter or animal fat to ease her baby's entry into its new world. Travail, a torment visited by God on the daughters of Eve, was perceived by Eliza-beth and her helping women with resurrection imagery. Childbirth labor was not only a sign of women's weakness and sin, but also a means for female redemption, as evidenced by a successful birth.[29]

When her child was delivered, it was important that at least one of Elizabeth's women was lactating, for her first milk, or colostrum, was con-sidered impure through the trauma of childbirth, and so the baby was suckled by a nursing neighbor or relative in its first few days of life. A new mother's possible breast infection was treated with lancing, warm wool compresses, and ointments of "parsley, wormwood, and chamomile stewed in butter."[30] There was also a ritual surrounding the cutting of the umbilical cord on a newborn: cut too long on a girl and she may become immodest; cut too short on a boy and he may experience sexual dysfunction.

Of course, not all births were successful, and infant and maternal mor-tality rates were high. Typically, women had five to eight children, and approximately one out of every two hundred mothers, or .5 percent, died in the birth process or soon afterward of infection, dehydration, or hemorrhage. Parish registers for seventeenth- and eighteenth-century women living in English villages, as researched by Laurel Thatcher Ulrich, showed maternal deaths actually rose with increased use of extraction tools and rudimentary hospitals. She determined a range from ten to twenty-nine maternal deaths per thousand births. For all of the infant deaths in these records, there was a 4.3 percent mortality rate, and of these, 40 percent were stillborn and the rest died within their first day.[31] In contrast, in twenty-first-century America, infant mortality is 0.7 percent of all births.

Elizabeth was relatively expert in caring for the sick in her community, equipped as she was with the apothecary knowledge she had learned from her father, along with some alchemical knowledge she may have discussed with her scientifically minded cousin, John Winthrop Jr., and it is possible that she too became an able midwife.

After a short and contentious marriage of only three years, Elizabeth's sister, Martha Fones Winthrop, and her newborn daughter died the August or September of 1634, having succumbed to the arduous process of childbirth. Her death inventory reveals that her assets included "a sea-green gown trimmed over with lace" which was likely inherited by Elizabeth, who may also have attended her labor. John Jr. lost his wife and first child and Elizabeth lost her only sister. Both of them, however, found comfort and solace in her death through the comparisons they made about her life, marriage, and motherhood to stories of women they knew from the Bible. Elizabeth's only surviving sibling now was her younger brother, Samuel Fones, who had stayed behind in England.

Elizabeth Feake's life in Watertown with Robert revolved around her domestic responsibilities of raising Martha Johana in addition to the birthing, nursing, and rearing of her four small Feake children, no doubt aided greatly by her maid named Sarah Sandbrock, as well as her new niece Judith and nephew Tobias. She educated her family religiously and secularly, and she planted, grew, and prepared the food that fed many people every day, including the family's farm laborers.

When she had to purchase items from others in her village, she bartered or used the local currency, which were tiny Indian-made beads created from the blue and white parts of shells. These were strung on sinew or animal tendons and the Dutch called them "seawant" and the English called them "wampam-peag." Long Island, which the Indians called, "Sewanhacky," was a major manufacturing source of these beads. The use of these beads as currency for decades in the Northeast is why we still refer to "shelling out" money in our modern day. These very small, handmade, hand-drilled, and hand-sanded beads were made from the purple edge of quahog clam shells and the inner spires of whelks. They were tooled by Indian women and children into cylinders about one quarter of an inch long and an eighth of an inch wide that varied in color from black, white, and blue to purple. The process of making these beads was difficult and time-consuming until the Europeans brought in hand saws and metal drills and started to mass produce them, which created inflation in their market. The Indians used them ornamentally on belts to create designs with the different colors and wove them into many other articles of clothing to signify standing or wealth. The trade of such bead-encrusted clothing was common as currency, too.

The Dutch on Manhattan set the trading rates for this market. The superior, smooth, high-quality version called "Manhattan seawant" traded in 1640 at four-to-one for a Dutch stuyver. What the Dutch perceived to be inferior, rough, coarse, and possibly counterfeit seawant from New England traded at six to a stuyver. These beads were commonly strung in six-foot-long strings called fathoms and Elizabeth might have paid up to ten fathoms "peag" for a brown bear skin blanket. Undoubtedly the Downings partially paid for their son's first Harvard tuition in wampam-peag fathoms. Rates were adjusted occasionally and by 1648, the English exchange rate for "peag" was eight white shells for a penny and four black ones per penny.

If barter was desired instead of currency, Elizabeth traded any item she could produce, such as eggs from her chickens, ducks, or geese; dried herbs; fruit preserves; spun cloth; sewn items; or her medical assistance with other families in her highly interdependent little village. She might agree to trade some of the food she had cooked to have someone else wash her family's clothes for a day by hand in a boiling kettle, or she might exchange a day spent at her spinning wheel or weaving loom in return for half a barrel of flour made from wheat ground at Watertown's watermill. Her seasonal chores included helping with the care and breeding of the Feake family livestock, milking their cows and churning the animals' milk for cream and butter, and making cheese. She helped plant wheat, barley, corn, potatoes, pumpkins, parsnips, onions, cabbage, squash, peas, turnips, carrots, beans, and many medicinal herbs. She preserved foods in jars and barrels, brewed beer, made cider, baked and grilled wild meats, fished, gathered shellfish, raised poultry, and helped tan all kinds of animal hides for personal use or trade. Her home lot may have contained one or more outbuildings such as a pighouse, henhouse, washhouse, smokehouse, or brewhouse, in addition to an outhouse and a hand-dug well for fresh water.

Her cooking fireplace was up to nine feet wide, which allowed her to create many small fires and ember piles at one time on the hearth or floor to vary the temperature for different foods, and to fry, roast, boil, or simmer several dishes at the same time. She stood at this large chimney in her long skirt and apron, moving from one fire to another and courting disaster with every step she took. Many women died from the burns they suffered when their clothes caught fire as they worked in such perilous conditions.

To create a variety of dishes, Elizabeth adjusted pots hung on hooks to alter their distance from the ever-burning ember beds, and checked her baking without thermostats or standardized measurements. Frying, boiling, roasting, and baking occurred all year long, and keeping a fire going in the household fireplace required constant attention day and night, every day of every year. Lack of attention to the fires in these large, medieval-style fireplaces that were only roughly "catted" or daubed with mud or clay mixed with straw often resulted in the chimney itself catching fire, and quickly burning down a house that had taken weeks of grinding labor to build.

Processing meat required Elizabeth to participate in the annual fall slaughter, which included killing some of the smaller animals by herself.

Delaware Indians wearing seawant-decorated clothing, *THOMAS CAMPANIUS HOLM, DESCRIPTION OF THE PROVINCE OF NEW SWEDEN, NOW CALLED BY THE ENGLISH, PENNSYLVANIA IN AMERICA* (M'CARTY & DAVIS, 1834)

To preserve the meat through winter, she soaked these skinned and eviscerated carcasses in a salty brine. Bacon was packed in salt for two or three weeks, then hung from a pole in an activity called "hanging bacon," and then was placed inside the chimney for smoking. She was a comprehensive colonial multitasker, turning herbs into medicines, milk into butter, and livestock into lunch to ensure the survival of her family.[32]

Ever the industrious Bathsheba, she would have joined with other women to produce woven cloth for farm and family, including planting flax, and combing, coloring, spinning, and weaving it, followed by fashioning it into an article of clothing. Contrary to popular perceptions about Puritan fashion, which was always more simple and conservative than some excessively flamboyant English clothing, Elizabeth dressed herself in a wide range of pre-synthetic greys, blues, greens, and reds, sometimes embellished with exquisite handsewn embroidery or lacework topped off by an assortment of wide-brimmed hat styles. Since the sheer difficulty of creating clothing in the New World greatly limited choices after one's British-made clothing wore out, it was not unusual for each person in earliest America to own only two or three complete outfits to wear throughout each year.

Needless to say, articles of clothing came few and far between, and cloth of all kinds was highly valued by the English and the Indians, who came to prefer it for some uses over animal skin, although at first the Indians, for reasons unknown today, would not accept cloth that had the color white anywhere in it. Europeans trapped and hunted wild native animals and prepared their hides for trade and family use, and undoubtedly leather, suede, and furs made up a large part of Feake family fashion and were made into household objects of all kinds, including bedding, carpets, and coverings that were sometimes lice-infested. Animals hunted in America's Northeast included elk, deer, moose, bear, wolf, bobcat or mountain lion, beaver, and raccoon, among other fur-bearing mammals, and may have included an occasional seal from Long Island Sound. When the Europeans arrived, Native Americans had no domesticated animals, save their dog companions, which are thought to have been bred from domesticated wolves.

The English shipped boatloads of livestock, including oxen, cows, sheep, hogs, and horses, from Europe for farm use, and "every fresh cargo of farm beasts was a victory in their war for survival, not only for their dietary value, but also for the muscle power that could extend the farming area of the settlement."[33]

CHAPTER FOUR

Mustermasters Daniel Patrick and John Underhill

ELIZABETH AND ROBERT'S NEIGHBORS FOR THE NINE YEARS THEY LIVED in Watertown were Captain Daniel Patrick, his Dutch wife Anneken van Beyeren, and their three children. Daniel Patrick and his Bay Colony comrade, Captain John Underhill, were Winthrop's military disciplinarians, and they had been hired by him to train the local militia and engage in military actions against any force that could threaten the colony's success in the region. They were proud of their aggressive ability to address wide-ranging threats to the new English settlements and in doing so these men sometimes came to decide upon their own tactics for use in the field. They, with fellow soldier John Mason, committed the Mystic Massacre for the English in 1637. In riding roughshod over regional Indian populations, and eventually destroying the Pequot as a Dutch trading power in the process, these men soon came to break the boundaries of acceptable behavior both inside and outside of the Bay Colony's community.

THE PEQUOT WAR AND THE MYSTIC MASSACRE
The Mystic, Connecticut, Massacre in 1637 was America's first tri-cultural collision involving the Dutch, the English, and the Indians.

The Dutch had established forts in Connecticut long before the English arrived, and they had been conducting profitable fur trading along the Connecticut River near Hartford with the Pequots, the Indian group that populated most of eastern coastal Connecticut. Through this relationship, the Pequots gained greater status, prestige, military advantage, and increased access to European goods over their rivals, the Narragansett in Rhode Island. When the jealous Narragansett became angry with this European-induced power shift, they petitioned the Dutch for equal trading rights. The Dutch, who sought to trade with the largest pool of Indian partners possible, then quickly mandated that all Indian groups, including the Narragansett, could trade at their Hartford fort, which effectively broke the Pequot's trading advantage. The Pequots, who were intent on maintaining their edge, then began killing any other Indian who approached Hartford's Dutch fort. In retaliation, the Dutch killed a Pequot leader named Tatobem to show just how serious they were about their new open trade policy.

In return, and to logically uphold their custom of "a man for a man" in just retribution, the Pequots killed one notorious and disreputable Englishman named John Stone, whom they erroneously thought was a Dutchman. In an increasingly messy and small-scale tit for tat, the next time some Pequot approached the Dutch fort to trade, the Dutch killed another one of their sachems or "chiefs" for their killing of Stone, and now the affronted Pequot, who had the rules changed on them by the Dutch, found themselves at war not only with the Narragansetts, but also with the Dutch.

Despairing of this situation, the Pequot then turned to trade with the English in Boston, who imposed another new set of European rules upon them. While John Winthrop had regarded the Pequot as "just and equal in their dealings, not treacherous," he demanded that the Pequot turn over those who had killed John Stone. The Pequot balked at this and pointed out that Stone had kidnapped two Indians. While John Winthrop largely agreed with the merits of the Pequots' complaint, he referred the resolution of the problem over to his colony's clergy.

Unfortunately for the Pequot, these clergymen advised against Winthrop's lenient intent, because they viewed the Indians in general as having far more comprehensive, cosmic, and diabolical motivation for existing unknown and unevangelized within the new world. Speculation had run rampant in America and Europe for years about who the American Indian actually was, and theories ranged from suppositions that they were remnants from the lost tribes of Israel, Syrians, or Egyptians, to wide and humorous musings of far-flung, exotic, and sometimes mythical places of origin. Even today, there are those who hypothesize that the Ohio Mound-Builders' ancestry is from another planet.

In comparing themselves to the Indians, the Puritans found the widest gulf between them was their religious difference, rather than their race, in that the English had difficulty grasping what the Indians' religion really was. The post-medieval Boston clergy, who darkly and uniquely saw the Indians as servants of Satan that universally threatened the Puritans' utopian cause, influenced Patrick, Mason, and Underhill to believe that Indians were led by the devil to destroy the Puritans' existence and purpose in America.

The Pilgrim William Bradford from the Plymouth Colony also supported this belief, writing that the Indians sought the devil's aid in repelling the English. Roger Williams, a known friend of the Indians, also wrote Winthrop to warn him—in this era that gave some credence to magical methodologies—that the Pequots were planning to use sorcery against the English. English mistrust of the Pequots fatally deepened, however, when the Pequots committed three sequential acts of refusing to turn over John Stone's murderer, failing to make a requested payment to the English, and killing a Massachusetts Bay Colony agent named John Oldham on Block Island for tangentially related reasons. This litany of perceived Indian offenses caused the clergy's ominous perspectives to gain greater traction within the Bay Colony community.

A rising fear existed that regional Indian groups could easily consolidate and overwhelm them, for the English had not accurately assessed the overall size and strength of the Indian populations in Massachusetts, Rhode Island, and Connecticut. In pondering a worst-case scenario, they referenced Cromwell's recent brutal battles in Ireland with their excessive casualty rates, and, closer to home, they dwelled on the Massacre of 1622, when the Virginian Indian named Powhattan killed 347 European men, women, and children in one day, exterminating fully one third of the Jamestown settlement's population.[34] An English survivor of the Virginia Massacre lectured them that this onslaught was the result of "long forbearance and too much leniency of the English towards the Virginian savages," a message received with fear by Europeans living near Boston.

To avenge John Oldham's death on Block Island, John Winthrop partially agreed with his clergy and ordered his soldiers to raid an Indian village and kill the men but spare the women and children for use as hostages to barter for the return of John Stone's murderer. Winthrop saw this raid as a limited incursion, rather than a full-scale war, and a just solution for the previous Indian-English skirmishes. The Connecticut Colony at Hartford and some citizens of Plymouth on Cape Cod considered it an over-reaction, and properly feared the further Indian retaliation that was to come. As they predicted, the Pequots did retaliate with an attack on Wethersfield, just south of Hartford, where they killed nine people and captured two young women. Other Indian raids throughout Connecticut brought the total European body count up to thirty, which for the time was considered a statistically significant loss of European life.

The Pequot, in gearing up to avenge their legitimate grievances, let bygones be bygones and arranged a new alliance with their old enemies, the Narragansett. With this consolidation of Indian groups, the English opted for larger-scale war as a reaction to events they perceived to threaten their very existence, colored by their metaphysical beliefs about a possible Satanic-Indian alliance and nudged along by their lust for more land.

Captains John Mason and John Underhill hadn't initially planned to burn hundreds of Indians alive in the largest event of the Pequot War, but tragically, it turned out that way in the end.[35] In this particular catastrophe for northeastern America's native people, John Winthrop's governing council of magistrates directed the colony's mustermasters to attack a large Pequot community living at Mystic, Connecticut, to send them an unforgettable message of English power and strength. Daniel Patrick was to join the organizing English forces, but he had only reached Providence from Boston by the designated attack date, so Mason and Underhill, who never really liked him, went on without him.

The village that Mason and Underhill attacked was heavily fortified, a large circular enclosure that contained many Indian long houses, each measuring up to one hundred feet long and twenty feet in width. In a typical, palisaded or fenced-in Indian village such as this, multiple long houses were lined up parallel to each other "street fashion," with the twenty-foot face fronting the "street." The Pequots made them by inserting long, thin, peeled hickory saplings into the ground at evenly spaced intervals, forming the footprint of the final structure. A Dutchman named Adrien van der Donck observed:[36]

The sapling poles are then bent over and fastened to one another, so that the frame looks like a wagon or an arbor as are put in gardens. Next, strips like split laths are laid across the uprights from one end to the other . . . This is then covered with very tough bark. For durability, everything is peeled so no worms can get in . . . In sum they arrange it so that their houses repel rain and wind and are also fairly warm, but they know nothing about fitting them out with rooms, salons, halls, closets or cabinets.

From one end of the house to the other along the center they kindle fires, and the space left open, which is also in the middle, serves as a chimney to release the smoke. They may be sixteen or eighteen families in a house, more or less according to the size of the house. The fire is in the middle and the people on either side. Everyone knows his space and how far it extends. If they have room for a pot and a kettle and whatever else they have, and a place to sleep, they desire no more. This means that often 100 or 150 and more lodge in one house. Such is the arrangement of a house as they commonly are found everywhere, unless they are out hunting or fishing, when they merely put up a makeshift shelter. In the villages and castles they always do solid and good work.

As sites for their castles they prefer a high or steep hill near water or on a riverbank that is difficult to climb and often accessible on one side only. They always make them flat and even on top. This they enclose with a heavy wooden stockade constructed in a peculiar interlocking diamond pattern. First they lay a heavy log on the ground, sometimes with a lighter one on top, as wide and as broad as they intend to make the foundation. Then they set heavy oak posts diagonally in the ground on both sides to form a cross at the upper end where they are notched to fit tighter together. Next another log is laid in there to make a very solid work. The palisades stand two deep and are strong enough to protect them from a surprise attack or sudden raid by their enemies, but they do not as yet have any knowledge of properly equipping such a work with curtain, bastions, and flanking walls, etc. They also build some small forts here and there on the level and low land near their plantations to shelter their wives and children from an assault, in case they have enemies so nearby that they could be fallen upon by small parties. They think highly of their forts and castles built in that fashion, but these actually are of little consequence and cause them more harm than good in a war with the Christians. In such a castle they usually put twenty or thirty houses of up to a hundred feet and some even longer, like those measures by our people at up to 180 paces. Seeing that they manage with so little space in the castles, as related above, they cram such a multitude of people inside that it is unbelievable and leaves one amazed when he sees them come out.

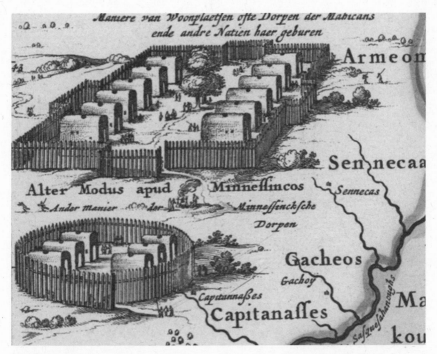

Detail of palisaded Indian village from a map called Novi Belgii Novaeque Angliae made by Justus Danckerts in the mid-1650s. It was engraved as a copy of Nicholas Visscher's 1651 composite map (i.e., the 1650 map of J. Jansson and the 1650 New Amsterdam view of J. Blaeu). LIBRARY OF CONGRESS

In 1637, Mason, Underhill, and their men sailed out of the Connecticut River and put in east of Stonington, Connecticut, passing the Indian scouts at the Mystic fortress, who were relieved to see them sail past. Landing up the coast from the village, the soldiers backtracked on foot to the Indian fort that evening and prepared for a surprise, land-based, morning invasion. Their first plan was to kill the inhabitants by sword so as to disrupt their capacity to fight, and reserve the village for plunder. When the assault began, up to 150 Indian warriors valiantly fought back, earning admiration and praise from John Underhill, who wrote, "Most

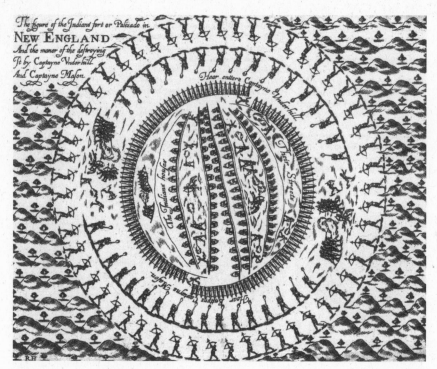

John Underhill's drawing of the Mystic massacre

courageously these Pequots behaved themselves ... Many courageous fellows were unwilling to come out and fought most desperately through the palisadoes ... and so perished valiantly. Mercy did they deserve for their valor, could we have had the opportunity to bestow it."

Impressed but increasingly worried that a well-matched and protracted battle would allow another nearby Pequot group five miles away to arrive with reinforcements, Mason hastily abandoned the idea of saving the village for plunder and gave the order to surround the fort, preventing any Indian from escaping, and set fire to it. The fire, which immediately swept through the large wooden and thatched community, burned three hundred to six hundred Indians alive that tragic day. Underhill and

Mason were censured for their overwhelming and brutal action by some of the English, but they were more largely celebrated and sought-after by other European-American communities for their perceived proven ability to provide long-term protection from the Indians.

Underhill's ego inflated with this "victory," and to increase his newfound celebrity he sent a report entitled "News From America," to England and detailed it with the drawing shown above. Reflected in his report was his justifying belief that he had been a soldier of God, destroying Satan's agents. He compared his efforts to the wars of King David by explaining that, "when a people have . . . sinned against God and man, God does not respect these people, but harrows them, and saws them, and puts them to the sword and lets them have the most terrible death that may be. Sometimes the Scripture declares that women and children must perish with their parents . . . We had sufficient word from the light of God for our proceedings."[37] Like other Puritans, Underhill defined himself by contrasting his position in the world with that of others; he and other Europeans of his time searched for differences that set them apart and "proved" their superiority.

Reaction to and justification for Underhill's actions varied, but it was generally endorsed. John Mason claimed the act was necessary for self-preservation, and a contemporary observer, Philip Vincent, believed the Indians deserved such treatment for their aggressiveness toward the English. Cotton Mather, the minister of the Bay Colony at the time, questioned the Indians' very humanity; he opined that Satan had placed the Indians far from England in America on purpose, to hide them from the gospel of Christ, thus prolonging the devil's existence on earth, and delaying Christ's second coming. This threat would continue, he believed, until they were converted or removed.

A modern reviewer of these military events has noted that within the context of the time, Mason and Underhill's strategy was neither novel nor unconventional. The Pilgrim Colony at Plymouth also found no fault with Underhill's actions,[38] which further affirmed his belief that he was authorized biblically to act as he did, and which prompted him to engage in larger and more dangerous endeavors in the future.

Puritan doctrine was not conducive to converting the Indians religiously as the French Catholics were industriously doing in Canada for the Puritans saw little evidence these people were likely candidates for being "Elect." Native Americans were accepted into Puritan society as long as they partially assumed or accepted European standards of social civility, but, "the English, including Winthrop, neither sought nor found any merit in native customs and values."[39] Winthrop listed the religious conversion of the Indians fairly low on his list of priorities for his new colony, and little effort was made toward achieving this objective in the settlement's earliest years.

In the aftermath of the Mystic Massacre, surviving Pequots were pursued southward by Daniel Patrick. A large and final engagement occurred in Southport, Connecticut, where several hundred Pequots took refuge with the Sasqua Indians there by hiding within a great swamp now bisected by US Route One and I-95. Surrounded by Patrick and his soldiers and unable to escape from the swamp, eighty Indian men were killed, their families were distributed to other, non-Pequot Indian groups, and many of the fittest were sold into slavery in Bermuda. As noted by historian Steven T. Katz, this comprehensive destruction of the Pequot community was an act of both cultural and physical genocide to these people.

John Underhill and Daniel Patrick received greater civic censure for their sexual proclivities in the Bay Colony than they did for their military tactics. In 1638, the year after the Mystic Massacre, Boston magistrates questioned Underhill on how he, a married man with children, came to be found behind closed doors with his neighbor's wife on a Sunday.[40] The court recorded his ludicrous account that:

> . . . *the woman was very young and beautiful, and had a jovial spirit and behavior. He went to her house daily, and was at different times*

58

found there alone with her, the door being locked on the inside. He confessed it didn't look good, because it had the appearance of evil in it, but the woman was in great trouble of mind and liable to be tempted to do wrong. He went to her to comfort her, and that when the door was found locked upon them, they were in private prayer together.

His sexual escapades continued unabated at the Bay. He was again called into court,

. . . for committing adultery with the wife of one Joseph Febar, a cooper, and also for attempting the like with one Jane Howmes, the wife of a Robert Howmes of Cambridge, Husbandman, and also for reviling the Governor and other Magistrates, threatening revenge and destruction to the country, and writing slanderous lies to the State of England for that end. All of which he, the said Captain Underhill confessed, but not in such measure of humiliation, as might satisfy the church, in the truth of his repentance, answerable to his crimes, his confessions being mingled with sundry causeless self-justifyings, and some falsehood as saying he never abused the Scripture to draw any to sin. Whereas it was proved that he had incited some to folly or lewdness upon pretense to knock them off from their own righteousness, as the aforesaid Jane Howmes to whom he had confessed that, so he could knock off the said Febar's wife from her own righteousness.

He afterwards confessed his adultery, and in the year 1640 before a great assembly in Boston, on a lecture day in the courthouse, sat upon a stool of repentance with a white cap on his head, and with many deep sighs, a rueful countenance, and abundance of tears, owned his wicked way of life, his adultery and hypocrisy, and many expressions of sincere remorse, and besought the church to have compassion on him, and deliver him out of the hands of Satan. Yet the church considered his confession insincere and cast him out of their communion.

Church elders skeptically considered Underhill's assertion that his religious conversion had happened when he discovered the joys of smoking tobacco.

Winthrop lamented on Underhill's particularly false morality in that: [41]

> *All his confessions were mixed with such excuses and extenuations, as did not give satisfaction of the truth of his repentance, so as it seemed to be done more out of policy, and to pacify the sting of his conscience, than in sincerity. But however, his offences being so foul and scandalous, the church presently cast him out; which censure he seemed to submit unto, and for the time he stayed in Boston.*

Six months later church officers reinstated Underhill to church fellowship upon the proper acknowledgement of his many sins, but Daniel Patrick remained unrepentant.

DANIEL PATRICK

Daniel Patrick cheated on his twenty-year-old Dutch wife, Anneken, in much the same way John Underhill had cheated on his Dutch wife, Helena de Hooch. Patrick was accused of sexual assault on young Elizabeth Sturgis in Watertown, Massachusetts, when she wrote Governor John Winthrop Sr. with claims that Patrick had groped her repeatedly:[42]

> *First I, Elizabeth Sturgis, do affirm that when I lived with my Master Cummings, I was sent to Captain Patrick's to help his wife, and having business in the cellar, he came down presently after me, and took me about the middle and would kiss me and put his hand into my bosom, at which I was much amazed at his courage to me, being but young. Yet striving with him, he let me go. . . . Secondly, sometime after I was living at home with my Father, I went into*

the lot to gather some sucking stalks and he came suddenly upon me, and asked whether I (had accused him of doing those things). I said I had not meant to hurt him, and would speak no more about it. Then he offered to kiss me. I refused. He said unless I would kiss him, he would not believe that I would not speak of it again. Thirdly, sometime after I was married . . . he asked me to see his wife, which I did, and suddenly he came in and desired me to go into the next room to speak with me about our plantation and when I was there he came to kiss me. I desired him to forbear and told him such things were not fit, but he would and did, and would have me sit in his lap, but I did not. Then he told me it was lawful to express love to one another. Then I rose up to go away but he said I should wait since he had sent for sack, and I should drink with him. I told him I must be gone. He told me if he had time and opportunity he would convince me of the legality of his actions. I still desired to be gone, and he told me not to be offended, for if I loved him as much as he loved me, I would not take it so ill but would rather pity him rather than be offended. Then he was at me to meet him in the evening, in the way, where he would further labor to convince me of his love, but with much ado, I got away and presently made my Father and all the house acquainted with what had happened, and dared not go out into the way, at night, for fear.

Patrick wrote the governor to defend himself and variously noted that he had threatened Elizabeth's husband if he should spread the story, that it was his wife who was at fault, that she had no witnesses, and that it was only her word against his. Governor Winthrop was not placated by Patrick's further defenses that Elizabeth Sturgis's husband had it in for him, and that the governor shouldn't believe a word that she wrote. Henry Bond, a nineteenth-century historian, thoughtfully explains that: [43]

The governments of Boston and Hartford, Wethersfield and Windsor were harsh disciplinarians and the new world settlers chafed under the same corporal punishment system they disliked in Europe. In Massachusetts Bay Colony, common men felt themselves oppressed; the government was a meddlesome interference with themselves as individuals. They had come to America from a land of bondage, and to encounter all the annoyances which they had before in their new home, was of special aggravation to them.

Chapter Five

The Feakes and Patricks Leave the Bay Colony

When the English in Boston traded the threats they faced from their own in Europe for those they faced from their own in America, they were only jumping out of one frying pan and into another. As the restive English pushed further west and south from Boston, they now confronted the wildly divergent worldviews of the Indian and Dutch, who expected them to conform to two new sets of rules in addition to their increasingly inadequate old ones.

As the English population near Boston increased, John Winthrop saw new settlements establish themselves further away from Boston. These included the Connecticut Colony at Hartford and the New Haven Colony in New Haven. John Winthrop was upset with this southward migration, worried that the Puritans' model society was becoming spread too thin for effective control, and that his desired cohesive theology was becoming fragmented, as a variety of civil governing models were being instituted. His concept of a singular model society that could serve as an example for England to follow was becoming endangered. Restive settlers such as Roger Ludlowe, who disputed tenets of Winthrop's theology, explored and settled large tracts in Connecticut and had unsupervised interactions with Native Americans, which Winthrop believed had the potential to hurt a unified English response if the English faced more warfare. As Winthrop's jurisdictional control decreased, inter-colony skirmishes arose.

Roger Williams, a former Bay Colony man, should have been a Pilgrim instead of a Puritan, for he advocated for full separation from the Church of England. In disputing Winthrop though, he rightly pointed out that Puritan tenets that empowered just a few, the "Chosen" or "The Elect," to think and act for themselves were philosophically and logistically at odds with the needs of people who had to create a brand-new society, far removed from their governing authorities. He pointed out that the power of a few over many was as bad as the power of one over others, as had been the case in England, especially when the society in question lived in a wilderness that required them to govern for themselves. Williams, an insightful Indian sympathizer, also believed that lands granted to the colonists by the king of England were unjust because they had not been purchased from the Indians; simply, the land was not the king's to give away. Winthrop banished Williams, as he later would Anne Hutchinson, because he had the potential to disrupt Winthrop's fragile new civil government and his philosophical objectives.

An eager English population quickly moved beyond the Shawmut peninsula and founded Watertown to the west where the Feakes and Patricks lived, along with Charlestown and Newton. Anxious to explore further, settlers heard irresistible stories about the richness, beauty, and extent of the Connecticut River Valley and by 1634, English Massachusetts had spawned English Connecticut.

There were two major English settlements in Connecticut; at Hartford and New Haven. Hartford was located on the Connecticut River and was natively named "Sicaogg" by the local Indians called the Sequeens, perhaps pronounced the "Sekeens." The English first named Hartford "Newtowne," but then quickly changed it to Hartford to commemorate the English birthplace of John Stone, the shady personality who served to ignite the Pequot War with the English.

The Dutch wistfully named their Hartford fort "Huys de Hoop," or the "House of Hope," and this outpost was an important engine that drove the Dutch fur trade. The small fort, which housed only fifteen soldiers at most, was located on modern Dutch Point in Hartford, and appropriately near today's Huyshoep Avenue. This location took advantage of Pequots' production and control of wampum or seawant and it gave the Dutch a currency to trade for fur trapped by the more inland Mohawk, who attached great value to the beads, perhaps that of a spiritual nature. The Dutch traded hard European goods like kettles, copper sheets, and woolen "duffels," a canvas-type cloth, to the Pequot for seawant, and then in turn traded Pequot seawant for Mohawk-hunted fur pelts. Dutch defenses and manpower were weak near Hartford however, and English people quickly settled all around the Connecticut River without encountering much if any Dutch resistance. New Haven, further south of Hartford, was also originally settled by the Dutch for trading, and they had named it "Rhoodebergh" or "Red Hill" for the large red mountain that continues to distinguish this town geologically.

Once the Dutch had more or less capitulated in their effort to control the Connecticut River at Hartford and Indian resistance had become more manageable, a few English Watertown settlers founded the town of Wethersfield, only a short distance south of Hartford on the west bank of the Connecticut River. Adventurous Wethersfield settlers further split away from the Hartford area and settled Stamford, in southwestern Connecticut, which they logically called the "Wethersfield Mens' Plantation" before they rechristened it Stamford.

John Winthrop's resistance to English expansion throughout Connecticut factored in the technicality that neither Hartford nor New Haven had been granted a governing charter from the Crown, as had Boston. If such expansion was ever to be seriously challenged by the Dutch, the English king could interfere and more closely investigate the principles and practices of his American settlements. In fact such an authorized governing charter took almost twenty more years to occur, and it was not until 1662 that Saybrook, Hartford, and New Haven Colony territories merged under a Crown-approved charter that identified the large region (now collectively called Connecticut) as a distinctive English territory.

When Elizabeth's sister, Martha Fones, died three years after her marriage to John Winthrop Jr., the newly widowed John Jr. returned to England to meet with many of his academic friends who were scientists, geologists, and medically interested men and to find a new wife. There he discovered the vivacious, eighteen-year-old Elizabeth Reade. The couple, who would remain married for the next thirty-seven years, returned to Boston the following year and by 1645 at the age of forty, John and his new wife founded the town of New London at the mouth of the Thames River on the Connecticut coast. Natively, New London was called "Nameag" at the time and the modern-day Thames River in New London was called the "Pequot" for the Indians who controlled the majority of coastal Connecticut. John Winthrop Jr. also named his new farm "Pequot," and the regional area "Groton" (Connecticut), in honor of his family's English home.

While his home and farm buildings were being constructed, John Jr. moved his growing family to Fisher's Island in Long Island Sound in the fall of 1646, and was cajoled into accepting election as a magistrate of Massachusetts, which still had jurisdiction over the area of Connecticut. Men of John Jr.'s education, status, and positive personality were in strong demand in the new colonies, and he was widely admired and respected.

Robert and Elizabeth Feake also began entertaining the idea of moving away from Watertown to further explore the country as had many of their neighbors. Elizabeth hoped they could live near John Jr. and Elizabeth in Wethersfield (confusingly also called Watertowne at first). The thought of living near John Jr., who was her friend, closest relative, and medical expert in the region, appealed possibly because of Robert's further mental debilitation. If a move to Weathersfield did not work out, the Feakes also considered moving to Concord, Massachusetts.[44] John Jr. did in fact choose not to move to Wethersfield since the deadly skirmish related to the Pequot

War had broken out there in the spring of 1637. Commenting on their relocation plans to John Jr., Robert Feake referenced his increasing mental issues that would ultimately cause him to abandon his young family:[45]

> *To the Worshipfull John A. Winthrop, Esquire, at Connecticut, give this. Watertown, this 5th July, 1636*
> *Loving and Kind Brother . . . I confess that we are to blame that we have not written to you all this time, but I suppose that you knew of occasions and distractions we have been in by reason we were altogether unsettled, you would then excuse us & bear with us for it. Assure yourself it is not of want for love to you or unmindfullness of you. You write to us to know our minds, which, when I received your letter I did not know my own mind, but . . . we are resolved again for Connecticut, & therefore I have now sent my man to mow grass there for to winter my cattle, and to get what housing he can there, . . . I propose, God willing, in the Spring to come there with my wife and family. I should be glad to hear that you will be set down there too, that if God please, we may enjoy your company there to dwell, which I do protest would be great comfort to me . . .*
> *Your truly loving brother, Robert Feke*

Robert and Elizabeth were not fully committed to moving in 1636 and they remained in Watertown three years longer. Their neighbor, Daniel Patrick, was restless remaining near Boston where he had suffered multiple public humiliations that overshadowed his military value. It was during this time that he chose to take out some of his resentment on John Winthrop by signing the petition[46] that supported the views of Anne Hutchinson, whom Winthrop would soon banish from the Bay.

ANNE HUTCHINSON

Within the Bay the debate continued about how Puritanism should be most properly practiced. Reformists argued over how their ministers should be ordained, the reasons for and against infant baptisms (which addressed the larger question of when one's Elect status was conferred by God), and the standards to which a revelatory experience must conform to qualify as significant enough to merit church membership.[47] They argued over the required level of purity for their church and the degree of depravity they assigned to the Roman Catholic Church. They also addressed discrimination among non-church members, because colonists who were not Elect resented paying taxes to support the ministers and churches of the Elect, as well they might, for it was like having to pay dues to a country club they could not access.[48]

Anne Hutchinson was accustomed to confronting authority such as Winthrop's, for her father, Thomas Marbury, had been jailed in England for his many dissenting religious opinions. Proud of her heritage and her Elect status to a fault, Anne's argument was both theological and political in nature since religion and politics then were inseparable. She held that her adherence or disobedience to man's laws had no effect on her Elect status nor would the number of times she attended church, the number of good works she accomplished, the number of gifts of charity she bestowed to the church or to individuals, or the number of hours she devoted to studying the Bible.[49] She also asserted that no minister was needed to interpret one's state of grace; it was an act of self-realization and a minister was just an obstacle between an individual and God. She took this view, according to biographer Charles Adams, because the Puritans held that the Bible—not the church or church administrators—was the ultimate authority and expression of God's word. The danger in Anne's thinking, however, was the danger inherent in John Calvin's concept of predestination, which was that one's human outcome is pre-programmed by God and no events in life will alter one's course. Anne accordingly proposed that since she was Elect, she would achieve salvation regardless of her adherence to man's laws. Many libertines have also found cover for their amoral behavior by taking refuge in this interpretation of Calvin's concept, and one can see why Daniel Patrick and John Underhill found justification for their actions through it.

John Winthrop and his ministers were less strict in their interpretation of Calvin and allowed the idea that through diligent good works on earth *plus* adherence to man's laws one expressed one's high status with God and with one's community on earth. Indeed, Winthrop needed people to come together and help each other selflessly in building their new society and, as in modern times, he could not allow divisive class distinctions within his community that exempted some people from following society's rules.

Anne, an adamant, outspoken, and confident person, was brought to court for vehemently contesting those ministers who allowed that good works would improve one's status. She pushed John Winthrop to his limit when she additionally claimed, to the disapproval of all of the clergy, that she had the unique metaphysical power of being able to perceive the Elect state in others.[50] She claimed outright that she was above the law as one of the Elect, by saying, "As I understand it, laws, commands, rules and edict are for those who have not the light which makes plain the pathway," which meant that since she was predestined to achieve salvation, early Boston's rules just didn't apply to her.[51] This quote oddly adorns the base of her statue in Boston in casting her as an early feminist. She was a feminist in that as a woman, she was one of the first to fight for religious freedom as she argued for alternate religious interpretations. She can also be said to have championed free speech in her public preaching; women were prohibited from this activity because of the very old grudge men held against women when Eve corrupted Adam in the Garden of Eden. Her lectures attracted large crowds of people and she garnered a number of prestigious supporters. The quote used on her statue, however, references neither of these achievements; its context is her promotion of greater social segregation and division.

She fiercely lobbied for greater class distinction for the Elect, and even demanded separated building entries and church services for the Elect and the non-Elect. She argued against combined church attendance of the Elect and non-Elect, for the futility of preaching to "the thorns among the lilies," as the thorns had no hope of ever changing their status.

Winthrop knew it was critical to maintain order and discipline in his fledgling colony, and was quite pragmatic about it. He advocated for a greater inclusiveness, that people should work with those in whom the smallest measure of godliness could be detected, and to "cover the rest with love." Anne's other controversial assertions were that she was a prophetess and able to predict the future, and that she had powers that far superseded those of ordained Puritan ministers. Winthrop assessed Hutchinson as a dissenter who posed a dangerous threat to the colony's governance and its theological cohesion, which was true enough.

But Winthrop made some unsettling assertions himself that redress Anne's unflattering social snobism and cast him as a heartless misogynist, or having an extremely male-centric worldview, even for his time. This unfairly removes him from the context of his culture, but his actions do mitigate one's unreserved affections. He gloated over a miscarriage of one of Anne's supporters named Mary Dyer and opined that her malformed fetus was proof of the devil's interaction with Anne and all of her friends. He tested the limits of modern sensibilities when he concluded that the mental illness of a woman within another colony was the result of too much education and he opined that women should know their place and never stray far from it. Anne Hutchinson and John Winthrop brought out the worst in each other, as they resorted to arrogance, anger, and condescension to further their competitive views and it is ironic that it was their very humanity that diminished them both in their obsessive quest to be the one who pleased God most.

John Cotton, one of Winthrop's magistrates, condemned Anne's disruptions and argued for her dismissal from the Bay because "her opinions fret like a gangrene and spread like a leprosy and infect far and near and will eat out the very bowels of religion and has so infected the churches that only God knows when they will be cured." Being in agreement Winthrop banished Anne, "the breeder and nourisher of all these distempers," and her large family from Massachusetts, along with others who agreed with her, which included John Underhill, Daniel Patrick, and their very young families.

CHAPTER SIX

"She lives where all good means are wanting"

KICKED OUT OF THE MASSACHUSETTS BAY COLONY FOR HIS LONG LEGACY of sexual offenses, topped off by his final act of insurrection by siding with Anne Hutchinson, Daniel Patrick began looking for a new job and a new beginning for his family in a territory far removed from Boston. He knew that Englishmen from Wethersfield had just established an offshoot of the New Haven Colony called the "Wethersfield Men's Plantation," now Stamford, which was located conveniently close to the Dutch on Manhattan Island. New Haven Colony's land purchasing agent, Captain Nathaniel Turner, had just purchased Stamford, or "all the land at Rippowams and Toquams,"[52] for this new settlement which would be under New Haven Colony jurisdiction and would receive whatever religious, economic, judicial, and military support New Haven could provide. The Stamford plantation was purchased on July 1, 1640, from Munsee Indian sachems named Ponus and Toquamske.

Daniel and his Dutch wife Anneken likely loved this greater proximity to the Dutch in a small English settlement far removed from a larger English settlement at New Haven. It was a location that was difficult to oversee by either its Dutch or English administrators, and it was a perfect situation for an antisocial soldier who found his wings clipped too closely by the Puritans. English-born Daniel was well versed in Dutch language, customs, and military tactics and had a wife who was fully Dutch but had lived among the English for many years; the two could live easily under either jurisdiction. Daniel may have moved close to Manhattan to become a mercenary, alternately selling his soldiering skills to New Netherland or to the fledgling Stamford settlement which, in reality, would receive little protection from New Haven forty miles away up the coast. Why the respectable Elizabeth and Robert Feake joined forces with this irresponsible, irreverent, and outspoken soldier is less clear.

Since the Feakes were "richly endowed with plowland and meadow" in Watertown,[53] employed a maid, and had received generous land grants in the first land distributions of the town, the decision to move with the Patricks and to jointly purchase new property with them in uncharted territory must have hinged on highly personal reasons. Perhaps Elizabeth's friend and neighbor, the cuckolded Anneken Patrick, who was six months pregnant at the time, pleaded with her friend Elizabeth to move away with her, as she needed Elizabeth's medical skills to see her through her impending birth, and was frightened to move alone with her loutish husband and small children into an unknown frontier. It's possible, but not probable, that Robert Feake supported Anne Hutchinson.

Robert was an educated gentleman and his family in England was well-to-do but religiously divided. His cousin, Christopher Feake,[54] was against the Puritans and he preached violently against the Puritan leader, Oliver Cromwell, in 1653, and was jailed in Windsor Castle for it, to the detriment of his wife and eight children. Robert, on the other hand, agreed with the Puritans' views and John Winthrop shared his library with Robert, including a treatise called *One Hundred Sermons on the Apocalypse*,[55] that had been owned by Adam Winthrop, John's father.

More likely is the possibility that an unstable Robert was encouraged and influenced by his friend and former military superior, Daniel Patrick, and felt safe and secure around him. The Feakes, perhaps ostracized in Watertown because of Robert's unraveling mental state, decided to move from Watertown under the strong arm and bluster of Daniel, their unruly friend and politically incorrect neighbor. Daniel may have felt unchallenged by Robert, a gentleman with issues who looked to him for guidance and protection in his unstable mental landscape. Elizabeth, for her part, perhaps saw Daniel Patrick as an uncouth yet able leader and only warily agreed to move with him deep into the wilderness of southwestern Connecticut to placate her husband and her friend.

Only eighteen days after New Haven's purchasing agent Nathaniel Turner bought Stamford for the New Haven Colony, Daniel Patrick independently bought half of nearby Norwalk, although he never fully paid for it, from an Indian named Mamechimo; Robert's nephew, teenager Tobias Feake, served as a witness. Daniel then pooled his remaining funds with Robert Feake to jointly purchase land the Munsees had called "Petuckquapoch," which was located two and one half miles southwest of the Stamford settlement.[56] A Stamford settler named Jeffrey Ferris had previously purchased land in this area from a Munsee named Keofferam, but Ferris was an absentee owner of this meadowland and he continued to live in the safer confines of the English Stamford settlement.

Elizabeth Feake bought all of Greenwich Point, then called "Monakeywaygo," with her own money. Daniel Patrick and Robert Feake jointly bought all the land between the "Asamuck" creek, which runs through modern-day Binney Park in Old Greenwich, Connecticut, and the "Patoumuck" creek, which flows to Tomac Cove near the modern Stamford/Greenwich boundary. Their purchase may have run inland for perhaps twenty miles or as commonly directed, "as far as an Indian can go in a day." The couples renamed Petuckquapoch "Greenwich," and it was separated from Stamford's English jurisdiction by the Patoumuck River, which "divided ye bounds between Capt. Turner's Purchase and this."

This territory, beyond the bounds of Turner's purchase of land for the New Haven Colony, meant that Greenwich was beyond the jurisdiction of the New Haven Colony. Greenwich, unlike Stamford, was only casually and informally associated with the New Haven Colony through a later verbal request for Indian protection by Robert Feake. New Haven magistrates, aware that the property was an easy sail from Fort Amsterdam, did not officially induct the town[57] as one of their sanctioned satellite colonies in 1640, realizing they ran the risk of overtly antagonizing New Netherland into military action.

The Patricks and Feakes began living their lives beyond the bounds of the Stamford settlement in Greenwich, uncertain as to whether New England or New Netherland would officially claim the right to rule their lives and property. They likely knew that New Netherland had been unable to secure its borders throughout Connecticut, and may have thought chances were reasonable that their Greenwich residency would be ignored by the Dutch. The Dutch, however, had noted the attractiveness of their claim by recording:[58] "The country on the East River [Long Island Sound] between Greenwich and the island Manhattens is for the most part covered with trees, but yet flat and suitable land, with numerous streams and valleys, right good soil for grain, together with fresh hay and meadow lands."

Wives rarely bought land independent of their husband's,[59] but Elizabeth emphasized her singular ownership of Monakeywaygo by renaming her land "Elizabeth's Neck." She likely purchased it with money she had earned through her midwifery and apothecary treatments and did so to safeguard her children's future inheritance, "for her heirs and assigns," the deed reads, in light of Robert's instability and the uneasy character of Daniel Patrick.

Daniel Patrick's decision to purchase property with the Feakes outside of Stamford settlement boundaries, to become an "outliver," was not by accident. He was forced to move beyond the territory authorized for purchase by the New Haven Colony for, as Governor Winthrop noted, he had not been released from his church in Watertown, Massachusetts, so was not free to join another, and therefore not entitled to be involved in Stamford's governance.

Stamford was a relatively well-organized community, with fifty-eight households by the early 1640s. The original Stamford settlement was clustered near the current intersection of Main and Atlantic Streets, where the Stamford Town Center shopping complex is now located.

The Patrick and Feake homesteads were very near Tomac Cove, within easy sight of Dutch scouts exploring Long Island Sound, and most likely the Feake and Patrick homes were built along the shore path that led from Greenwich Point to Stamford's harbor along today's Shore Road. Dutch explorer David DeVries wrote of sighting the Feake and Patrick homes in 1640 near Tomac Cove from Long Island Sound:[60]

The 16th weighed anchor, and sailed by two places which the English were building up [Stratford], and about noon arrived where two Englishmen had built houses. One of the Englishmen was named Captain Patrick, whose wife was a Holland woman from The Hague. After we had been there two or three hours, we proceeded on our voyage, and towards evening reached the Minates [Manhattan], before Fort Amsterdam, where we found two ships had arrived from our Fatherland.

When Elizabeth Fones Winthrop Feake, now thirty years old, arrived in Tomac Cove in a shallop, a large yet light masted row boat, she arrived with her first child by Henry Winthrop, ten-year-old Martha Johana Winthrop, along with Elizabeth Feake, aged seven, Hannah Feake, three, and John Feake, who was only a toddler of two years. Robert had brought along his teenaged nephew Tobias, but his sister Judith had married a man named William Palmer and she had stayed in Massachusetts to raise her family. The Patricks arrived with Daniel Patrick Jr., six-year-old Annetje, and four-year-old Patientia (or Patience); three months after their arrival, on October 21, 1640, baby Beatrice Patrick was born. Robert Feake Jr. was born one year after Elizabeth's arrival, and sometime in 1647 her sixth child, Sarah Feake, was born.

Baptismal records for the Reformed Dutch church that was located within the Dutch fort on the southern tip of Manhattan show that Daniel Patrick sailed there to baptize his children as Dutch citizens and two years later, on July 16, 1642, Robert Feake and Daniel Patrick sailed there again to baptize their newest sons, Samuel Patrick and Robert Feake Jr. Five years later on August 2, 1647, Sarah Feake was baptized there as well.[61] This would make Beatrice and Samuel Patrick, and Robert and Sarah Feake the first European children born within Dutch Greenwich.

Stamford also attracted the attention of the Dutch, who warily noted the proximity between Fort Amsterdam on the southern tip of Manhattan Island and this extension of the New Haven Colony, "from whence one could travel now in a summer's day to the North River [Hudson River] and back again, if one knows the Indian path."[62]

The Indians who lived in Petuckquapock, Toquams, and Rippowams had also found Greenwich and Stamford attractive for the past seven thousand years or so and they resented the new European presence. They were the Weichquaesgeck (Weck-as-gecks or Weck-as-queeks), a Munsee group who had migrated to America's Northeast from Delaware. Their hostilities toward the area's local Europeans had been exacerbated for years by poor Dutch management of their trading relationship in the "tri-state," or southern New York, Connecticut, and northern New Jersey areas. The Feakes and Patricks were particularly unnerved when an attack occurred soon after their arrival, which brought the ongoing Dutch and Munsee conflict to the forefront of the new settlement's concerns.

Governor Winthrop wrote of an Indian attack on an English woman in Stamford during Elizabeth and Robert's first two years in Greenwich:[63]

At Stamford an Indian [named Busheag] came into a poor man's house, none being at home but the wife, and a child in the cradle, and taking up a lathing hammer as if he would have bought it, the woman stooping down to take her child out of the cradle, he struck her with the

David Devries, Kieft critic and Indian diplomat and sympathizer JOHN THOMAS
SCHARF, *A HISTORY OF WESTCHESTER COUNTY* (PHILADELPHIA: L.E. PRESTON & COMPANY,
1886, 2 VOLS.) 1:35

sharp edge upon the side of her head, wherewith she fell down, and then he gave her two cuts more which pierced into her brains, and so left her for dead, carrying away some clothes which lay at hand. This woman, after a short time came to herself and got out to a neighbor's house, and told what had been done to her, and described the Indian by his person and clothes, etc. Whereupon many Indians of those parts were brought before her, and she charged one of them confidently to be the man, whereupon he was put in prison with intent to have him put to death, but he escaped, and the woman recovered, but lost her senses. A good time after, the Indians brought another Indian whom they charged to have committed that act, and he, upon examination, confessed it, and gave the reason thereof, and brought forth some of the clothes he had stolen. Upon this the magistrates of New Haven, taking advice of the elders in those parts, and some here, did put him to death. The executioner would strike off his head with a falchion, but he had eight blows at it before he could affect it, and the Indian sat upright and stirred not all the time.

Stamford hired the job-seeking, ex–Bay Colony, Mystic massacre mustermaster John Underhill in 1642 to protect them from further attacks. While Stamford society was well aware of Underhill's louche reputation, which made more than a few of them feel uneasy, they satisfied their moral consciences with the technical fact that Underhill had been reinstated by the Boston church and was again a "freeman," thus able to participate as a governor or magistrate of their small community. Their moral sensitivity was overridden by their great need to have him protect their families from a rising tide of native Munsee hostility that they perceived, perhaps inaccurately, threatened their very survival. The town offered him good wages, free housing, and land. John and his wife Helena may also have wanted to live closer to the Dutch on Manhattan, for John's sister, Petronella, lived in New Amsterdam and was married to a

Dutchman there named Ulrich Leopold. When John and Helena arrived in Stamford, they brought Deborah, Elizabeth, and newborn son John Underhill Jr. with them.

ELIZABETH FEAKE AND DANIEL PATRICK SUBMIT TO DUTCH SOVEREIGNTY

Just three months after the Feakes and Patricks purchased their land from the area's Munsees in 1640, Dutch director-general William Kieft of Fort Amsterdam took decisive action concerning their tiny unaffiliated settlement and demanded they acknowledge themselves to be within Dutch jurisdiction. Governor Kieft "sent the vandrager [an ensign] and soldiers and required them to submit to the government or avoid the place." He issued the following protest:[64]

> *I, William Kieft, Director-General of New Netherland, notify you, Captain Daniel Patrick, or whom it may concern, and belongs to their High Mightinesses, so that hereafter you may not pretend any cause of ignorance. We order and warn you in default thereof, we protest against all damages, losses and interests which may accrue therefrom.*
> *On the Island of Manhattan, in Fort Amsterdam, Oct. 15, 1640.*

The Dutch had decided to defend a northeastern mainland boundary, and they decided that this line would be the small creek that ran between the small, undefended, and unassociated Feake-Patrick property and the larger New Haven Colony–affiliated Stamford settlement. The Dutch had become distinctly uneasy now that English authorities associated with large defendable colonies had begun purchasing land and creating significant English settlements near defendable Dutch territory. When the New Haven Colony established Stamford, and claimed it to be under English jurisdiction, this meant they might defend it with small but effective English militias, which would further erode Dutch land claims and send a message of easy military capitulation. Without Dutch resistance, Manhattan, which was a simple half-day's sail away, might be the next English target. The affronted Dutch became determined to stop any further border erosion at Greenwich and the English in New Haven offered no objection or resistance to this Dutch action, having no significant military force at the time to stand up to them.

Daniel Patrick knew the arrangement that he and the Feakes had with New Haven Colony wasn't a strong claim for English jurisdiction, and he certainly did not want to incur a fine for his trespass. Thus, when he was brought before Kieft's lieutenants at the fort, he replied diplomatically to Kieft's missive:

> *We shall not do anything in the least which will contravene their High Mightinesses, the Lords States' rights to any lands of theirs in New Netherlands, yet . . . until the matter be more clear that this is the States land on which we live, we dare not give any other answer to this protest.*
> *Signed Daniel Patrick*
> *Witnesses; Willem Kieft, Ulderick Lupolt, Oloff Stevenson.*

When Daniel Patrick and Elizabeth Feake agreed to cede to Dutch jurisdiction, there really wasn't much choice. Robert Feake objected but Elizabeth and Daniel overrode him, recognizing his increasing mental instability, fearing the Dutch threat of force against them, and knowing their need for protection from the Indians. Effectively with a gun to his head, Daniel Patrick sailed alone to Fort Amsterdam on April 9, 1642, to sign and swear Feake and Patrick allegiance.[65]

> *Whereas we, Captain Daniel Patrick and Elizabeth Feake, duly authorized by her husband Robert Feake, now sick, have resided two years about five or six miles (Dutch) east of the Netherlands, subjects*

of the Lords State General, who have protested against us, declaring that the said land lay within their limits, and that they should not suffer any person to usurp it against their lawful rights; and whereas, we have equally persisted in our course, during these two years, having been well assured that His Majesty, King of England had pretended some right to this soil; and whereas, we understand nothing thereof, and cannot longer presume to remain thus, on account both of the strifes of the English, the danger consequent thereon, and these treacherous and villainous Indians, of whom we have seen sorrowful examples enough. We therefore, betake ourselves under the Protection of the Noble Lords States General, his Highness the Prince of Orange, and the West India Company, or their Governor General of New Netherland, promising, for the future to be faithful to them, as all honest subjects are bound to be. Whereunto we bind ourselves by solemn oath and signature, provided we are protected against our enemies as much as possible, and enjoy henceforth the same privileges that all Patroons of New Netherland have obtained agreeably to the freedoms.

In Fort Amsterdam, ninth day of April, 1642.
Daniel Patrick
Witness.
Everardus Bogardus
Johannes Winkelman

Kieft changed the name of their land from "Greenwich" to a Dutch approximation spelled "Groenwits"[66] (pronounced "Groonvits") to assert its Dutch jurisdiction more concretely. Now, the eastern border of Robert and Elizabeth Feake's property, the Patoumuck Creek, which flows to Tomac Cove through today's Innis Arden golf course, gained newfound importance. Not only did it mark the Feake-Patrick's eastern border with Stamford, but it became the defended border between New

Netherland and New England. In purchasing her land at Monakey-waygo, Elizabeth Fones Winthrop Feake had moved to the very edge of New England.

In acknowledging Dutch jurisdiction over the Feakes' portion of property, Elizabeth acted as a legally recognized entity for her incapacitated husband. Robert Feake's mental illness caused her to assume many duties usually accorded to a male head of household at the time, and she acted in the manner of a "deputy husband," a qualified and respected double for her husband. While womens' roles were primarily domestic, they were authorized by their culture to act as surrogate husbands when necessary, although some surely disliked doing so and others lacked the necessary skills.[67]

Wives had the right to assume responsibilities for the administration of their families' affairs, such as paying taxes, supervising assets and conducting property sales and acquisitions. Educated wives such as Elizabeth, who knew how to read, write, and run a business, were considered capable of managing properties that their male heirs would ultimately inherit. By the winter of 1647, perhaps caused by some untenable event that occurred near or after their infant daughter Sarah's death, Robert Feake and Elizabeth agreed it was necessary that he abandon her and their children in (Old) Greenwich and return to Watertown to be cared for by the deacon Samuel Thatcher. In making this decision, Elizabeth must have felt that she and her family were safer or more functional without him than with him, even though it meant she was left to carry on alone. Managing her family and her farm now without any male assistance, Elizabeth surely must have felt challenged by making such a profound decision, given the dangers of living near a hostile native population and living on the cusp of a jurisdictionally disputed border between English and Dutch societies. Soon, however, and to her great surprise, she would come to experience more direct and devastating attacks from those within her own family.

CHAPTER SEVEN

New Netherland

IN THE EARLY 1620S, A DUTCH CORPORATION HELD VERY DIFFERENT ideas about how northeastern America might best be used, and it focused on generating profit through fur trading rather than on religious experiments designed to improve the quality of life on earth and in heaven. The legislature of Holland, the States-General of the Netherlands, had granted West India Company the exclusive right to trade in America. In America's Hudson River area, the company planned to create profits through the export of animal pelts from America to Europe and it eyed a whopping amount of land for these operations that reached from Delaware to the Barnegat Bay in Maine.[68] The company named this huge swath of land "New Netherland," after its Dutch homeland, and its claim rested on the discovery and occupation of this land rather than on any specific grant of territory from a sovereign nation.

In 1624, on the southern tip of Manhattan Island, the Dutch established Fort Amsterdam and planned for the Hudson River, the Connecticut River, and the Delaware River to become profitable trade routes.

Dutch and English battles for northeastern American real estate began even before the Pilgrims arrived in Plymouth, for ten years before Winthrop's Puritans arrived in Boston the Dutch burghers, or executives, who controlled the West India Company got wind of the Pilgrims' original desire to settle in the Hudson River region, and they worked to scuttle this objective. Through orchestrated delays and faulty shipbuilding, the Dutch company caused the English Pilgrims to land much farther east of

Detail of Fort Amsterdam on map cartouche. Novi Belgii Novaeque Angliae, Justus Danckerts. LIBRARY OF CONGRESS

them, at Cape Cod in Massachusetts Bay, preventing any early English settlement near Manhattan.[69]

By 1640, when the Feakes and Patricks moved into southwestern Connecticut, the West India Company limited the money and manpower they supplied to defend this vast territory. It was making more money in its Caribbean, South American, and South African outposts and it didn't want to spend the large sums required to transition New Netherland in America from simple trading outposts into a complex and sophisticated Dutch society complete with churches, courts, schools, hospitals, and otherwise fully supported infrastructures.

The Dutch, stretched too thin even in their earliest days, were not able to cope with the vast scope of this new world, and could not defend the area around their trading outpost named "Fort Good Hope" at Hartford against the English. The Dutch also did not defend any border near their New Haven area trading fort, "Rhoodebergh" or "Red Hill," and by the early 1640s almost five thousand English people had settled within areas of the Northeast claimed as belonging to New Netherland. Enforceable Dutch power became most concentrated near Fort Amsterdam in Manhattan, along the Hudson River, and to a lesser extent in Albany, New York.

Adrien van der Donck, a West India Company critic who advocated for the Dutch to build full-scale communities in America, but ultimately lost his prescient argument, wryly commented on the attempts of the company's director to enforce Dutch land claims in interior Connecticut against a growing English population. He mockingly wrote, "The Director has caused several protests to be drawn up . . . commanding them to desist from their usurpations, and warning them off. But, it was like knocking on a deaf man's door, as they did not regard these protests, or even take any notice of them."[70] The eastern border between New Netherland and New England was steadily pushed closer toward the area of southwestern Connecticut until the line in the sand that would become New Netherland's eastern border was drawn with the Feake and Patrick purchase in Greenwich.

New Netherland's managing director at this time was the autocratic and often irrational William Kieft, who governed from 1638 to 1647. Kieft, as directed by the company, was only prepared and equipped to deal with the territory as a trading outpost and to run it on a shoestring. He tried, unsuccessfully, to maintain a tightly controlled trading environment, to keep company profits up, and to keep administrative matters firmly within company control. In theory, one had to be authorized by the company to conduct trade with the Indians, under highly specific conditions, with established rules. This was a good way to begin, and things worked fairly well for the company's first twenty years in America (though not for the local animal population), however the European population within Dutch-controlled communities remained quite small in comparison to the number of English people settling all around them. In far-flung regions that were hard to police, rogue traders swindled the Indians and the company out of payment, which set the stage for valid and dramatic accusations of theft, murder, robbery, rape, and increased trading hostilities.

Fur was extremely valuable for clothing, as woven cloth was still limited, handmade, and produced on a small scale. Only the extremely wealthy had many articles of clothing, and animal pelts were a valued supplement. Between 1624 and 1635, the number of beaver and otter pelts sold to Europe increased from forty-seven hundred to over sixteen thousand annually, with a rising price per pelt.[71] In November of 1624 the cargo of a ship sailing to New Amsterdam listed an amazing number of pelts trapped by the Indians including 7,246 beaver skins, 675 otter skins, 48 of mink, 36 of wild cat and assorted others; by 1656, more than eighty thousand animals were killed annually. Between June and September of 1657 alone, almost forty-one thousand beaver and otter pelts were shipped from New Netherland to Holland.[72] The Dutch themselves never actively trapped animals, but served as brokers and salesmen between Indian procurers and European purchasers.

The Visscher Map of New Netherland

Early Dutch maps show the mix of Dutch, English, and Indian names used to describe southwestern Connecticut in the mid-1600s. Nicholeas Visscher was a Dutch cartographer who had been hired by Adrien van der Donck some years after he lived near Albany, and on Manhattan, to create a map of New Netherland, as Van der Donck reported it. Visscher drew one of the earliest maps of America's Northeast in 1661, revised in 1665, which is called "Novi Belgii," or "New Netherland."

A close-up of this map focusing on the Greenwich and Stamford area shows a number of familiar and unfamiliar names. One can easily discern "Manhattans" for Manhattan, "Lange Eyeland" for Long Island, "Stamfort" for Stamford, and "Strotfort" for Stratford. You can almost hear the Dutch accent. A close-up view of southwestern Connecticut displays the additional words Siwanoys, Betuck-qua-pock, Naniechiestawack, and Groeobis.

Northeastern Indian scholar Robert Grumet offers evidence that the word "Siwanoy" was an Indian group name meaning "southerners," and was misplaced on the mainland in the region of southwestern Connecticut by Visscher. There is some deed evidence that suggests to Grumet that this Indian group should more properly be placed on

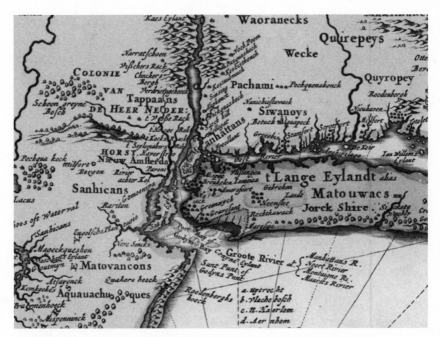

The Greenwich and Stamford area in 1650 as seen on the Novi Belgii map

eastern Long Island near the Shinnecocks, and there is one other Dutch map showing the name "Siwanoy" placed in the waters of Long Island Sound.[73] Adrien van der Donck, who commissioned the map based on his contemporary experience with these groups, reported, however, that the "Siavanoos" lived south of the Dutch on Manhattan and the word may refer to either the Shawnee or the Delaware. In either case, it seems clear that the printer misplaced the word "Siwanoy" on this map and that they did not live in the area of southwestern Connecticut. The Weichquaesgeck, however, definitely did live in the area including that of Greenwich, Connecticut. "Petuckquapock" was their name for the Feake-Patrick purchase, represented as "Betuckquapock," which is clearly seen next to Stamford.

The word "Groeobis," shown placed next to Stamford, is another type-setter's error in spelling the word "Groenwits," the Dutch renaming word for Greenwich. "Naniechiestawack" has a meaning that is not documented, and some nineteenth-century linguists suggest it may have been a large for-tified Indian village, called a "castle" by the English. (Nearby North Castle, NY, and other New England towns that were settled early with the word "castle" in their names presumably refer to these protected Indian villages.) From this map, one can see how modern place names changed from their original Dutch names: "Breukelen," for Brooklyn, and "Staten Eylant" for Staten Island, named after the Dutch governing body, the States-General. Notice the five-pointed fort of New Amsterdam at Manhattan's southern tip. Notice also on Long Island "Vlishingen," which is modern day "Flush-ing," and an over-large point at "Mispat," or Mespath on Long Island. Along the Hudson River you can see the locations of "Hellgat," Elizabeth Feake's future home, along with the words Weichquaesgeck and "Alip-konck," a large Weichquaesgeck village in Dobbs Ferry, New York.

Long Island Sound was called the "Oost" or East River by the Dutch and it was called the tongue-twisting "Manunketesuc" by Sound-shore groups of Indians. The Hudson River was called "Muhheahkkunnuck," or Mahican-ituck, the Mahican's river, or alternatively, the "River that Flows Both Ways," by Native Americans. The Dutch first called the Hudson the "Rivier Mauritius," which didn't stick, then the Noortrivier or "North River," until the English gained supremacy over the area, at which time it was called Hudson's River. In Elizabeth Feake's Connecticut, there was a Dutch, Munsee, and English name for everything.

INDIAN TURMOIL WITHIN NEW NETHERLAND

The Indians near Manhattan were convulsed with the changes thrust upon them by the European influx. Besides the introduction of alcohol, firearms, and new diseases into their societies, they now had to contend with dispossession of their lands, new systems of fur trade and land sales, new interracial relationships, political gamesmanship between the Europeans, and a new balance of power between Indian groups. As if this weren't enough, they had to continue managing traditional Indian warfare, now additionally layered with political and tactical complexity.

Munsee territory stretched over twelve thousand miles, from the Atlantic Ocean to one hundred miles inland of the Appalachian Mountains. It encompassed western Long Island Sound, southwestern Connecticut, southeastern New York, northern New Jersey, and northeastern Pennsylvania. The borders of these regions were fluid and porous and the Munsees welcomed other groups into their lands for trade and marriage. People who spoke a closely related dialect of Delaware called Northern Unami lived just to the south, in central New Jersey and adjacent portions of southeastern Pennsylvania. Those north and east of the Munsee spoke slightly more distantly related Eastern Algonkian Mahican and Quirippi languages.[74] The groups that came into contact with the Dutch near lands now known as Albany, New York, were the Mohawk, who lived in the upper Hudson River Valley.

Focusing on the region of southwestern Connecticut where the Patricks and Feakes lived, a group called the Tankitekes lived north and west of Greenwich in the Poundridge and Bedford areas of Westchester County, New York. The word Tankiteke meant "Little River," and it is believed to refer to a small tributary of the Housatonic.[75] Another possible Tankiteke site was where the Cross River unites with the Croton, near the present town of Katonah. Besides these villages, there were certainly many more. Indian groups[76] were composed of from fifty to three hundred persons living in one or more villages. Each band was independent of the rest, although there were variations and they would unite in larger groups in times of warfare, food scarcity, or other emergencies. Individuals had allegiance to their smaller bands and these extended family groups were the political groups with which the Europeans negotiated.

THE WEICHQUAESGECK

The Weichquaesgeck that lived in the greater Manhattan area spoke Munsee, the northernmost dialect of the Eastern Algonkian language called Delaware.[77] The group's name was first printed as "Wikagyl" on a map sketched by Adrian Block in the early 1600s and the Europeans mangled this difficult name with a wide variety of spellings. The Weichquaesgeck interacted intensively with the Dutch on Manhattan, and their name may mean "from the end of a bog or swamp," or it may have been derived from the words "wigwos heag," or, "people from the birch bark country,"[78] birch being valuable for housing, boat building, and fire-making. Some settlers shortened this name to "the Wickers Creek Indians," and the area where Wickers Creek enters the Hudson River in Dobbs Ferry, New York, or "Alipkonck," was one of their largest sites. As described by David DeVries in 1642, two years after he stopped in Greenwich to lunch with Daniel and Anneken Patrick, the most important Indian trading path into and out of Manhattan Island from Westchester County is now part of Route 9 as it runs along the Hudson River. It continued from the upper west side southward through Central Park to reach Manhattan's tip, and it was called "The Weichquaesgeck Road."

At the time of Dutch and English settlement, areas near Manhattan Island were controlled by three dominant Indian groups: the Raritan on the New Jersey side of the Hudson River, the Montauk on eastern Long Island, and the Weichquaesgeck, on the mainland in Westchester County. These and other Connecticut and Westchester groups were "subservient to the enforced dominations of the Mohawk Iroquois, who compelled them. . . . to pay tribute to their military superiority."[79] The Weichquaesgeck feared the Mohawk, with whom they were sometimes at war. The name "Mohawk," according to one Victorian linguist, meant "Man-Eaters" in Munsee.

When referring to Indians in general, the Dutch called them the "Wilden," "Wilden Menschen," or wild people, and the English called

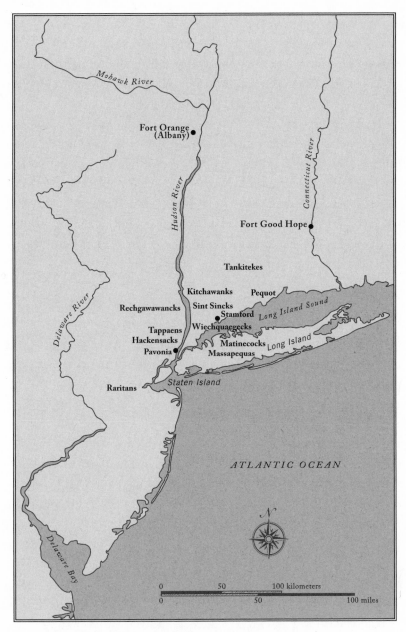

Indian group locations near Manhattan BASED UPON ROBERT S. GRUMET,
THE MUNSEE INDIANS, A HISTORY (NORMAN, OK:UNIVERSITY OF OKLAHOMA PRESS, 2009)

them "Savages." The Indians called the Dutch "Swanniken," from the time they first knew of them at one of their first settlements at Swanendael, in Delaware, and for reasons unknown they called Englishmen "Owanux," although Indians near Hartford noted that it was sometimes hard for the Indians to tell the English apart from the Dutch.

There was a system of tribute payment between groups at the period of initial European contact in the southern Connecticut, New York, and northern New Jersey region. Some Long Island tribes paid tribute to some Connecticut tribes, and some Munsee and upper Hudson Mahican groups paid tribute to more inland Mohawks. If tribute was deemed insufficient, late or lacking, warfare occurred. During the first contact period, warfare between tribes was sometimes exacerbated by Europeans who would engineer scenarios to pit tribes against each other, for the ultimate benefit of the Europeans.

Between Europeans and Indians, differing concepts of property ownership were a major point of contention. Europeans believed that through their system of paper deeds and the transfer of items, they had justly "purchased" property. Native Americans interpreted the European concept of "buying" land as a temporary loan of their land to them, or a deal that could be renewed or cancelled when desired. They believed that when they needed their land back again, they would have it, and that they could continue to use the land regardless of who "owned" it. This perception prompted Indians to request renewed payments for their properties, and caused European purchasers to insert language specifically banning them from entering or continuing to use their ancestral territories. This misunderstanding also gave rise to the derogatory term "Indian giving" suggesting Indian unfairness, which in reality was a European misconception. Indians initially valued the European items received in return for their land sales more highly than did European gift givers, perhaps imbuing these items with high spiritual value, but later they would come to demand additional and increased payment for their properties.

To further complicate matters of property ownership, there were instances of fraudulent deeds issued by Indians who had no power or right to convey, or who were drawn into sales when intoxicated, or were held prisoners by designing Europeans. In some situations, rival Sachems laid claim to land owned by their adversaries; but these instances were exceptions.

The Dutch stood behind their belief in the legality of their paper deeds and enforced permanent ownership. They were here to stay and they were not about to give back their bonanza. This was an enormous source of conflict for Native Americans, and unfair trading practices by unscrupulous European traders was another. Due to lax, spotty, arbitrary, and fraudulent enforcement of trading violations, situations that might have been handled as legitimate cultural misunderstandings became quickly manipulated to benefit one party over another. Fighting, murder, and revenge killings became common near Manhattan in the 1640s, and those once thought friendly could turn into assassins in an instant. Hostilities between Indians and Europeans that began near Manhattan quickly affected non-trading settlers far removed from the protection of Fort Amsterdam throughout New York, New Jersey, and Connecticut.

CHAPTER EIGHT

Contempt, the Father of Hate

INFORMATION ABOUT DUTCH ACTIVITY IN CONNECTICUT AND NEW York was unknown in America for almost three hundred years. In the 1800s, New York legislators despaired of their ignorance over earliest legal affairs and had a Dutchman named A. J. Van Laer translate some old Dutch documents that were collecting dust in Albany for almost two centuries. This created twenty-six handwritten volumes of somewhat inaccurate translations that were called the "Albany Records." Energized by this new, though imperfect knowledge, New York state legislators then commissioned state secretary John Romeyn Brodhead to search the archives of London, Paris, and The Hague for additional documents concerning New Netherland. Brodhead returned in 1845 with nearly five thousand additional documents "never before known to the historian."

On March 29, 1911, a devastating fire at the New York State Library in Albany destroyed many of these priceless, original documents. Those that survived continue to be translated to this day by Dr. Charles Gehring, director of the New Netherland Research Center.

Destined to survive fires, floods, neglect and the American Revolution, these records reveal a violent Indian war that was commissioned and conducted by William Kieft, the third director-general of New Netherland, and which deeply affected America's northeastern Indians.

Just as the Feakes and Patricks moved into southwestern Connecticut, violence between the Dutch and Munsee groups in New Jersey, Long

Delft tile of Dutch soldier found in Secretary Van Tienhoven's house privy near Fort Amsterdam in Manhattan THE DRAGOON © THE NEW YORK STATE MUSEUM ALBANY, NEW YORK

Island, Connecticut, and Westchester began to escalate. Dutch and English settlers were coming into increasing contact with the Native Americans here because the Dutch had recently relaxed trading restrictions. The company's directors in Holland had decided, from their experience of losing control of the Connecticut River to the English, that more people living in New Netherland, along with their greater tax revenues, would be key to long-lasting Dutch control of their claim.[80] New Netherland, which consisted of only a thousand people by 1640, needed a much larger population to survive and challenge the English. Manhattan was its only town, and it contained half of New Netherland's total population.

The Dutch passed the Freedoms and Exemptions Act of 1640[81], which conferred greater freedoms and the rights to existing fur traders and allowed for more people to participate in the industry. Accordingly,

New Netherland's population quickly doubled in the next few years. The predicted downside to passing the act was that the Dutch lost a large degree of control over trading procedures and practices. Traders swindling Indians over fur and land became more commonplace, and the strength of peace treaties, deeds, and currency value declined. Liquor and firearms were increasingly sold to the Indians, unprosecuted crimes became more frequent, and Indian aggressions increased in response. When Director Kieft made no redress to Indian complaints, the Indians began to enforce justice in the way that they saw fit.

When New Netherland's governance was quite functional in 1638, the Dutch provincial council fined a man for Indian assault and robbery; another man was ordered to restore wampum belts he had cut off an Indian woman by force. The Indians, who at first welcomed European interaction, were increasingly becoming antagonized, however, by a noted increase in unfair European practices, erratically applied justice, and the unusually arrogant actions and demands of Director Kieft's administration. Seeking ways to generate new revenues to pay for the escalating costs of running of New Netherland since the Dutch West India Company had begun to choke off its funding, Kieft concocted one harebrained scheme, for example, to recover the costs of his fort and the payment of his soldiers by taxing the Indians whom he considered had made these expenses necessary, to their enormous outrage.[82]

He then ordered an expedition of eighty soldiers, led by the fort's secretary, Cornelius van Tienhoven, to attack the Raritans in New Jersey on July 16, 1640, in retaliation for the killing of hogs owned by the West India Company and for their unsuccessful hijack of a yacht ironically named *Peace*. Kieft accused the Indians of the swine slaughter, when in reality Manhattan-based Europeans had been the perpetrators. David DeVries accurately stated that Kieft "wished to charge upon the savages what his own people had done." Van Tienhoven managed to shirk responsibility for many Raritan deaths by leaving his soldiers alone with the Indians, whereupon several were murdered. With Van Tienhoven's knowledge, however, the sachem's brother was taken prisoner on the sloop back to the fort, where he was tortured by a soldier with a split stick of wood to his genitals.[83]

In August of 1641, the most incendiary event in a brewing conflict, now known as Kieft's War, occurred when a Weichquaesgeck man on his way to Fort Amsterdam to trade was robbed and killed. His small nephew had hidden himself away during the assault and was an eyewitness to his uncle's murder. When grown, the young Indian man avenged his uncle's death by killing a Dutchman named Claes (pronounced "class") Cornelius Swits who was a rademaker, or wheelwright, whom he recognized as the murderer. As the wheelmaker bent to take some items from a chest in his home near Deutels Bay on Manhattan (now Turtle Bay on Manhattan's Midtown East Side), the adult Indian nephew killed Swits and kidnapped his wife and six children.[84] (He must have decapitated him, for Dutch records note that Swits's head was found ten years later.) A report of a supervisory Dutch committee called the "Orphan Masters of New Amsterdam," formed in response to care for the large number of orphans and widows left destitute through the violence of Kieft's War, said that Swits's widow, Aryantie, her children, and those of another man were taken by the Indians and held. The report noted that "The widows and children are still with the savage barbarians," and the men's cattle had been found wandering. While the Swits family eventually was released, Kieft demanded that the murderer's elders give him up, but they refused. This Indian was a chief's son and could not be returned, they argued; and besides they claimed, he had left the area and gone far away to the Tankitekes in modern-day southwestern Connecticut or southeastern Westchester County.

In April, Daniel Patrick wrote the Dutch to say he had heard the Tankiteke chief say "he was sorry twenty Christians had not been murdered,"[85] and suggested that the Swits murderer was hiding near Greenwich.

On September 1, 1641, the Raritan in New Jersey retaliated for the torture of their chief's brother and the deaths of their own, and attacked the DeVries farm on Staten Island, killing four of David DeVries's men and burning his house and barn along with the home of David Pietersz. Kieft offered payment to Indians who would retaliate for him and some took him up on this offer.

A sachem, or chief of the Tankitekes, named Pachem, sought to de-escalate matters by bringing a dismembered human hand hanging on a stick into Fort Amsterdam, claiming it was the hand of the chief who had killed the Staten Island men, and boasting that he had taken revenge for the Dutchmen "because he loved the Swannikens who were his friends." This may have just been a ploy by the chief to prevent further Dutch attacks on his people, but it didn't work as Kieft sent out two further forays of soldiers to try again to track down Swits's murderer. The Indians, frightened by how close the soldiers had come to them in one of these instances, asked the Dutch for a peaceful solution. Kieft again demanded the murderer be surrendered. The Indians agreed, but failed to surrender him.

Kieft became increasingly frustrated that his demands for the murderer's return were ignored by the Munsees and he threatened further military incursions to find him. Settlers living well away from the fort and southwestern Connecticut became alarmed at Kieft's unrelentingly hostile and aggressive approach to solving the murder, for he was endangering their lives. Kieft, they alleged, was directing a war from the safe confines of his militarized fort while their widely dispersed homesteads were far removed from Manhattan and were essentially defenseless. They argued that their lives and prosperity depended on maintaining good relationships with the Indians, which Kieft seemed intent on jeopardizing, and pointed out that the West India Company itself desired peaceful relations. Kieft was roundly charged with failing to act in the community or company's best interest. As their fears increased, the settlers laid all responsibility for the more violent, random, and additional settler deaths directly at his feet.

In March of 1642, Kieft began to feel uneasy with all the finger pointing, and convened a Council of Twelve Men[86] ostensibly for their advice, but also to apportion blame if need be. They considered the options: If Dutch authority remained challenged, it would set a dangerous precedent with the Indians; this in turn would be interpreted as weakness, and more assaults could follow. Nevertheless, a show of force could lead to a wider war.

Contrary to Kieft's desire for the latter choice, the twelve men urged him to delay further punitive expeditions and ask for the surrender of the Swits murderer three additional times. The settlers were anxious for a peaceful resolution but realized that if this failed, a military option had to send a decisive and final message to the Indians, to break the cycle of endless retaliations. Additional requests were made, but the Swits murderer remained at large. Unsure and apprehensive about the consequences, Kieft's council never granted him permission to forcefully attack the Weichquaesgeck, so the imperious Kieft promptly dissolved his Council of Twelve Men and warned them never to meet again without his permission. The settlers' fears of more surprise attacks only intensified with this disturbing new edict.

That year, two more Europeans were killed by the Hackingsack Indians in New Jersey. The Indians offered to pay Kieft for this crime, as was their custom, but they continued to refuse to surrender any perpetrator. The Indians blamed the Dutchmen who had sold the culprits liquor.

THE PAVONIA/JERSEY CITY MASSACRE

In February 1643, Kieft hoped to turn an incident of inter-Indian warfare between the Mohawks who lived near the area we now call Albany, New York, and the Weichquaesgeck who lived north and east of Manhattan Island to his advantage, but his actions led to a broader war and a more committed opposition. When armed Mohawks began to wage a war for unpaid tribute from groups of Munsees who lived in the Tarry-town and Dobbs Ferry, New York, areas, seventeen Munsees were killed by the Mohawk and many of their women and children were taken prisoner. In the dead of a February winter, frightened survivors fled to Dutch homesteads on Manhattan Island for protection. Many colonists, including David DeVries, fed and protected these people for two weeks, and Kieft even sent them some corn. The Munsees begged for the Dutch to attack the Mohawks on their behalf, but this request was refused. The Munsees then returned to Westchester where they were terrorized once more, causing them to gather again in Dutch homes on Corlaer's Hook on the Lower East Side of Manhattan, and in New Jersey in the Hackensack area.

The perfidious Kieft and his sidekick secretary, Cornelius van Tienhoven, perceived this large Indian massing to be the perfect opportunity to achieve justice for the unresolved Dutch murders. David DeVries, opposed to Kieft's plan, reported that the director had made up his mind to "break the mouths" of the Indians, referencing the time when untamed horses get used to having hardware placed in their mouths. Some men who agreed with Kieft signed a petition that argued for war at Pavonia. A majority of other settlers were opposed to escalating the violence and rightly predicted that the outcome would bring nothing but further destruction of their farming and trading efforts. DeVries, a frequent critic of Kieft who may have exaggerated events to justify his grievances, wrote frustratedly:[87]

> But it appeared that my speaking was to no avail. He [Kieft] had, with his co-murderers, determined to commit the murder, deeming it a Roman deed, and to do it without warning the inhabitants in the open lands, that each one might take care of himself against the retaliation of the savages, for he could not kill all the Indians. When I had expressed all these things in full, sitting at the table and the meal was over, he told

*me he wished to go to the large hall, which he had been lately adding
to his house. Coming to it, there stood all his soldiers ready to cross the
river to Pavonia to commit the murder. Then I spoke again to Governor
Willem Kieft; "Let this work alone. You wish to break the mouths of the
Indians, but you will also murder our own nation, for there are none of
the settlers in the open country who are aware of it. My own dwelling,
my people, cattle, corn and tobacco will be lost. He answered me, assur-
ing me that there would be no danger; that some soldiers should go to
my house to protect it, but this was not done. So was the business begun
between the 25th and 26th of February, 1643.*

In the Pavonia Massacre, 129 soldiers slew 120 Indians, including
women and children, and this grotesque action did serve to more strongly
unite surrounding regional Indian populations against all local Europeans, as predicted by Kieft's critics. DeVries continued his narration of the
Pavonia massacre in a highly inflammatory style, hoping to incite the
anger of Hollanders in Europe to revoke Kieft's authority.

*I remained that night at the Governor's, sitting up. I went and sat by
the kitchen fire, when about midnight I heard a great shrieking, and
I ran to the ramparts of the fort, and looked over to Pavonia. Saw
nothing but firing, and heard the shrieks of the savages murdered in
their sleep . . . When it was day, the soldiers returned to the fort having
massacred or murdered eighty Indians, and considering they had done
a deed of Roman valor, in murdering so many in their sleep.*

Incensed by Kieft's actions, DeVries borrowed further language from
an anti-Kieft pamphlet, possibly written by former Staten Island owner
Cornelis Melyn, the *Breeden-Raedt*, or "Broad Advice," which woefully
lamented on the same attack:[88]

Young children, some of them snatched from their mothers, were cut in pieces before the eyes of their parents, and the pieces were thrown into the fire, or into the water; other babes were bound on planks and then cut through, stabbed and miserably massacred, so that it would break a heart of stone; some were thrown into the river and when the mothers and fathers sought to save, the soldiers would not suffer them to come ashore, but caused both old and young to be drowned. Some children of from 5 to 6 years of age as also some old infirm persons, who had managed to hide themselves in the bushes and reeds, came out in the morning to beg for a piece of bread and for permission to warm themselves, but all were murdered in cold blood and thrown into the fire or water. A few escaped to our settlers, some with the loss of a hand, others, of a leg, others again holding in their bowels with their hands, and all so cut, hewn and maimed that worse could not be imagined; they went indeed in such a state that our people supposed they had been surprised by their enemies, the tribe of the Maquaes [Mohawks]. After this exploit, the soldiers were recompensed for their services, and thanked by Director Kieft in person.

The author ends his diatribe against Kieft with a most tragic final tale:

I am told for a fact that a certain skipper Isaac Abrahamsen, having saved a young boy, and hidden him under the sails, in order to give him to Melyn towards morning, the poor child, overcome with cold and hunger, made some noise and was heard by the soldiers, 18 German tigers [Dutch-hired mercenary soldiers], who dragged him from under the sails in spite of the endeavors of the skipper, who was alone against 18, was cut in two and thrown overboard.

The Director robbed and murdered where ever he could, and in the manner already related 1600 savages were killed in the years 1643 and 1644; some of them were settled among the English, at a distance of 10 to 20 miles [40 to 80 English] from us, who were most of them

surprised in their sleep, many of them never having seen a German,
much less them ever having done them any harm.

Kieft remained firmly entrenched in his genocidal ideology despite a peace treaty he soon signed with a small number of Indian groups. In July 1643, through DeVries's diplomacy, Kieft was informed by a chief that many orphaned young warriors were urging additional attacks. Kieft's insensitive solution was to tell the chief to kill his troublesome warriors, and that he, Kieft, would pay him for doing so. The astonished sachem declined Kieft's advice and warned him of continuing vengeance by the highly frustrated Indian people.

In Connecticut, the sachem named Pachem, who had previously declared that the Swannikens were his best friends and who may have been protecting the Swits murderer, did what settlers most feared and began inciting Indian groups to join together and inflict a massacre on the Europeans. Sporadic incidents also continued with an August 7th Indian attack on Dutch trading ships on the Hudson, which killed or captured twelve persons. Four farms near Manhattan were torched by Indians, killing fifteen Dutchmen. All of these actions were reported to English Governor Winthrop in Boston, as the violence spread into Connecticut.

A Wiequaesgeck man named Mianus or Mayane was so angered over European presence in the area that he jumped three armed men by himself in 1643. In this incident, Mianus, who likely lived in modern-day Riverside, called "Mianos Neck" by the English, killed one of the men and injured another. Mianus himself was beheaded in this struggle, and his head was brought to Fort Amsterdam to prove that Indian anger had now erupted in Greenwich.

ATTEMPTED ASSASSINATION
After the Pavonia massacre, Kieft affirmed his reputation as a first-class weasel and distanced himself from his plan to put the attack in motion.

He attempted to shift all responsibility for the cruel and undeserved deaths of women and children onto those who had signed the petition for war. These signers were now being lambasted as murderers within New Amsterdam and were being ostracized within the community. Signer Maryn Adrianson, in particular, became furious at Kieft on March 22, 1643, for his cowardly disavowal of all responsibility, and was incensed that other settlers blamed him for the escalating violence, instead of Kieft. For this, he and two friends tried to kill Kieft twice in one afternoon. Adrianson recounts:[89]

> *Leaving his house in a rage with a sword and a loaded and cocked pistol he came to the house of the Director, and went to his bedroom. Pointing his pistol at the Director to shoot him he said, "What devilish lies have you been telling of me?" Monsieur la Montaignes, [the Fort's physician and Kieft friend] being at the time with the Director, caught the pan [part of the gun's firing mechanism] with such quickness, that the cock snapped on his finger preventing through God's mercy, this atrocious design. Meanwhile the Fiscal and several others had come into the chamber. They disarmed Maryn and took him to prison.*
>
> *About an hour later, Jacob Stangh . . . armed with a musket and a pistol, came to the Fort, where the Director was walking up and down. He was informed of their coming and retreated to his house, which he barely had entered, when Jacob Stangh fired at him, so that two bullets passed through the door into the wall. The sentry before the door immediately fired at Jacob Stangh and killed him, God having in his mercy saved a second time within an hour and a half the Director and the community from a dreadful murder.*

Rattled by these events, Kieft convened a second council, this time composed of eight men, to decide how to handle a situation that was spiraling out of control. They decided that any available settler was to be enlisted, armed, and trained for war because the West India Company refused to pay for additional mercenaries to aid those living near Manhattan. Against an estimated force of 1,500 Indian warriors, the Dutch mustered only fifty to sixty soldiers and 250 colonists.[90]

Kieft hired John Underhill away from Stamford, recognizing him as a most effective man in the fine art of Indian massacre as proven by his actions at Mystic six years earlier. John Winthrop angrily commented on John Underhill's employment history in leaving Boston for Stamford, and then leaving English Stamford for Dutch Manhattan, seeing a kind of treason in it against the English who had recruited him to America. He may also have been upset that by leaving Stamford, Underhill could no longer protect his niece and daughter-in-law Elizabeth Feake and her family. Winthrop groused:[91]

Captain Underhill, finding no employment here that would maintain him and his family, and having good offers made him by the Dutch Governor, (he speaking the Dutch tongue and his wife a Dutch woman), had been with the Governor, and being returned desired the church's leave to depart. The church, understanding that the English, at Stamford near the Dutch had offered him employment and maintenance, after their ability, advised him to go thither, seeing they were our countrymen and in a church estate. He accepted this advice. His wife, being more forward to this, consented, and the church furnished him out, and provided a pinnace to transport him; but when he came there he changed his mind, or at least his course, and went to the Dutch.

Underhill leaped at the chance to work for Kieft, as he had been stymied by Stamford's stipulation that any officer under him had to be a "freeman," or church member. This was a consequence of Stamford's jurisdiction by the very orthodox New Haven Colony who followed biblical rules for governance. Underhill was accustomed to more liberal

Massachusetts Bay Colony rules, which did not require church membership for the military, and Stamford's strict regulations were unheard of among the Dutch.

In April 1643, the Dutch, working diplomatically and militarily now, arranged a peace treaty between the Hackingsacks and the Tappaen. Similar agreements were made with the Reckgawawanks of northern New Jersey, the more northerly Kitchawanks by Croton Point and the Sint Sinks near Ossining, New York. The simply worded agreement was that "All injuries done by the tribes to the Dutch or by the Dutch to the Indians shall henceforth be forever forgotten and forgiven."[92] However, the Weichquaesgeck about Stamford and Greenwich, Connecticut, and in Pelham, New York, where Anne Hutchinson's family now lived, remained enraged.

THE HUTCHINSON DEATHS

August was a deadly month. An Indian attack on English Lady Deborah Moody at Gravesend in Brooklyn on Long Island was repelled by forty colonists. Settlements at Mespath and Newtown on eastern Long Island were terrorized, as was a farm on Newark Bay and on August 20, 1643, the sensational murder of Anne Hutchinson and her family occurred.[93]

Led by a sachem named Wampage, some Weichquaesgeck attacked the Hutchinson property named "Anne's Hook." The location of their homestead was likely somewhere near or within the modern-day Pelham/Split Rock Golf Course, close by the Hutchinson River Parkway and the Hutchinson River in Westchester County that are named in Anne's honor. Her house was situated somewhere between two freshwater creeks in this area that are now extinct. After she and her family were banished from Boston, they first relocated to Rhode Island, and upon the death of her husband there she moved deeply into Dutch New Netherland with a large part of her family to put herself further away from still critical English communities.

Split rock at top of ramp intersection of the Hutchinson River Parkway and I-95 northbound in Westchester County, New York. The Hutchinson home is believed to have been located nearby, on the present-day Split Rock Golf Course. PHOTO: BEN PIANKA

To begin the attack, legend has it that Wampage first signaled Anne's young son to tie up their large dogs. His men then herded all the livestock into the Hutchinson barn and set it on fire, killing all the animals inside. They then killed Anne, her son-in-law, some servants, and five of her youngest children, her five older ones being elsewhere. One can only image how Anne, in realizing that violent and unforeseen death was about to occur to her family, reconciled her vaunted Elect status to the litany of horrors now playing out upon her property. Settlements outside Fort Amsterdam were newly stunned and traumatized at the magnitude of this event, and urged Dutch authorities to take immediate and overwhelming action.

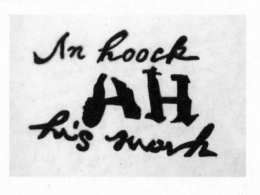

Ann Hoock's mark ROBERT BOLTON, *A HISTORY OF THE COUNTY OF WESTCHESTER, VOL. 1:130*. (NEW YORK: ALEXANDER S. GOULD, 1848)

A famous but unsubstantiated footnote to this story is that Anne's young daughter Susan hid herself in the wide crack of a boulder called the "Split Rock," which can still be seen near the intersection of I-95 northbound and the Hutchinson River Parkway. Taken captive from the split rock at the age of nine, Susan was renamed Autumn Leaf by the Wampage and his group because of her flaming red hair. It is documented that she lived with the Weichquaesgeck for nine years after her family's deaths, and when she was eighteen she was returned to Stamford[94] having forgotten her English and not wanting to leave her Indian family. She did eventually regain her language and married Englishman John Cole in 1651. With him she had eleven children and died in Rhode Island in 1713 after eighty years of living a most interesting life.[95] As was custom for successful warriors, Wampage forever

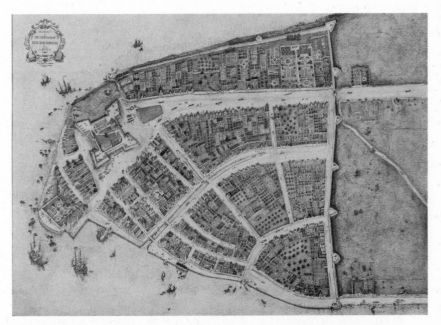

The wall of Wall Street placed during Kieft's War to protect the town of New Amsterdam on the southern tip of Manhattan Island REDRAFT OF THE CASTELLO PLAN, NEW AMSTERDAM IN 1660, 1916 BY JOHN WOLCOTT ADAMS (1874–1925) © COLLECTION OF THE NEW YORK HISTORICAL SOCIETY USA / THE BRIDGEMAN ART LIBRARY

after called himself "Annhoeck," signing land deeds years later with this name.

On October 1, 1643, Indians who didn't participate in the New Jersey groups' peace treaty continued battling the Europeans near Manhattan and they killed a man named Jacob Stoffelsz on his farm, after luring his protective soldiers away. They kidnapped his young son and took him up the Hudson to their encampment at Tappaen. David DeVries was asked to obtain the release of the boy, which he did but that same month, DeVries returned to his boyhood home in Holland, having had enough dangerous interactions with soldiers, Indians, and lethally incompetent administrators to last him a lifetime.

Europeans on Manhattan had become so afraid of the increasing violence that they erected a heavy wooden palisade or stockade fence across the southern tip of the island to protect themselves from marauding natives. Water surrounded all other sides of the settlement, which was considered defensible enough and this palisaded fence line that was erected is recognized today as Manhattan's "Wall Street."

In December of 1643, the people of Fort Amsterdam plaintively appealed to Holland for more protection:[96]

We poor inhabitants of New Netherland were pursued by these wild Heathens and Barbarous Savages with fire and sword; daily in our houses and fields have they cruelly murdered men and women; and with hatchets and tomahawks struck little children dead in their parents arms . . . or carried them away into bondage; the houses and grain barracks are burnt with the produce; cattle of all descriptions are slain or destroyed . . . Almost every place is abandoned. We, wretched people must skulk, with wives and little ones that still survive, in poverty together, in and around the fort at the Manhatas, where we are not safe. We are powerless. The enemy meets with scarce any resistance. The garrison consists of but 50 or 60 soldiers unprovided with ammunition. Fort Amsterdam, utterly defenseless.

In 1643, a Frenchman visiting the area noted:[97] "While I was there . . . [the natives] actually killed some two score Hollanders, and burnt many houses and barns full of wheat."

The war raged on. Throckmorten's farm (from which the name "Throg's Neck" is derived) was attacked, and its buildings burned, while the people escaped in their boats. The position of the Dutch was perilous in the extreme. Some propose that at this time, had the Indians been able to confederate and collectively mass, they may well have been able to rout the Europeans for a time from their beachhead on Manhattan.

These events instilled the will in many regional settlers to eliminate the Indians before they themselves became eliminated, an idea that allowed for pre-emptive strikes, particularly toward large massings of Indians that they believed rightly or wrongly had the potential to overwhelm European populations. Kieft and his council had decided that the time for overwhelming force against the Indians had come and that any strikes in the future would have to be sizeable, swift, and severe. The Indians were given no further chance to negotiate and force was the only answer that Kieft called to mind.

Chapter Nine

The Indians Near Manhattan

ADRIEN VAN DER DONCK WAS BANISHED FROM NEW NETHERLAND TO Holland in 1652 for criticizing Kieft, the West India Company, and its directors for poor management of vital Indian trading relationships and for the company's lack of a long-term commitment to its North American settlements. He used his involuntary time spent in Holland to history's advantage, however, when he wrote extensive descriptions of the American Northeast and the native Munsee he had encountered near the Hudson River and in Westchester County. Left untranslated for hundreds of years, the first English language translation of Van der Donck's complete report was published in 2008. From his long-neglected *Indian Observations*, we finally hear Van der Donck's extensive reports about the native people who lived near Manhattan in the time of Dutch contact. In this significant abridgement of these observations, Van der Donck comments on the Indians he encountered in the 1630s and 40s:

> *They were well proportioned, slim, nimble and supple, and they could run with striking stamina, able to carry large and heavy packs for long distances. Congenital defects and deformities were seldom seen among them. None were blind or cross-eyed, except those injured by smallpox, accident or war. No fools, madmen, maniacs or lunatics were witnessed. Their hair was jet-black, sleek, uncurled and coarse,*

and their bodies had very little hair. Men and women had handsome, graceful and fine faces with black brown eyes and snow-white teeth.

In taking food and drink they were not wasteful, excessive, frivolous, or lavish, and they ate according to the season. Their usual drink was water and occasionally grape juice, which they never turned into wine; this was accompanied by fresh meat or fish. Liquor was unknown to those who did not move among the Dutch, but those who did were easily made drunk by small amounts of alcohol, which they consumed greedily. Their food was normally meat and fish of every kind depending on the time of year and where they were. They cooked meat and fish simply in water, without any herbs, salt or lard other than that which was naturally present in it. They were ignorant of stewing, braising, baking, frying, and rarely heated or grilled anything unless hunting. The women beat or pounded corn and baked cakes of it. They added grits to boiled meat to make a broth, but their most common fare was a corn meal porridge known as sappaen. They ate this almost daily and always consumed it when visiting others. They also ate a lot of boiled Turkish beans and fruit. They observed no customary or fixed meal times, eating anytime they were hungry. They had tremendous control over their hunger and could get by with very little for up to four days. Exceptional treats for their guests included beaver tails, fatty meat, rockfish heads, and cornmeal covered in a fatty broth. They also enjoyed eating boiled chestnuts stewed in gravy and fat. When going on long trips, they provisioned themselves with small bags containing parched meal made of roasted corn.

In their dress and ornament, they all generally wore the same kind of clothing, except for some young men. The women were inclined to ornament themselves more than the men. Boys up to twelve or thirteen went about quite naked; girls covered their private parts from infancy. Around their waists they all wore a belt made of leather, whalefin, whalebone or seawant. They pulled a length of cloth between

113

their legs and hung it off the belt. Before they had cloth, they used ani-
mal skins for this purpose. On women, the cloth came halfway down
their legs, and the wealthier ones decorated this loincloth entirely with
seawant, so that it became quite valuable. On the upper part of their
body they draped a red or blue duffels cloth over their right shoulder,
tied it in a knot at the waist, and allowed the remainder to hang
down to their feet. By day this served as a cloak, and by night, as a
bed and blanket.

Other reports include mentions that they also wore mantles of woven
turkey feathers. The explorer Verrazano, who visited the waterways near
Manhattan in 1524, reported that the Indians were dressed out with feathers of birds of various colors, which was corroborated by Henry Hudson
in 1609. Verrazano reported that "two kings" came aboard his ship, "more
beautiful in form and stature than can possibly be described"; one man
was forty, the other, twenty-four. The older man had a deerskin around his
body, artificially wrought in damask figures. His head was without covering, his hair was tied back in various knots; around his neck he wore a
large chain ornamented with many stones of different colors. The younger
man was similar in general appearance. Their eyes were "black and sharp,"
and their expressions "mild and pleasant."

Van der Donck continues:

Men and women's shoes and stockings were made of deer or elk skin.
Men went mostly bareheaded but women pulled their hair back and
folded it a hand length long like a beaver tail. Over this they wore a
kerchief, often exquisitely decorated with seawant. They wore neck-
laces, headbands, belts, earrings and bracelets of seawant. The women
painted their faces slightly or not at all and presented a very stately,
quiet, steady and yellowish appearance. The men painted themselves
all over, but mostly in the face in all kinds of vivid colors. Some also

wore a circular headdress of very long and fine deer hair, dyed red, which looked like a saint's halo.

In winter, women and children rarely left their shelter. In addition to covering themselves with cloth, deer, elk, weasel and bear fur jerkins, they further shielded their bodies against the cold with bear and raccoon fat that had been rubbed onto the skin.

The Indians did marry and usually had one wife, except for the chiefs, who may have had three or four at the same time, generally the handsomest and most diligent women. In a divorce, the children followed the mother. It was considered honorable and laudable the longer a marriage lasted. During marriage, prostitution and adultery were considered disgraceful, particularly by women. They thought it even more vile when done in the light of day or in open fields where someone might watch. If a woman was single, she did as she pleased, provided she accepted payment. Free favors were scorned as scandalous and whorelike.

When pregnant, whether in or out of wedlock, Indian women very carefully guarded against anything that could injure their unborn children. When their time came near, they prepared a potion of local roots and herbs. Then they commonly went into the woods, even in the depth of winter, where they gave birth unaided. For this they preferred a quiet, sheltered spot near running water. They erected a simple screen or hut of matting, and brought provisions with them. If the child was a boy, they immersed it straightaway in a nearby stream and left it there for quite some time, even in freezing weather. The child must be hardened from the first, they said. Then they warmed and watched the infant carefully lest it die accidentally. After a few days, they returned to their home and family. During the time of their impurity, they were averse, distant and shy; they kept apart and seldom let themselves be seen by men.

Foul and improper language was despised. Kissing, romping, pushing and similar playful frolicking or fondling was unlikely to be seen.

115

When someone died, all around took great care in committing the dead body to the earth. After a few days and nights of vigil and lamenting, they carried the corpse to the grave, where they did not lay it down, but supported it by a stone or block of wood as if sitting in a chair. Then they placed money, a pot, a kettle, a dish and a spoon with some provisions in the grave in case there was need in the next world. Next, they stacked wood all around the corpse to keep the earth away from it and over the grave they built a great mound of wood, stone and earth with a wooden enclosure on top like a little house. A set period of lamentation was observed by the women. The women called out the name of the departed with hideous howling and strange gestures, beat their chests, scratched their faces and displayed every bodily sign of mourning. When a mother lost a child, her lamenting exceeded all bounds, for she wailed and ranted the whole night through as though she was stark mad. Mourners shaved their heads and burned their hair on the grave at a specific time in the presence of kin. To put the death behind them, they disliked making mention of it, talking or asking about it, and felt that doing so meant hurt and injury. When a woman's husband died, she shaved her head and blackened her whole face, as a man did when his wife died. Mourners did not marry for a year.

The Indians were notably calm, unaffected, and of few words. The little they did say was long considered, slowly spoken and long remembered. Cursing, swearing and scolding were foreign to them, unless they learned it by mixing with the Dutch. They scorned any pain inflicted on them and took pride in singing until they succumbed. Strongly independent, they did not tolerate domination. They resented being struck, unless they did wrong, and then they endured it passively. Delicacies in food and drink did not tempt them. Cold, heat, hunger and thirst they bore remarkably well, and they disregarded hardship.

The women did all the farming and planting. The men hardly concerned themselves with it unless they were very young or very old.

They grew no wheat, oats, barley, or rye, and were unacquainted with plowing or spadework and did not keep their land tidy. They planted corn and beans, pumpkins and squashes, and tobacco for their own use. Their plots were not fenced off from the open field and they gave little attention to them. They regarded their methods as better than those of the Europeans, which, in their view, involved far too much bother, care and effort for their liking.

The Indians were in the habit, and Europeans adopted this practice, of burning the woods and plains and marshlands that were not too wet, once a year in the fall. Portions that were missed got their turn later in March or April. It facilitated hunting, because impediments, like a crackling underfoot that alerted game, were removed for the hunter. It thinned the forest, killing new undergrowth, cleared the forest of old deadwood and increased the game since it restricted the animals' movements and enabled them to be tracked in burned areas. Bush burning was an extraordinary and spectacular event. The fire burned so fiercely and spread so fast that it was terrifying to watch. When the fire raged near houses, homesteads and wooden fencing, one had to be careful lest they suffered damage, which happened before people watched out for it. Such a fire was a spectacular sight when one sailed on the rivers at night while the forest was ablaze on both banks. It was a delightful scene to look on from afar.

When swearing an oath, the Indians took the Sun as their witness, which they regarded as all-seeing. They had great affection for the Moon, the governor of all growth, yet they did not worship or pay homage to it. The other planets and stars they knew by name, and through that knowledge, and by other signs, they were weather-wise.

They did know something of God, and they were in great fear of the devil. When they went out fishing or hunting they customarily threw a portion of the catch into the fire and said, "There, devil, you eat that." When one berated them for some wicked act or speech on the grounds that it incurred the wrath of God in heaven, they replied, "We do not know that god, or where he is and have never seen him; if you know and fear him, as you say you do, how come there are so many whores, thieves, drunkards, and other evildoers among you? Surely that God of yours will punish you severely, since he warned you of it. He never warned us, and left us in ignorance; therefore, we do not deserve punishment."

Once a merchant went to trade with the Indians in 1639 and got into a discussion on religion. After he and a chief had downed four or five glasses of wine the chief related this insightful story of his conversion back to Indian ways:

> I was so well instructed in your religion that I used to say mass to my people. Once the place in which the altar stood accidentally caught fire and the people rushed forward to quench it but I held them back saying the God standing there is almighty and will shortly make the fire go out by itself. Then we waited, but the fire burned on until it consumed the altar. Ever since, I have disliked religion and esteem the sun and the moon much more for they can warm the earth and make the crops grow and your God cannot save himself from fire.

The Indians said the soul animates and rules the body from which springs all the vices and virtues. When separated from the body at death, the soul travelled to a region to the southward if the person was good and virtuous. If those in life were wicked and evil they went to a completely different place with no comforts.

When they heard voices or sounds coming from the woods in the dead of the night that we might reckon were made by wild animals, they said in amazement, "What you hear calling there are the souls of wicked persons who are doomed to wander about and haunt the woods in the night and at unseasonable times." For fear of them, the Indians would not go anywhere at night, unless in a group when they must; otherwise, they took a torch. They were frightened of evil spirits, who, they believed remained intent on hurting and terrifying them. When we said the devil was evil, cunning and wicked, they agreed and maintained that every scourge, misfortune calamity and infirmity is inflicted by the devil. Since the devil is so malicious and merciless towards them they have no choice but to fear, yet to keep on friendly terms with him, to throw a morsel in the fire to please him.

They said the lord of heaven is not alone up there, but has with him a goddess or woman who is the fairest the eye has ever beheld. With this beauty he passes his time and forgets, and the devil plays the lord on earth and does whatever he pleases.

(Excerpts reprinted from A Description of New Netherland, *by Adriaen van der Donck and edited by Charles T. Gehring and William A. Starna by permission of the University of Nebraska Press. Copyright 2008 by the Board of Regents of the University of Nebraska.)*

CHAPTER TEN

Munsee Massacres Launched from Old Greenwich

THE DUTCH LAUNCHED A NUMBER OF FORAYS AGAINST THE INDIANS in 1643 and 1644 from Tomac Cove in Old Greenwich, Connecticut, which were described in unique documents that New York State Secretary John Brodhead had retrieved from The Hague in the early 1800s. One of these actions resulted in what might have been the largest massacre of Native Americans in the Northeast, surpassing some of the estimates given for those four hundred who were killed in Mystic, Connecticut, by John Underhill and John Mason some seven years before. This largest genocide resulted in the deaths of five to seven hundred Munsees who were burned alive by John Underhill and his troops one freezing February evening in 1644.

The first foray launched in 1643 was to retaliate for Mianus's or "Mayn Mayane's" attack on three armed "Christians" in Greenwich earlier that same year. The Dutch reported:[98]

> One hundred and twenty men were sent thither under the preceding command. The people landed at Greenwich in the evening from three yachts, marched the entire night, but could not find the Indians, either because the guide had given warning or had himself gone astray. Retreat was made to the yachts in order to depart as secretly

as possible. Passing through Stamford some Englishmen were encountered who offered to lead soldiers to the place where some Indians were.

The soldiers were frustrated at not finding any Indians on this first stomp through the rocky Greenwich wilderness at night, and they became even more enraged when they returned to John Underhill's house in Stamford and Daniel Patrick ridiculed them there for their failure to locate any inhabited village. Believing that Patrick had warned off the Indians himself and had sent them on a wild goose chase, a great argument ensued between Daniel Patrick and a soldier named Hans Frederick. The harrowing details of Patrick's assassination were recounted by Governor Winthrop in his journal on December 1, 1643 (Old Style).[99] Winthrop's anger toward Patrick is evident in his recount and it stemmed from his unhappy interaction with the offensive soldier in Boston and the dangerous influence he exerted on his niece and daughter-in-law Elizabeth Feake to move away from the Massachusetts Bay Colony and into this most dangerous area of southwestern Connecticut. Winthrop disgustedly recorded:

About this time Captain Daniel Patrick was killed at Stamford by a Dutchman, who shot him dead with a pistol. This captain was entertained by us out of Holland (where he was a common soldier in the Prince's guard) to exercise our men. We made him a Captain, and maintained him. After, he was admitted a member of the church of Watertown, and a freeman. But he grew very proud and vicious, and for though he had a wife of his own, a good Dutch woman and comely, yet he despised her and followed after other women; and perceiving that he was discovered, and that such evil courses would not be endured here, and being withal of a vain and unsettled disposition, he went from us, and settled down not twenty miles from the Dutch, and put himself under their protection, and joined to their church, without being dismissed from Watertown: but when the Indians arose in those parts, he fled to Stamford and there was slain. The Dutchman, who killed him was apprehended, but made an escape; and this was the fruit of his wicked course and breach of covenant with his wife. With the church, and with that state [New Netherland], who had called him and maintained him, and he found his death from that hand where he sought protection. It is observable that he was killed upon the Lord's Day in the time of the afternoon exercise (for he seldom went to the public assemblies). It was in Captain Underhill's house. The Dutchman had charged him with treachery, for causing 120 men to come to him upon his promise to direct them to the Indians, etc. but deluded them. Whereupon the Captain gave him ill language and spit in his face, and turning to go out, the Dutchman shot him behind in the head, so he fell down dead and never spoke. The murderer escaped out of custody.

Patrick's assassination was undoubtedly a shock and severe economic setback for his family, but some others did not mourn long over his passing. When John Underhill imprisoned Patrick's murderer, he placed the man in his own home in Stamford and, while he and his wife Helena sat downstairs in this very tiny building, the soldier escaped out of an upstairs bedroom window. It's possible this man may have been the same Hans Frederick who had killed men before during a brutal mutiny on the Dutch ship named *Batavia* in 1629.[100] It may also have been that John Underhill held a grudge against Daniel Patrick from the time of the Mystic massacre, for when Daniel Patrick showed up late but with a boat at the end of these proceedings, he refused to loan it out to ferry the wounded home, which incensed his fellow soldiers.

A second foray from Tomac Cove found a well-protected village that was uninhabited:[101]

Sixty-five men were dispatched under [George] Baxter and Peter Cock, who found them [Indian houses] empty, though thirty Indians could have stood against two hundred soldiers, inasmuch as the castles were constructed of plank five inches thick, nine feet high, and braced around with thick plank studded with port holes. Our people burnt two, reserving the third for a retreat. Marching eight or nine leagues further, they discovered nothing but a few huts, which they could not surprise as they were discovered. They returned, having killed only one or two Indians, taken some women and children prisoner, and burnt some corn.

Kieft Appeals to Winthrop for Assistance

By late 1643 Kieft and his Council of Eight Men found themselves in a situation so dire that they begged the West India Company for more soldiers, but the company shrugged off their requests in that it could not afford to send more forces after losing some other conflicts in South America. Kieft even begged for John Winthrop to become involved, and offered to pay him twenty-five thousand guilders if the English governor could provide a force of 150 men. In a sign of desperation, he actually threw in Fort Amsterdam as collateral. Winthrop ignored Kieft's entreaty and said he considered the request, "a plot of the Dutch Governor to engage the English in the quarrel with the Indians, which we had wholly declined, as doubting the justice of the cause."[102] The New Haven Colony also turned away Dutch pleas for assistance, but sanctimoniously promised they would reconsider in the spring if the situation seemed to be worsening.

Captain Underhill traveled to Stamford from Manhattan and received new intelligence that the older Cos Cob Indian hostage, who had previously failed to lead Dutch troops to an inhabited village, was offering to lead the Dutch again to another large massing of the Munsee people who had recently gathered to celebrate the new moon of February. The Indian's offer was to prove his loyalty to the Dutch and to show that his former failure had not been his fault. In leading the Europeans to find the Wiechquaesgeck, the Cos Cob guide completely cast his lot with the Europeans, for his own would surely kill him for this treachery.

Kieft's mismanaged use of force and diplomacy had worsened the Indian situation for Manhattan-area Europeans who clamored even more loudly and relentlessly for a resolution to the endless cycle of European-Indian murder and revenge.[103] While some Dutch farmers, traders, and soldiers had killed small numbers of Indians and the Indians avenged themselves with small-scale but shocking murders in return, no settler or West India Company soldier felt comfortable with the idea of large-scale Indian slaughter, which Kieft proposed as the solution to their problems. To discourage this idea, the Council of Eight Men tried to make Kieft personally lead any expeditionary force against large Indian massings, such that he would fully assume responsibility for such offensive ideas. Kieft declined this personal involvement and decided instead to hire John Underhill for the job, one of the few men in the region with the stomach to pursue such endeavors. Underhill accepted Kieft's assignment and took up the old Indian man's new offer to lead the Dutch again to a new large assemblage of Indian people. With this traitor's help Underhill launched the third, largest, and most violent foray yet from the Feake-Patrick property, in February of 1644:[104]

> One hundred and thirty men were accordingly dispatched under General Underhill and Ensign Hendrick van Dyke. They embarked in three yachts, landed at Greenwich, where they were obliged to pass the night by reason of the great snow and storm. In the morning they marched northwest up over stony hills, over which some were obliged to creep. In the evening, about eight o'clock, they came within a league of the Indians, and inasmuch as they should have arrived too early and had to cross two rivers, one of two hundred feet wide and three feet deep, and that the men could not afterwards rest in consequence of the cold, it was determined to remain there until about ten o'clock. Orders

having been given as to the mode to be observed in attacking the Indi-
ans, the men marched forward towards the huts, which were set up in
three rows, street fashion, each eighty paces in length, in a low recess
of the mountain, affording complete shelter from the northwest wind.

The moon was then at the full and threw a strong light against
the mountain, so that many winter's days were not clearer than it
then was. On arriving, the enemy was found on the alert and on their
guard, so that our people determined to charge and surround the huts,
sword in hand. The Indians behaved like soldiers, deployed in small
bands, so that we had, in a short time one dead and twelve wounded.
They were likewise so hard pressed that it was impossible for one to
escape. In a brief space of time, one hundred and eighty were counted
dead outside the houses. Presently none durst come forth, keeping
themselves within the houses, discharging arrows through the holes.
The General, seeing that nothing else was to be done, resolved with
Sergeant Major Underhill, to set fire to the huts. Whereupon the Indi-
ans tried every way to escape, not succeeding in which they returned
back to the flames, preferring to perish by fire than to die by our hands.

What was most wonderful is, that among this vast collection
of men, women and children, not one was heard to cry or to scream.
According to the report of the Indians themselves, the number then
destroyed exceeded five hundred. Some say, full 700, among whom
were also 25 Wappingers, our God having collected together there the
greater number of our enemies, to celebrate one of their festivals. No
more than eight men in all escaped, of whom even three were severely
wounded.

The fight ended, several fires were built in consequence of the great
cold. The wounded, fifteen in number were dressed and sentinels were
posted by the General. The troops bivouacked there for the remainder
of the night. On the next day, the party set out much refreshed in good
order, so as to arrive at Stamford in the evening. They marched with

great courage over that wearisome mountain, God affording extraor-
dinary strength to the wounded, some of whom were badly hurt[105]
and came in the afternoon to Stamford after a march of two days and
one night, with little rest. The English received our people in a very
friendly manner, affording them every comfort. In two days they
reached here. A thanksgiving was proclaimed on their arrival.

This massive holocaust, five times larger than the Pavonia massacre, shocked and stunned regional Munsee populations and resulted in very few European deaths. It was no doubt a body blow psychologically and militarily to the Indians that essentially ended any further large-scale battles of Kieft's War. The Europeans who participated in the massacre did not boast or write of it in any personal documentation yet discovered. Maintaining a low profile surely helped prevent any personal Indian reprisals, but it did not completely stop further small and sporadic skirmishes, which continued for many years.

John Underhill remained in a highly agitated and aggressive state a week after his massacre when, on March 17, 1644, he wreaked havoc in a tavern near Fort Amsterdam, slashing up the entire room with his sword and breaking all its mugs and crockery when asked to quiet down or quit the premises. A witness reported:[106]

Three men and their wives had been dining at the New Amsterdam
tavern of Philip Gerritssen, when Underhill, George Baxter, and the
drummer of their militia noisily arrived. The diners asked the soldiers
to drink in another room, which they did, but the soldiers soon asked
those in the adjacent dining room to join them. Upon their refusal,
reports one of the diners, Underhill and his companions, "with drawn
swords, knocked to pieces all but three of the mugs which hung from the
shelf in the tavern, as may be seen by the marks which remain in the
shelf and by the cuts and hackings in the posts and doors; furthermore

endeavoring by force, having drawn swords in their hands, they came into the room where the invited guests were. This was for a long time resisted by the landlady with a leaded bludgeon and by the landlord by keeping the door shut, but finally John Underhill and his companions, in spite of all opposition, came into the room, where he made many unnecessary remarks, having his sword in his right hand and scabbard in his left said (to one of the men who was a minister), 'clear out of here or I shall strike at random.' Presently some English soldiers came likewise to assist him, whereupon Underhill and his companions became guilty of gross insolence, so that the fiscal and the guard were sent for and . . . Underhill was ordered to depart . . . to prevent further, more serious mischief, yes, even bloodshed, we broke up our pleasant party before we had intended."

Immediately after the great genocide of 1644, twenty-three families from Stamford, a third of its total population, moved across Long Island Sound to Newtown and Flushing on Long Island to put distance between themselves and the surviving Wiechquaesgeck.[107] Daniel Denton, the son of Stamford's Richard Denton, who may have been a participant, wrote, perhaps facetiously, that it was amazing to him how the Indian populations had declined so quickly in the region near this time. Remaining Indians in the area requested a formal cessation of hostilities from Underhill in Stamford on April 16, 1644.[108] The captain, after signing this peace treaty however, killed even more Indians on Long Island that same month, and two months later Kieft asked him to continue.

In April 1644, seven savages were arrested at Hempstead on Long Island for killing two or three pigs, although it was later found that some Englishmen had done it. Kieft sent John Underhill and fifteen or sixteen soldiers to Hempstead, who killed three of the seven in a cellar. He then put the four remaining Indians in a boat, two of whom were towed behind in the water by a string wound round their necks. The soldiers drowned these two men and the two unfortunate survivors were detained as prisoners at Fort Amsterdam where they were brutally tortured. A critic of the events, perhaps David DeVries, wrote up Kieft's brutality in the most inflammatory manner possible to drive home his point that Kieft must be recalled:[109]

When they had been kept a long time in the corps de garde, the Director became tired of giving them food any longer and they were delivered to the soldiers to do with as they pleased. The poor unfortunate prisoners were immediately dragged out of the guard house and soon dispatched with knives of from 18 to 20 inches long which Director Kieft had made for his soldiers for such purposes, saying that the swords were for use in the huts of the savages, when they went to surprise them; but that these knives were much handier for bowelling them.

The first of these savages having received a frightful wound, desired them to permit him to dance what is called the Kinte Kayce, a religious use observed among them before death; he received however so many wounds that he dropped down dead. The soldiers then cut strips from the other's body, beginning at the calves, up the back, over the shoulders and down to the knees. While this was going forward, Governor Kieft, with his counselor Jan de la Montaigne, a Frenchman, [and Fort physician] stood laughing heartily at the fun and rubbing his right arm, so much delight he took in such scenes. He then ordered him to be taken out of the fort, and the soldiers bringing him to the Beaver's Path, he dancing the Kinte Kayce the entire time, threw him down, cut off his partes genetales, thrust them into his mouth while still alive, and at last placing him on a mill stone cut off his head . . . What I tell you is true, for by the same token there stood at the same time 24 or 25 female savages who had been taken prisoner at the N.W. point of the fort; and when they saw this bloody spectacle they held up their arms, struck their mouth, and, in their language exclaimed: "For shame! For shame! Such unheard of cruelty was never known, or even thought of among us!" The savages have often called out to us from a distance: "what scoundrels you Swanneken are, you do not war upon us, but upon our wives and children who you treacherously murder; whereas we do no harm to either your wives or your children, but feed and take care of them, till we send them back to you again.

And further, Director Kieft, not content with this causing the hunted savages to be surprised, engaged some English spies to accompany his soldiers as guides, into places unknown to our people, by which many poor inoffensive savages were cruelly and traitorously massacred."

That fall, on October 17, 1643/4, Underhill attended another meeting at Fort Amsterdam with Kieft and his council. There they planned yet another hostile attack, this one on "Mamarunock," an important Kitchawank sachem and the same chief with whom Underhill had signed a peace treaty in Stamford in April. Underhill and Kieft's plans were stymied however, when the West India Company refused to fund this expedition.

For over 250 years until the early 1900s, Captain John Underhill was celebrated for his efforts to eradicate the Indian. John Greenleaf Whittier created a lengthy poem entitled "John Underhill," which suggested that the personal shame, embarrassment, and loss of face and standing that Underhill suffered in Boston provoked him to conduct large-scale feats of European "protection" to regain his reputation as a valuable and unique person.

Greenwich and Stamford settlers celebrated Underhill's destruction of the Wiechquaesgeck, and were grateful to him for it. Years later, Robert and Elizabeth Feake's daughter Elizabeth married John Underhill as his second wife and they had five children together. The Feakes and the Underhills would become even more tightly entwined through many marriages of their offspring in future generations.

A report to Holland explained the subdued but still troubled aftermath of these tragic episodes:[110]

The winter passed in this confusion mingled with great terror; the season came for driving out the cattle, which obliged many to desire peace. On the other hand, the Indians seeing also that it was time to plant maize, were not less solicitous for a cessation of hostilities, so after some negotiation, peace was concluded in May 1643/44. This truce was broken when Wappingers, north of the Weichquaesgeck, hijacked a boat with 400 hides coming from Ft. Orange [Albany] killing nine, including two women, and taking one woman and two children prisoner.

Colonists continued to demand protection, for which Kieft additionally taxed them and continued their ire against him. The spring planting season of 1644 helped to bring about a lull in hostilities, despite Kieft's horrific interventions. His iron fist approach to creating a subservient Indian population had the effect of escalating regional violence, which colonists predicted, and made the region a hostile place for the Munsee, which was Kieft's intention, short of complete annihilation. Kieft neither eliminated the Indian population entirely, nor did he entirely scare them into total subservience. He did cause untold European and Indian deaths however, from which the Europeans eventually recovered, but the Indians never did. Area settlers begged for Kieft's replacement, urging the West India Company to send someone who could rebalance the Indian relationship and restructure settlement policies to create communities with political representation, "so that the entire country may not hereafter be at the whim of one man, again reduced to similar danger."

The company did finally replace Kieft as the director of New Netherland, although it took longer than anyone hoped. When Peter Stuyvesant arrived in 1648, company directors carefully advised him against Kieft's policy of ethnic cleansing. On Kieft's long journey home to Holland that same year, he shipwrecked near Swansea and drowned, taking a suspicious fortune of 400,000 guilders to the bottom of the sea with him, along with many important papers concerning his years of mismanaging New Netherland. Perhaps God does exact retribution after all.

The company counseled Peter Stuyvesant to institute "a lenient Indian policy," and remarked disapprovingly, yet poetically, on Kieft's disastrous management:[111]

A Lenient Policy Towards the Indians is Directed—7th April 1648
We shall first reply to your Honor's report on the condition of our terri-
tory there, in which you complain that the soldiers are very disorderly
and without discipline. It looks as if the slackness of the late Director
and the neglect of duty by the preacher have been the cause of it and we
expect your Honor to redress it, even as a tree which has been growing
some time and has run wild, must be pruned with great care and bent
with a tender hand, to be brought into a good shape; . . . of the native
inhabitants of these territories; that they must be governed with kind-
ness and the former wars incline us to believe it; we would have pre-
ferred to avoid these wars, . . . under our present circumstances a war
would be utterly unadvisable.

Chapter Eleven

Her Case Is Very Dangerous

How William Hallett met Elizabeth Feake is not recorded,[112] but Elizabeth finally found the right man for herself and her family. In William she found a strong, clever, and capable person who helped her survive a coming firestorm of destructive intent that would have broken weaker unions. One year after Elizabeth buried her sixth child, baby Sarah Feake, in the loneliness of an entirely unpopulated Old Greenwich in 1647, William Hallett surveyed the situation of Elizabeth attempting to raise five children alone on her West India Company property without Robert Feake or Daniel Patrick around, and a jurisdictional inability to rely on English Stamford for protection from Indian attack. Anneken Patrick was raising her family here alone as well after Daniel's assassination but had the assistance of Toby Feake to sustain her. William and Elizabeth changed at some point from acquaintances to deeply committed life partners. Realizing that her long-term survival lay not only in the abstract philosophies of her father-in-law but in the aid, comfort, and counsel of William Hallett, Elizabeth agreed to their marriage. On a journey to New Haven to marry in a manner that was recognized by English authorities, however, the couple was shocked to discover that New Haven forbid such a marriage to them. Because Robert Feake was insane but still living,[113] yet had abandoned his family by consensual agreement, their quest to marry became a saga of politically and economically motivated impossibility.

William Hallett was born in Bridport, Dorset England in 1616, and was the son of Richard Hallett and Alice or Agnes Alford. His father had died when he was twelve. He and his sisters—Alice, Elizabeth, Hannah, and Susannah—may have arrived in America under the supervision of William's well-off uncle, Andrew Hallett Jr., who arrived in Boston with his own large family and who became the patriarch of today's large Massachusetts branch of the Hallett family. William was an intrepid, personable, and intelligent man, who, in his later will, would describe himself as a yeoman—a middle-class landowner of a hundred or more acres who farmed his own property—a title that differed socially from a gentryman or gentleman like Robert Feake, who began life with wealth inherited from his family's merchant business.

Divorce, or "unwiving" oneself, was extremely rare in England at this time. By the end of the sixteenth century, England was the only Protestant country to have no divorce law and this lasted for three more centuries until 1857. There were, however, practical ways to separate couples in untenable situations, including private separations, desertions and elopements, wife "sales," declarations of annulment, or quite rarely, divorce granted by an act of Parliament. Decrees of separation and annulment had been occasionally granted in England, but they had never been granted in marriages producing children.

The reformist Puritans considered that marriage was a legal contract, and as such, it could be broken or amended. In the colonies, a woman could legally divorce with great difficulty, but only if there was abuse, neglect, cruelty, desertion, and if it was she, not her husband, who had committed the adultery.[114] Generations of Puritans held that "the absolute property of a woman's chastity was vested not in the woman herself, but in her parents or her husband." Those few people who received a divorce were allowed to remarry, but only with governmental approval, which represented a change from established English law. Within American Puritan communities, the family was considered the fundamental

Reverend John Davenport (1597–1669/70) YALE UNIVERSITY ART GALLERY

basis of civilized society, the church ranked second, and the state of the commonwealth came in third in the order of one's earthly priorities.

Repeating her history of proceeding without consent and refusing to face the future alone, Elizabeth and William Hallett began living together without the benefit of a recognized English marriage. The same New Haven magistrates who denied her a legal marriage now felt snubbed by her boldness and promptly began accusing her of adultery.

Accusing Elizabeth Winthrop Feake of adultery after denying her redress began the opening act of a Puritan power play that would pit the Winthrop's Massachusetts Bay Colony against New Haven Colony in a skirmish to prove one's theological supremacy over the others'. New Haven Colony, which functioned under the management of Theophilus Eaton and John Davenport, followed a more conservative, biblically adherent style than did John Winthrop Sr.'s Massachusetts Bay Colony, which considered adultery and other crimes on a case-by-case basis. John Winthrop had experience with adultery within his own family before, with his illegally married Irish uncle, and in an argument about the construction of Puritan punishments that obliquely addressed Elizabeth's situation, he cited Bathsheba as an adulteress whom her king had pardoned as a rebuttal to New Haven's sterner stance. He reflected that, "as upon the law of adultery, it may be a question whether Bathsheba ought to die by that law," because "God himself varieth the punishments of the same offenses, as the offenses vary in their circumstances."[115] He was really reaching with this point, for the king who pardoned Bathsheba, King David, was Bathsheba's lover in question. Prosecuted cases in the Bay Colony were usually watered down to lesser charges of attempted adultery, "uncleanness," or "lasciviousness."[116]

The New Haven and Hartford men, however, perhaps wanted to make an example of how even those with connections and high status, such as the niece and daughter-in-law of Governor Winthrop, could fall if one did not hew to their stricter interpretations. By denying her legal remedy and making an example of the Boston governor's family member, the New Haven and Connecticut Colony, which followed the prescribed penalties of the Capital Laws regardless of an accused's particular situation, sought to affirm their strength, authority, and superior moral authority for all in New England to observe and Elizabeth Fones Winthrop Feake had just become their Puritan political pawn.

Elizabeth and William visited New Haven multiple times to explain their situation, but received no relief for their troubles. In choosing William Hallett over the laws of the English, Elizabeth chose dangerously, for she knew that the death penalty could be a possible consequence, particularly for a woman, since Anne Hutchinson's disruptions still influenced colonial discipline of female dissent. In defiance of Connecticut's capital laws, Elizabeth gambled on her Dutch jurisdiction and the powers of her influential family to protect her.

The unresolved marital state of Elizabeth Feake and William Hallett caused turmoil in the infantile judicial systems of the Connecticut and Massachusetts colonies, which had difficulty addressing the multiple legal issues her case created. Her closest male relatives, Toby Feake and her brand new son-in-law Thomas Lyon (who had recently married Martha Johana Winthrop), seized on her unauthorized and unorthodox situation to own and control her property, as did the Dutch and English politicians, who argued over her land to extend the boundaries of their societies.

Elizabeth's aunt Lucy Downing wrote to her brother John Winthrop to urge him to do whatever he could to help their "Bess":[117]

February 24, 1642/3,

Some things I have desired long to speak to you about my poor cousin Feakes. I have not had opportunity to write to her since she left the Bay, nor have I heard of her but by others; and that only which was not like to be for her good or our comfort. And now I hear Patrick is cut [killed] of which makes me hope that by the use of some good means there might be more hopes to receive her. I beseech you to neglect no opportunity in your power. I speak only in respect of the difficulty of distance she is in, and the multiplicity of business you are burdened with, yet every one is not her mother's child. . . . And as far as I can hear, her case is very dangerous in respect she lives where all good means is wanting.

Legal issues of transactional authority, real estate title, and inheritance became particularly contentious when Elizabeth Feake and William Hallett sold some land out of the joint Feake-Patrick holdings. Title and subdivision rights were difficult to discern at the time, complicated by competing Dutch and English jurisdictional claims. Robert Feake's vagaries as to whom, how, and when he had granted his wife and William Hallett the authority to act on his behalf in regard to ownership and disposition of property became the subject of his sanity depositions. Under questioning, he prevaricated as to whether he had given his children some of it, whether Martha Johana Winthrop was to inherit some, and whether Elizabeth had authority over other parts of it. He seemed to waffle over whether he had given Elizabeth full authority or not, and whether he minded the relationship and acting authority of William Hallett.

Elizabeth's male family members, Toby Feake and Thomas Lyon, were angered by the couple's sale of their inheritable property and they appealed to New Haven Colony officials to resolve the situation, even though New Haven held no jurisdiction over their land. Purchasers of the property in question appealed to the Dutch to guarantee title to their properties, as their real estate lay within the defended jurisdiction of New Netherland, and their letter cast a light on the suspicious nature of English-Stamford vs. Dutch-Greenwich politics of the day.[118] The Greenwich land purchasers worried that Elizabeth's marriage dispute would serve as a pretext for New Haven officials to seize their land, which lay within Dutch jurisdiction, and in effect allow Stamford to "steal" Greenwich away from them.

They warned the Dutch of New Haven's intent, and gave notice of their opposition to English Stamford's plan.

Toby Feake married the widowed Anneken Patrick (and had a son named James Feake by her), and he was legally in line to receive Daniel Patrick's joint portion of any land sale proceeds. Toby, who pressed for additional claims since he was also Robert's ward and nephew, declared that the joint Feake-Patrick purchase was "owned" and managed unjustly by William Hallett and he charged that Elizabeth, by living with Hallett, had illegally passed her authority on to him, rendering Hallett an illegal male head of household with no ability to execute real estate transactions. In return, Elizabeth and William Hallett made Toby prove he was Robert's legal ward and prove that Robert still retained the right to pass land on to him.

Thomas Lyon, the Stamford man who had recently married Martha Johana, was also upset. He could have become the Feake family's acting male head of household if William Hallett had never intervened, in addition to gaining control over Martha Johana's inheritance. He speculated that if it was Elizabeth who was selling the land, she had no right to do so, since Robert had not properly passed his authority on to her. If he had, he opined, it was because Elizabeth had undue influence over Robert and had "seduced" him through his infirmity.

The first man (whose name is not recorded) to give a deposition as to Robert Feake's state of mind stated, to Elizabeth's detriment, that Robert was utterly incapable of making decisions, and was totally under the influence of his wife:[119]

This may certify whom it might concern respecting Mr. Robert Feeke sometime an inhabitant of Greenwich near Stamford . . . that the said Mr. Feeke . . . was a man whose God-fearing heart was so absorbed with spiritual and heavenly things, that he little thought of the things of this life, . . . We moreover considered . . . him as a man so unsettled and troubled in his understanding and brain, that although he was, at times better settled than at others, nevertheless in his last years, and about the time he agreed with his wife, respecting the division of their temporal property, he was not a man of any wisdom, or capable of acting understandingly like any other man in a manner regarding his own benefit, profit and advantage . . . [He] exhibited a more than ordinary respect towards his [recent] wife, and that he in our opinion was more easily to be seduced by her to do whatever she wished than what was wise or reasonable . . .

The second witness, Deacon Thatcher, who cared for Robert Feake in Watertown, also prevaricated about Robert's grant of authority to Elizabeth:

. . . for said Mr. Feake living with my family . . . giving out that his wife took the children, and therefore needed the property more than he . . . in leaving the property to their mother . . . The children possessed a natural and innate right to the property which belonged to their father . . . he became melancholy, and about fourteen days after was seriously ill, headstrong and crazy.

Thomas Lyon and Toby Feake fanned the flames of William and Elizabeth's social ostracism to gain support for their positions. When Martha Johana and Thomas Lyon first married, they lived with Elizabeth and her other children in Greenwich immediately after their marriage. Thomas Lyon spread a salacious and scandalous rumor of her living arrangement with William Hallett to the highest English authorities in New Haven. Lyon even wrote to Elizabeth's uncle, Governor Winthrop, to disparage her and to ask for clarification of Martha Johana's inheritance. He tried to inflame the governor's passions against Elizabeth by emphasizing her disgraced place in society and her new pregnancy by William Hallett as well as nastily insinuating that she might abandon her daughter Martha

Johana or become jilted by Hallett. It seems impossible to imagine that he and Elizabeth were on speaking terms when his first missive to the governor was written in August 1647.[120] His second letter the following spring showed that his intent to defame her had only escalated.

> *From Stamford, ye 14 April, 1648*[121]
>
> *Loving Grandfather, —My humble duty remembered unto you.*
>
> *Concerning my wife's mother, she hath dealt very harsh with me, withholding my right from me in several cases. The reason, as I conceive . . . I shall tell you. When I married first, I lived in the house with her because my father [Robert Feake] being distracted, I might be a help to her. Whereupon seeing several carriages between the fellow she now hath to be her husband and she the people also took notice of it (which was to her disgrace) which grieved me very much . . . And having offered diverse times . . . to help her to take care of her estate . . . that so she might regain her name, bring glory to God, and part with the fellow; yet nothing would prevail, but the more I desired her to part with the fellow, the more I see she were against me . . . However, I am sorrowful for the sad effect she hath brought upon herself in the general . . . others may take notice of her fall that so it may be gain . . .*

The matter was discussed between Governor Winthrop Sr. and Theophilus Eaton, the governor of the New Haven Colony and Lyon was miffed when he was told by Governor Winthrop to deny the rumors, rather than rebuke the couple. Instead of separating Elizabeth Feake from William Hallett, the governor, his sister Lucy Downing, and his son, John Winthrop Jr., continued to befriend and support them.

The magistrates of New Haven Colony, without jurisdiction, but also without Dutch interference, decided to enforce disciplinary action on William Hallett and Elizabeth Winthrop Feake, fully cognizant of Elizabeth's Winthrop family connections but also realizing that John Winthrop

Sr. was now gravely ill. Stamford authorities, as directed by over-reaching magistrates of the New Haven Colony who held no English jurisdiction over an English person within Dutch jurisdiction, leveled an untenable and frightening mandate on her: If William Hallett left, she and her children could remain in Greenwich unmolested, but if she continued to live with William Hallett and settled in New London, Watertown, or any English colony, two of her children and half of the Feake estate would be governed by English authorities, and Stamford authorities would have jurisdiction over her other two children, maintaining the property for Robert Feake. If she chose to leave Greenwich, the decree continued, she could not take her children or any assets of the estate with her. Her family would be broken apart and authority over it would be removed from her. Adding to her stress at this same time in 1649, thirty-nine-year-old Elizabeth gave birth to her seventh child, William Hallett Jr.

Governor Eaton of New Haven wrote John Winthrop Jr. on July 21, 1648[122] that he had directed William Hallett to straighten out all real estate and adultery issues surrounding the Greenwich property in New England's courts rather than those of New Netherland. William Hallett rejected this idea, since English Stamford was about to seize Elizabeth's land and take away half of her children.

Indian violence had also flared again at this time along the Greenwich-Stamford border. In October 1648, a well-liked Stamford man named John Whitmore, who likely lived near modern Whitmore Street on the Greenwich-Stamford border and grazed his livestock on the large, low-lying plain there, went out to feed his cattle one morning when he was jumped by some Indians and killed.[123] The Indians, called the "Toquattoes," presumably because they were from "Toquams," today's Shippan Point area of Stamford, refused to reveal what they had done with his body until a high-ranking sachem from out of town named Uncas forced them to do so. Stamford and the Greenwich settlers became newly alarmed over resurgent Indian attacks.

With Indian wrath recurring, and Stamford officials on their way to seize her children, Elizabeth and William fled overnight by boat from Greenwich to John Winthrop Jr.'s home in New London, accompanied by her many Feake children and their new infant Hallett stepbrother. An upset Governor Eaton wrote, "William Hallett in a secret underhand way, had taken the children, two cows, all the household goods, and what else I know not, and by water were gone away . . . the children went (if not naked) very unsatisfyingly appareled." And, "she had no right to take the children."[124]

Elizabeth was also forced to leave her daughter Martha Johana in Stamford to face her future alone with a sullen Thomas Lyon.

Chapter Twelve

Martha Johana Winthrop Lyon

ELIZABETH HAD WORRIED ABOUT HER FIRST CHILD, MARTHA JOHANA by Henry Winthrop, ever since she had married Thomas Lyon. She suspected that the continually complaining man had married her daughter mostly for her inheritance of their extensive Greenwich property and, failing that, had been neglecting or abusing her. Lyon had unwisely written to Governor Winthrop that Martha Johana, the governor's own granddaughter, had been "a hindrance to him" with her frequent illnesses and lack of strength. As it turned out, Elizabeth's worries were justified, but for an entirely different reason, and one that may unwittingly have been caused by her own medical recommendations.

While Elizabeth lived in exile and safety in New London with John Winthrop Jr., she expressed her mounting concerns about Martha Johana to him and they did what they could to protect her. John Jr. asked Theophilus Eaton (who was no friend to the Halletts) to check in on Martha Johana the next time he travelled to Stamford. This was, perhaps, also a way to elicit some sympathy for the family from the family's most determined Puritan prosecutor.

John Winthrop Jr., who was Martha Johana's uncle, was Connecticut's acting surgeon-in-chief of sorts, a true renaissance man who was renowned and respected in Massachusetts and Connecticut for his alchemical knowledge and medicinal abilities, in addition to his governmental efforts and interests in determining New England's mining and geological promise.[125]

He treated hundreds of people for every illness known to man in this era and likely discussed various treatments with Elizabeth, who was undoubtedly part of his statewide network of local female practitioners whom he advised. Eaton replied to Winthrop that he was "altogether a stranger to Thomas Lyon and his wife; till now, I have not heard the least intimation of her weakness or his neglect. From your information, I shall now enquire, and consider what the case may require."

That same year, Martha Johana came down with severe digestive difficulties and a weakness in her limbs. She did, however, also manage to give birth to a second child named Mary Lyon, who survived whereas her first child had not. Based on her uncle's continued enquiries concerning her welfare, Martha Johana explained her situation. She refers to the birth of her child, and assumes blame for Thomas Lyon's difficult life. She also reveals the poverty-stricken nature of her life while living within the Stamford settlement:[126]

> *To my loving and kind Uncle, Mr. John Winthrop, at Pequot, this dd.*
> *From Stamford, ye 23 March, 1648/9*
> *Most Loving and Kind Uncle and Aunt,*
> *My humble duty remembered unto you. . . . I humbly thank you for your great love and care toward me in that you have sought to know how it is with me. Mr. Eaton being here I have sent by him plainly and nakedly how it is. I hope he will acquaint you. For my own part I am weaker than ever I was and not able to do anything, scarce to take my own vittles when it is set by me. I likewise have a very bad stomach, but . . . because of my breeding my stomach is very choice and dainty, which causes me to suffer the more, my husband being not able nor at leisure to get me what I would. Here is no help to*

*be got, neither by neighborhood nor servants, my husband being forced
to do all both for himself and me, which is great hindrance and loss. I
entreat you, good Uncle, consider my condition as it is and help me a
little with some of your cast off clothes, for I know not how to do when
the Lord please to give me another little one. For my husband's part,
he does what he can for me and I am sorry he should suffer so much
for me, for he drinks water that I might drink beer, eats Indian [corn]
that I might eat wheat, and fares hard & works hard that I might not
suffer; but you may consider partly his condition that he cannot do as
he would. . . . Remember my duty to my Mother. I sent a letter to her.
I hope she hath received it . . . In haste, I rest*

> *Your humble and dutiful cozen,*
> *Martha Johana Lyon.*

Her next three letters are written in three different hands, meaning
she dictated her responses to her husband as well as to some others. In the
first letter she apologizes for costing Thomas Lyon money to hire a wet
nurse for the baby and for being a burden to him.[127]

*To the Worshipful her very loving Uncle, Mr. John Winthrop, at
Pequot, [New London] give this I pray.*

> *Stamford, dated this Second of September, 1649*
> *Right Worthy Uncle,*
> *. . . the late great God hath . . . given me a comfortable deliverance
> of a daughter who is a hopeful child & likely to live; & myself is well
> up again, thanks be given to God in & through Christ Jesus for it. I
> am forced to put it out to nurse by reason of my infirmity & because
> help is not to be had, so that my husband is at great charges for the
> nursing of it, . . . Concerning my husband's carriage to me I have no
> cause to complain, but rather to bless God that hath given him a heart*

to go through so many troubles with so much patience; for he is very
loving and kind to me & tender over me, so that I want for nothing
that lies in his power . . . Your humble and dutiful niece,
   Martha Johanna Lyon
   My husband also remembers his duty and service to yourself & my
Aunt & the children & love to the rest.

She wrote her uncle again seven weeks later telling him about her six-month-old daughter Mary and asked him to send more "white copperas," or iron sulfate, to apply to an oozing sore. John Winthrop Sr. had originally supplied her with some for the treatment of her malady; iron sulfate had been used since the Middle Ages to treat iron-deficiency anemia. It was also used to make ink and dyes, such as indigo, set permanently into fabric. Her many requests for it indicate that her use of it for her wound was endorsed by John Winthrop Jr. and Sr. and also by her mother.[128]

Worthy Sir & My Dear Uncle,
   . . . my little daughter whom God hath given me, now about half a
year old. We call her name Mary. She is well in health (through mercy)
& a thriving child for one bred up without the breast, as this hath
been. My husband and I are in good health. For myself, I am very hale
in body, saving that my weakness in my limbs abides with me; but it
increases not, so far as I find which is a great mercy . . . I had of my
grandfather some white copperas, which I found very good for my sore,
as drying up the humors flowing from it; but now it is almost gone &
I know not how to get a supply in these parts. I humbly entreat you, if
you can, to get & send me some of it, or anything else that you know of
that may be good for me in that respect . . .

In February of the following year, when she was twenty-one, she wrote Winthrop again and even more insistently for more "copperas" and now

146

for red lead, or lead tetroxide, which Elizabeth also had been supplying. Besides being used as a paint fixative when combined with linseed oil, red lead was used to treat ulcerations and ringworm topically, but it is highly toxic to humans when inhaled or ingested. In contact with open tissue, its effects can be quite fatal. Using it frequently on an open wound, Martha Johana would have experienced vision disorders and hypertension, and her skin would have had a gray pallor. A very sick Martha Johana struck a sad and forlorn note in her last letter when she mentioned Elizabeth and William's move away from Greenwich to get closer to Manhattan:

> *To her loving and kind Uncle, Mr. John Winthrop, living at Pequot, this dd.*
>> *From Stamford, the 17 February, 1650/1*
>> *Most loving and kind uncle and aunt,*
>> *. . . I am in good health and my child also. I would entreat you to send me some white copperas and red lead, and what may be fit for service, for I yet remain as I were and have need of some and know not what to do for some. My mother's is all spent. I pray you to do what you can, because of my own particular need of it. My mother is well and removing farther off from me . . .*

Martha Johana Winthrop Lyon, the only child of Elizabeth and Henry Winthrop, died sometime before 1654, when she was twenty-three and it is unknown whether Elizabeth felt safe enough to sail to English Stamford to attend her daughter's funeral.

CHAPTER THIRTEEN

"She is resolute in her course"

ON JULY 21, 1648, JOHN WINTHROP JR., WHO WAS HARBORING ELIZABETH Feake and William Hallett and their children in New London, or "Naumeag," received notice from Governor Eaton[129] of the New Haven Colony that William Hallett was to prove what part of Greenwich belonged to him. This letter also noted—to his horror—that an arrest warrant had actually been issued for the couple and that they were commanded to appear soon in Hartford at the Connecticut Colony court. Governor John Haynes of the Connecticut Colony in Hartford was so intent on his quarry that he even criticized John Winthrop Jr. for protecting the couple at his New London plantation named "Pequot," since New London was under Connecticut Colony jurisdiction. His court had found:[130]

> . . . that one Hallett, with one that was Mr. Feakes' (Pheax) his wife, are now come into, and live in the Plantation of Pequot, and . . . have committed in other places, and . . . at the present, that foul sin of adultery which is odious to God and man. And therefore this Court cannot but take notice of it. It is therefore ordered, that there be a warrant directed to the Constable of the same town to apprehend the said parties and to bring them up to the next particular Court in Hartford, which will be upon the first Thursday of the next month.

John Haynes, Connecticut's first governor, was committed to his moral mission, and he had the actual warrant delivered to John Winthrop Jr. on March 18, 1649 (Old Style):[131]

> *There is cognizance taken by our Court, of some parties resident with you that are of ill fame, as one that was the wife sometimes of Mr. Feake, & who it seems did confess herself an adulteress, (which is upon record at The Dutch), and now pretends marriage with another man, how true or legal is not well known. I am therefore to acquaint you that she with some others is sent for by warrant to appear at the Court here, to answer according to the tenure thereof. We could do no other but seek to do justice in such horrid facts, if truth, unless we should lay ourselves & others under guilt.*

Both Eaton and Haynes had ignored Elizabeth's continued pleas for a compassionate resolution to her situation, and chose instead to condemn her. "I shall pass by her injurious writings to myself,"[132] sniffed a dismissive Eaton to Elizabeth's repeated pleas for leniency in a letter dated January 4, 1648/9, "desiring God may give her true repentance for greater miscarriages, but her departure from Stamford with the children, (as I am informed) was altogether without allowance, and . . . she stole away . . . I pity her, and the children. . . .

John Winthrop Jr. likely spent many meals in New London conferring with Elizabeth and William Hallett in deciding what to do, and his solution was truly insightful, ingenious, and original. He completely bypassed his own English bureaucrats and struck a deal with the Dutch to have the very English Elizabeth divorce Robert Feake within New Netherland because she was, technically, a Dutch citizen, and her land lay indisputably within Dutch jurisdiction. Winthrop negotiated with William Kieft to accomplish this and Kieft agreed—most likely to keep the peace with

Winthrop personally, whom he wanted as an Indian fighting ally—while taking a swipe at the English from New Haven, whose aggressive territory acquisitions he detested. In discussing Elizabeth's case[133] Kieft noted that he was giving her special dispensation and reiterated New Haven's divorce stipulations that the Feake children should be split up with some cared for by English Stamford, that the property was to be saved for Robert Feake and his heirs, and that William Hallett was to be banished from Elizabeth's bed. The Dutch never however enforced any of these terms, as it was all a smoke screen meant for the Halletts' protection. With this maneuver John Winthrop Jr. challenged the New Haven and Connecticut colonies' claim of jurisdiction over the couple and their property because they were English subjects. For their part, the English refused to recognize Kieft's Dutch divorce of Robert and Elizabeth Feake as legal within New England, and they kept up the pressure on the couple to surrender themselves to the English.

Peter Stuyvesant replaced William Kieft that same year as the director of New Netherland, and so John Winthrop Jr. had to establish a relationship with the Dutch all over again on behalf of Elizabeth and to address many other matters concerning the dual Dutch and English ownership of the area we know today as Connecticut. First addressing the brand new director as "Peter Stephenson," Winthrop acquainted Stuyvesant with his cousin's situation and asked him to allow his father to deal with it personally. He proposed to remedy the situation, such that the Hallett case "shall be disposed of by the direction of my father and the English magistrates according to the English laws in your behalf."[134] In other words, with Stuyvesant's permission, the Winthrops were proposing to exert English jurisdiction over their own family members who lived within New Netherland.

Stuyvesant's reaction was an emphatic message to warn off any English plans, politically or personally, to exert jurisdiction over Greenwich. In his first three months in America, Stuyvesant strengthened the Dutch

Governor Peter Stuyvesant (1592–1672) C. 1660 (OIL ON PANEL) BY HENDRICK
COUTURIER (FL. 1648–D.C. 1684) (ATTR.) © COLLECTION OF THE NEW YORK HISTORICAL
SOCIETY, USA / THE BRIDGEMAN ART LIBRARY

title to Greenwich by buying all the land that ran along the coast from the Mianus River to Stamford's Mill River, and in a document called "Deed to Westchester County, Eastern Half,"[135] he confiscated all of the Feake-Patrick-Hallett land in the process. His purchase of this property from some Westchester Munsees, overseen by a widely travelled sachem named Seyseychhimmus, meant that Westchester Indians now controlled the area of southwestern Connecticut, since Mianus had been killed. Stuyvesant's purchase, which included all of modern-day Riverside and Old Greenwich, ran right up to the Mill River doorstep of Stamford's English settlement. The price of this property at the time was "six fathoms of duffels [canvas cloth], six strings of wampum, six kettles, six axes, addices [adzes], ten knives, some iron, coals, one gun, two staves of lead, two lbs. of [gun] powder, and one coat of duffels." In this deed we find that the Munsees called the Mianus River the "Kechkawes," (Kech-ka-wess) and the English called it "Greenwich Bay." We also learn the Munsees' name for Stamford's Mill River was the "Seweyruc."

Stuyvesant's purchase was described to West India Company administrators by Fort Amsterdam secretary Cornelius van Tienhoven as a strategy to strengthen the Company's title to the territory and to block further English encroachment toward New Amsterdam. Van Tienhoven wrote:[136]

The village of Greenwich belonging to their High Mightinesses, being the furthest place where the Director and Council exercise authority, in the name of their High Mightinesses the States General and of the West India Company, is separated from the English village of Stamford, by a small stream; so that the English along the main north coast cannot approach nearer New Netherland, without being obliged to settle between Greenwich and New Amsterdam, where there is an interval of about seven leagues of country: And to prevent that, Director Stuyvesant purchased these lands last summer from the native and right owners thereof, and paid for them, on account of the West India Company.

New Haven, Stamford, and Connecticut colony men groused and grumbled over this clever Dutch chess move but did nothing militarily to refute it. John Winthrop Jr. backed off and acknowledged Dutch jurisdiction over Greenwich. He then asked Stuyvesant to allow the couple to come back to Greenwich so that they could work their land and support their family. Winthrop himself could not continue to provide for them in New London, he noted, in addition to his own large family. He also assured Stuyvesant that Robert Feake had approved of William Hallett to manage his property:[137]

> There was an agreement made with William Hallett for the management of her estate (which Mr. Feakes, before his going into England told me at Boston that he fully consented to, knowing him to be industrious and careful, which I find since her being here to be very true,) that you will be pleased to let the estate be again returned into her hands, not knowing any other way how it can be improved to the comfortable maintenance of her and the children, who for present for want of it are in a necessitous condition; and also that you will be pleased to grant him liberty to return again within your jurisdiction that he may gather up the scattered estate & improve the land at Greenwich, which may add much to their comfortable subsistence . . .

He mentions that Robert Feake had gone to England and had returned. While it is not known why he went, most likely he went seeking medical treatment or was part of a lawsuit concerning a Feake family inheritance dispute. It is also possible that he went to attend the public trial of his cousin, Christopher Feake, who had railed against Cromwell and was subsequently imprisoned in the Tower of London. It was, in fact, not uncommon for those who came to America during the wave of the Great Migration, the ten years between 1630 and 1640, to return or remigrate back to England when religious conflict there and the climate of imminent threat had decreased due to Cromwell's governmental gains.

The trend to return was perhaps most notable for non-farming people, such as shopkeepers or academics, who found it difficult to make a living in America without a developed infrastructure, and who may have still had important assets and business networks left in England. Recent scholarship by Susan Hardman Moore[138] indicates that while many remained in America, by the 1640s and 1650s the flow of people between England and America had reversed from the trend of the 1630s and more people were going back to England than coming to America. Moore estimates that perhaps as many as one in four or 25 percent of America's English population returned to England permanently by 1660. These included well-to-do and connected emigrants, such as Elizabeth's aunt and uncle, the Downings, who stayed only ten years or so then returned to England to more successfully participate politically in Cromwell's Protestant reformation within their mother country. Others, less fearful of bodily harm, returned to the families they had left behind, more profitable businesses, and the management of significant assets they still owned in England.

On a comical note, while the Halletts lived in New London with the Winthrops, they took steps to protect their hastily abandoned items in Greenwich by asking James Hallett, who was likely a relative of William's, to retrieve them.[139] Unfortunately, James, who had been branded on his hand for past English thefts, was caught stealing from the Feake-Patrick property in Greenwich, likely by Toby Feake or Thomas Lyon, and was taken prisoner to Fort Amsterdam. The items stolen were acknowledged to be trivial, but he was punished for a litany of interesting Dutch offenses such as: running off with a tavern keeper's serving girl on Christmas Eve, leaving New Netherland without a proper pass, and stealing an Indian's canoe. The penalty for James Hallett's offenses was to saw wood for the administrators of Fort Amsterdam for a year while reporting back to the jail every night unless he posted bond and repented. His sentence was reduced by his apparently good behavior. He further provoked the Dutch, however, when he assisted "one James Rootrock, who was confined for theft, to escape at night from jail ... and also to carry off Hans Rootrock's wife and run away with her," probably to reunite her with her husband, who might have been a friend of James's. For this offense, the Dutch sentenced him to be "severely whipped with rods," and upped his labor sentence. He was also sentenced to be locked with a chain to a post and made to saw the wood indefinitely. James Hallett skipped town instead of serving this sentence and was recorded as "a fugitive." He unfortunately never appears in the records again to entertain us.

John Jr.'s many entreaties to Peter Stuyvesant to allow the Halletts back to Greenwich were ultimately successful. Stuyvesant may also have allowed the couple a Dutch remarriage or John Jr. may have married the couple in a New London ceremony, for Elizabeth now signed herself "Elizabeth Hallett." It's also possible that a Greenwich farmer named Andrew Crab, a brother-in-law of Stamford resident Robert Coe, married them. Crab had moved from Wethersfield to Stamford and then into Greenwich. He was accused by New Haven Colony authorities of performing "illegal" marriages, specifically one between Dutch Manhattan teenager Maria Verleth and Johannis van Beeck in "Groenwits" in 1654 without the proper posting of banns, which were written notices of marriage intent, and without permission from Van Beeck's father.[140] That Crab married these two teens may suggest that he had married people before and that Greenwich at this time was a known haven for runaway Dutch teenagers.

The Halletts were overjoyed with John Winthrop Jr.'s success on their behalf, writing many letters expressing their sincere and grateful thanks to him. On May 8, 1649, they also sold their six-acre New London home lot and thirty acres of pasture land to him for £10.[141] As they sailed from New London back to Greenwich, Elizabeth told her cousin that in their haste "We have left your table board and frame and bellows-board upon the cow house, and the rack in the yard."[142] The irony, and political adroitness, of John Winthrop Jr. to circumvent his colony's own English laws

Pro 2 Prov: VI. 11

Loving brother I acknowledg my self exceeding
obliged vnto you and therefore shall take this and
all other opertunities to manifest my thankful-
nes; I wrot 2 letters to you before one by
richard smith, the other by my cosen felt
that miscaried with his bote; through the
mercy of god we are in health and peace
att greenwich we have made a quiet end
about the estate wᵗʰ mʳ feke we have bought
all his land and right in greenwich ____
the dutch governour hath purchased all
land along the cost yet I vnderstand the
person you spake to vs to bui land for may have
land inough of him on better termes then any
other hath had; he would gladly see your
self my husband and my self desire to tender
our hearty loue and best respect to your self
and my sister our loue to mʳˢ Lake my
cosens and the neybours and shall euer rest

greenwich this
of feb 1649 new stile

your vnfained loning sister
Elizabeth Hallet

Letter in Elizabeth Hallett's hand ALLYN BAILEY FORBES, ED. THE WINTHROP PAPERS,
BOSTON, MASSACHUSETTS HISTORICAL SOCIETY, 1947.5:358–359

to find safety for his cousin's family by having New Netherland reinforce Dutch jurisdiction over them was a stroke of brilliance and great irony. It also supports John Winthrop Jr.'s reputation for intelligence, compassion, and innovation, while acknowledging his disinclination to further Connecticut or New Haven's strict ideology. He is also credited with later offering up an important piece of rationale that largely put a stop to witch trials in Connecticut.

Elizabeth wrote him a month later from Greenwich, profusely thanking him for his work to restore them, John Jr. being "the instrument of my present well being," and stating that the Dutch continued to hold their coastal acreage.

Once arrived back in Greenwich on February 12, 1649, Elizabeth told John Jr. that the Dutch governor's jurisdiction was still in effect and that she had resolved the real estate issues with Robert Feake peacefully:[143] "Through the mercy of God we are in health and peace at Greenwich. We have made a quiet end about the estate with Mr. Feke; we have bought all his land and right in Greenwich. Ye Dutch Governor hath purchased all ye land along the coast . . . Your unfeigned loving sister, Elizabeth Hallett."

Further communications between the two noted that the Dutch continued to treat them well, and that Stuyvesant extended John Jr. his good wishes and about this time, Elizabeth's uncle and John Winthrop's father, John Winthrop Sr., the former first governor of the Massachusetts Bay Colony, died in Boston from a lengthy illness.

CHAPTER FOURTEEN

The Halletts Abandon New England for New Netherland

The Halletts' return to Greenwich was very brief. On September 19, 1650, after much bickering between Stuyvesant and the English about the location of the border between New Netherland and New England, Stuyvesant agreed to a meeting in 1650 to clarify the situation. The Treaty of Hartford resulted in some terms that stemmed directly from Elizabeth Feake Hallett's case and Stuyvesant's promises to the Winthrop men that he would, ironically, protect the couple from their own English people.

The Dutch had hoped to deal with the English in England to establish boundary lines between the two colonial societies in America. By 1648, however, Charles I, the king of England, had been imprisoned by Cromwell and England was embroiled in its civil war. The Dutch had no clear English negotiating partner, and the chance to ratify an American boundary in Europe seemed remote. Tempers flared on the Connecticut border issue when a Dutch ship, the *St. Beninjo,* from the Caribbean, bypassed the Dutch tax office on Manhattan to trade with English colonies in New Haven and Virginia, despite warnings from the Dutch governor that the Dutch ship should trade only within Dutch ports in America.

Stuyvesant tried to set up a meeting with John Winthrop Sr. to discuss trading regulations that would benefit both societies and to define a border that was less contentious. His relations with the Bay Colony

158

leader had always been more cordial than his interactions with those at New Haven or the Connecticut Colony at Hartford, most likely because he and Winthrop had little geographic contact. After many delays, including John Sr.'s death in 1649, a meeting between the Dutch and the English was finally held at Hartford. The West India Company cautioned Stuyvesant to try to keep the peace with the now more powerful English because company resources were not allocated for any war against them.

Negotiations between Stuyvesant and New England colony representatives resulted in a curious compromise concerning Greenwich. When Stuyvesant left the meeting, a strange island of Dutch sovereignty had been created, which encompassed all the land between the west bank of the Mianus River and Tomac Creek and included all of modern-day Riverside and Old Greenwich. Stuyvesant also agreed that the new hard boundary between New England and New Netherland was the west bank of the Mianus, but that no further Dutch settlements would be built anywhere between Rye, New York, and Darien, Connecticut. This twelve-mile zone limited widespread Dutch population increase, with its attendant protections, and severely isolated Greenwich's existing settlers, including the returned Hallett family. It also demonstrated that Dutch sovereignty in the region had now become seriously unstable. The treaty's terms concerning Greenwich were specifically that:

> *The bounds upon the main to begin at the west side of Greenwich Bay being about four miles from Stamford and so to run a northerly line twenty miles up into the country and after as it shall be agreed by the two governments of the Dutch and of New Haven provided the said line shall not come within ten miles of Hudson's River. And it is agreed that the Dutch shall not at any time hereafter build any house or habitation within six miles of the said line. The inhabitants of*

Greenwich to remain until further consideration thereof be had under the government of the Dutch.

The Halletts were now uncomfortably wedged between the threatening English to their east in Stamford and a far more tenuous Dutch jurisdiction for six miles east and six miles west of them. Stuyvesant's negotiating results inflamed West India Company critic Adrien van der Donck, who had been prohibited from returning to America from Holland by Stuyvesant to limit his scathing criticisms of New Netherland's governance. When he heard the Treaty of Hartford's terms, he howled that Stuyvesant had "given Greenwich away to the English." Although his objections were not completely accurate, they surely did come close. Van der Donck's sympathetic allies painted the meeting in its worst possible light and reported to him that during the treaty negotiations, the English treated Stuyvesant like "a Prince" by flattering him, and then hoodwinked him by "a sweet and right subtle line."[144] Stuyvesant's critics wrote that the English actually bypassed the director and negotiated only with George Baxter, Stuyvesant's English secretary, instead. They said that when Stuyvesant was later charged with giving up Greenwich, he first claimed ignorance of the fact, and then claimed betrayal by Baxter to save face. In reality he realized New Netherland's strength had deteriorated to the point where he could barely enforce any claim, and that his best option was to forestall the inevitable as long as he could by limiting Dutch development instead of giving up the region outright. He also knew the company turned a deaf ear to the prescient but unprofitable demands of Adrien van der Donck.

The Halletts recognized that limited jurisdiction renewed the threat of their English prosecution, and they decided to immediately move more deeply into Dutch territory for their greater safety. Hallett wrote of his worry over these treaty negotiations and his pre-emptive plans to John Winthrop Jr. in October 1650:[145] "We hear that New Haven has propounded to our Governor to have Greenwich under them. We know not what is done as yet. I have sold my house and land and intend in the spring to remove nearer to Manhattan."

For three years following the Treaty of Hartford agreements, Stuyvesant complained of recalcitrant and mulish English administrators who were not upholding the treaty's tenets because they were allowing some English settlers to move into the twelve-mile no-Dutch-build-zone. English authorities tried to make the case that they originally owned Greenwich with the fantasy of a 1638 agreement with sachems that represented territory from New Haven to Manhattan, but this effort went nowhere. Stuyvesant accused the English of demonstrating "an insatiable desire of possessing that which is ours, against our protestations, against the law of Nations." He complained of New Haven Colony's "offensive affronts, and unpleasing answers," and "sundry usurpations," in a long list of grievances.[146] He reiterated specific Hartford Treaty agreements that:

> If any English . . . bought and paid for any lands within the limits and jurisdiction of New Netherland . . . [such as] upon Long Island by Captain Howe and at Stamford by Mr. Feakes . . . that the inhabitants of Greenwich shall remain under the Government of the Dutch, . . . and to show we have been kind governors of these people we have not meddled with or interrupted any of the subjects of Greenwich nor the place itself, nor have placed any magistrates therein; but left them as Neutrals at this time.

He reiterated Patrick's oath of fidelity to New Netherland that was "freely submitted," failing to mention the escort of Dutch soldiers sent by Kieft in 1642 to enforce this submission. For the time being, Dutch jurisdiction over the area effectively trumped any claim of an older Indian allegiance to the English.

Worried that the weakened Dutch sovereignty would embolden the New Haven Colony to bully the Halletts and reactivate their adultery warrant, John Winthrop Jr. again negotiated with Stuyvesant to allow William Hallett to buy a farm deep within New Netherland and remove the family from Greenwich. Stuyvesant agreed to let them have a property of twelve cleared acres across the East River from Manhattan in October 1650. Fearing for their lives, the Halletts moved once more just a year after their return to Greenwich from New London.

In November 1650, Elizabeth and William executed the sale of their remaining Greenwich property to Stamford resident Jeffrey Ferris. Even

The border between New Netherland and New England in Greenwich shifted four times in the sixteen years between 1640 and 1656.

1640: Original Feake and Patrick joint purchase of Petuckquapoch, renamed Greenwich, then Groenwits. Patoumuck Creek is the border between Greenwich and Stamford. In 1642, soldiers from Fort Amsterdam enforce Dutch sovereignty over Greenwich. Patoumuck Creek now also becomes the border between New England and New Netherland.

1648: Stuyvesant purchases all the land from the Mianus (the Kechkawes) to Stamford's Mill River (the Seweyruc) to block English Colony encroachment toward Manhattan. Stuyvesant seizes all Feake and Patrick land along the coast in this action.

1650: Treaty of Hartford terms: The border between New Netherland and New England is moved west to the west bank of the Mianus River from its previous boundary of Stamford's Mill River. Land and people living in a six-mile zone on either side of the west bank of the Mianus River remain under Dutch jurisdiction, but additional Dutch development is prohibited. Stuyvesant assumes further English settlement is prohibited, as well.

1656: The border between Greenwich and Stamford reverts to the original border of Patoumuck Creek. In 1665 New Netherland falls to the English and New Amsterdam becomes New York.

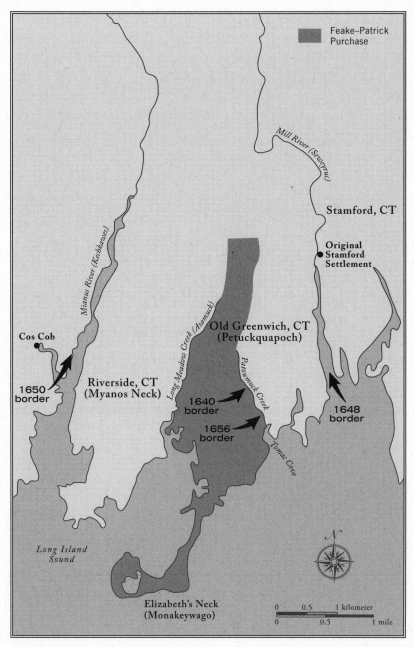

Feake–Patrick
Purchase

Mill River (Seweyruc)

Stamford, CT

Original
Stamford
Settlement

Mianus River (Kechkawes)

Long Meadow Creek (Asamuck)

Cos Cob

Old Greenwich, CT
(Petuckquapoch)

Riverside, CT
(Myanos Neck)

Patormuck Creek

1650
border

1640
border

1656
border

1648
border

Tomac Cove

Long Island
Sound

Elizabeth's Neck
(Monakeywago)

N

0   0.5   1 kilometer
0   0.5   1 mile

The changing eastern mainland borders between New Netherland and New
England.

though jurisdiction of their Greenwich land was held by New Netherland, it's possible that they executed this agreement under the auspices of English authorities, as Ferris, a Stamford resident, lived under English jurisdiction.

A year later, from Long Island, in 1651, Hallett wrote John Winthrop Jr. about the continued legal wrangling over Greenwich's nationality and the very good property they had purchased that was near the East River whirlpool called the Hellgate in modern-day Astoria, and the continuing Indian threat to the settlers living near them.[147]

> *Worthy Sir,*
> *. . . Our habitation is by the whirlpool which the Dutchmen call the Hellgate, where we have purchased a very good farm through the Governor's means that had fine housing and 12 acres of ploughed land fenced in, and a good meadow and other land sufficient for our use. The Lord hath been very bountiful to us, beyond our thoughts, so that we live very comfortably according to our rank. In the Spring, the Indians killed 4 Dutchmen near to our house, which made us think to have removed to some town for refuge, and through God's mercy every plantation was willing to receive us, which they expressed by writing us to dwell with them. Yet now the Indians are quiet and we think not yet to remove . . .*
> *Your truly loving cozens,*
> *William and Elizabeth Hallett*

Elizabeth's relief at being accepted into Long Island society completely and without condition, in that "every plantation was willing to receive us," is evident. Once established within New Netherland, her social ostracism had ended.

The jurisdiction of Greenwich continued to be Dutch until 1656, when Dutch power had declined and it was no longer a threat to English expansion. New Haven officials could finally order Greenwich to accede

Letter in William Hallett's hand selling Greenwich holdings to Jeffrey Ferris
GREENWICH LAND RECORDS. BOOK ONE.

to English jurisdiction sixteen years after the original Feake-Patrick purchase of 1640. In pressing New Haven to take control of Greenwich in 1655, Stamford complained of its wantonness. A court reporter wrote:[148]

> *The Deputies of Stamford have propounded that they have and do still suffer great inconvenience and damage by Greenwich, who pound their cattle off the common, besides their disorderly walking amongst themselves, admitting of drunkenness both among the English and the Indians, whereby they are apt to do mischief, both to themselves and others; they receive disorderly children or servants who fly from their parents or masters lawful correction; they marry persons in a disorderly way, besides other miscarriages; and therefore, if the court sees meet, they desire some cause may be taken to reduce them to join with Stamford in this jurisdiction, and they rather because they pretend to shelter themselves under the commonwealth of England, who we are confident will not approve of such carriages.*

In smugly assuming title over their new real estate, English authorities rewrote the 1650 Treaty of Hartford's terms to their advantage, stating that the treaty had rewarded Greenwich to the English. This verified Stuyvesant's old charge that the English had an "insatiable desire to possess that which is Dutch." New Haven authorities twisted history[149] when they

> *. . . considered of the several particulars, and remembered how Greenwich at first was by Mr. Robert Feake, the first purchaser of the said lands, freely put under this jurisdiction, though after Captain Patrick did injuriously put himself and it under the Dutch, yet after, it was by agreement at Hartford with the Dutch Governor in 1650, to be resigned to New Haven jurisdiction again, and since, we hear that the Dutch do exercise no authority over them; all which*

being considered, the court did agree and ordered that a letter should
be written to them from this court, (which they desire the Governor
to draw up), and sent now by the Deputies of Stamford, requir-
ing them according to the justice of the case to submit themselves to
this jurisdiction, which if they refuse, then the court must consider of
some other way.

This inaccurate remembering undoubtedly contributed to 1700s historian Benjamin Trumbull's erroneous assertion that Greenwich was founded by New Haven, a myth that persists to the present day. Trumbull correctly reports the terms of the Treaty of Hartford in his 1797 book, *A Complete History of Connecticut*, which states that Greenwich was to remain under the Dutch, but then immediately contradicts this text and states that "The purchase [of Greenwich] was made on behalf of New Haven, but through the intrigues of the Dutch Governor and the treachery of the purchasers, the first inhabitants revolted to the Dutch," which implies that Daniel Patrick somehow reversed Greenwich jurisdiction. Trumbull's personal preference for the town to have been English instead of Dutch, regardless of the facts, is further revealed when he also wrote,[150] "The Dutch were always mere intruders. They had no right to any part of this country" and "The English ever denied their right." His assertion, along with that of the New Haven Colony men, that Greenwich was founded under the auspices of the New Haven Colony, was only wishful thinking.

After years of resistance, the actual subjugation of Greenwich to the New Haven Colony in 1656 was not without furious, spirited, long-running, and hilarious opposition by two very cranky Greenwich residents: Andrew Crab, the same man who conducted illegal marriages for errant Dutch teenagers in Greenwich, and his wife. This voluble and histrionic couple, who clearly had no problem with challenging authority, fought adamantly against a New Haven takeover of Greenwich, and swore that

Benjamin Trumbull CONNECTICUT HISTORICAL SOCIETY, HARTFORD, CONNECTICUT

they would only be governed from England, directly. Narratives report that Mrs. Crab physically charged visiting magistrates, and railed at them in no uncertain terms, in "the most foul and insulting language," that New Haven just wanted to steal Greenwich. New Haven officials tried two cases against the Crabs: one concerning their opposition to New Haven's jurisdiction over them and another for Mr. Crab's penchant for marrying people without authority. Of significant detriment to the merits of the Crabs' arguments were the records of the couple's extremely lax church attendance. There was a third suit brought against Mr. Crab by Greenwich landowners Heusted and Reynolds, charging him with stealing a colt and painting a star on its face to disguise it. The horse theft resolution pages are missing in the records of New Haven Colony, but other records indicate that fines were levied for the couple's abusive behavior toward New Haven authorities.

Chapter Fifteen

Hellgate

AFTER LEAVING GREENWICH, THE HALLETTS MOVED DEEPLY INTO Dutch territory, far away from Puritan reach, to modern-day Astoria, Queens, next to a turbulent waterway named the Hellgate. They made their home on a point of land on the furthest reach of western Long Island, which they called "Nassau Island," where the currents from three large waterways—the East River, the Harlem River, and Long Island Sound—intersected over a shallow and rocky shoal. In the 1600s when the tides changed here, these waters swirled viciously and noisily and caused a famously dramatic and exceedingly treacherous whirlpool. The name "Hell Gate" was a corruption of the Dutch word "Hellgat," which meant "bright passage," which was originally applied to the entirety of the East River, a highly valued shipping lane as it allowed access to the Hudson River via the Bronx River and Long Island Sound. By the late nineteenth century, many ships, some say a hundred a year, foundered in the shallow strait where the violent currents of the three waterways collided.

Gracie Mansion, the traditional home of modern New York City mayors, was erected on the shore opposite from the Hallett farm so that its mayoral residents could have exciting views of this unusual, natural spectacle. The Triborough Bridge, recently renamed the RFK Bridge, now spans the whirlpool area.

The Halletts named their property, formerly known as Jacques Bentyn's farm, "Hellgate Neck" and "Halletts Cove," and when the family

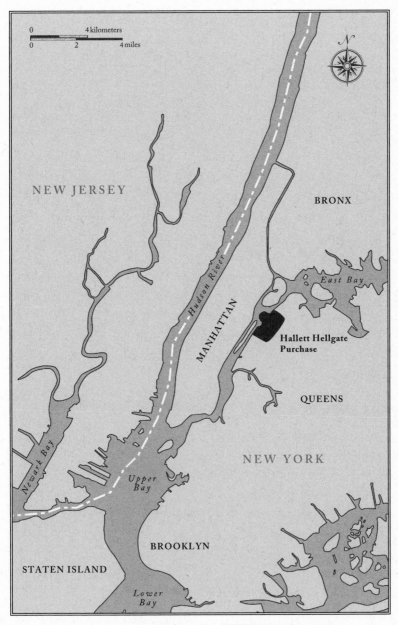

The Hellgate passage and Hallett's Point, now Astoria, New York

flourished there it was called Hallettville. Today the Hallett name is still in evidence throughout the neighborhood. Here, Elizabeth gave birth to her eighth and last child, Samuel Hallett, on Hallett's Point in 1651, when she was 41.

Close by their home was the Dutch settlement named "Vlissingen," now "Flushing," where many of their Stamford neighbors had fled, seeking safety after John Underhill's great massacre of the Munsee in 1644. The Halletts' friend and English secretary to Director Stuyvesant, George Baxter, urged John Winthrop Jr. to consider moving to live near the Halletts and this community, but John Jr., a future governor of English Connecticut, dismissed the invitation to become so fully Dutch. William Hallett also urged John Winthrop Jr. to leave New England and join him and Elizabeth in New Netherland, that it would be "much to the comfort of your poor kinswoman & myself."[151] William invited John to bring along the Indians that lived with him, and reported that he, Elizabeth, and all their children were in good health at Hellgate.

Many years later, author Washington Irving was also a resident of the Hellgate area on Long Island, and his description of this natural wonder is delightfully evocative.[152]

About six miles from the renowned city of the Manhattans, in that sound or arm of the sea and the Nassau, or Long Island, there is a narrow strait, where the current is violently compressed between shouldering promontories, and horribly perplexed by rocks and shoals. Being, at the best of times, a very violent, impetuous current, it takes these impediments in mighty dudgeon; boiling in whirlpools; brawling and fretting in ripples; raging and roaring in rapids and breakers; and, in short, indulging in all kinds of wrong-headed paroxysms. At such times, woe to any unlucky vessel that ventures within its clutches!

This termagant humour, however, prevails only at certain times of tide. At low water for instance, it is as pacific a stream as you would wish to see; but as the tide rises, it begins to fret; at half tide it roars with might and main, like a bully bellowing for more drink; but when the tide is full, it relapses into quiet, and, for a time, sleeps as soundly as an alderman after dinner. In fact, it may be compared to a quarrelsome toper, who is a peaceable fellow enough when he has no liquor at all, or when he has a skin full, but who, when half-seas-over, plays the very devil.

In fact, Irving, as an elderly man, died after exhausting himself by trying to sail a small boat home from Manhattan through this passage when the usual daily ferry had ceased operations.

On September 24, 1876, the US Army Corps of Engineers used fifty thousand pounds of explosives to blast the dangerous rocks and destroy the whirlpool. The destruction of Hell Gate shoals was said to be the largest man-made explosion in history until the Atomic Age. Though impossible to perceive today, the Astoria area was attractive to Elizabeth and William for its great natural beauty, fertile soil, and the entertainment of the whirlpool. It was recorded that,[153] "The whole north shore of this town from Flushing Bay on the east to King's County line on the west affords some of the richest and most varied scenery in the world . . . the softness and the beauty of the scenery is unsurpassed by any other which can be found . . . The scenery upon the Thames at Windsor scarcely compares with this, in all that can delight the eye, or satisfy the most extravagant fancy."

THE HALLETT HOMESTEAD BURNS IN THE ESOPUS WAR OF 1655
Beautiful though it may have been, the area was still a dangerous place to live. War with the Indians had reignited, particularly near the town of Kingston, New York, on the Hudson River. These significant conflicts were called the Esopus Wars, Esopus being Kingston's natively given name. Fallout from these hostilities affected many settlers on Manhattan and on western Long

Island. It seems the Halletts did not escape turmoil in this rough and rugged new world, even deep within Dutch territory. The Weichquaesgeck and other Long Island Indians, perhaps the Canarsie, successfully burned down the Hallett homestead and farm buildings on Hallett's Point on Long Island in 1655, five years after their removal from Connecticut. Peter Stuyvesant himself recounted the burning of the Hallett home while he was waiting for the tide to change one day at Hallett's Cove:[154]

> *Having gone ashore during the ebbing of the tide, and this side of the Hellgate where William Hallett's house and plantation formerly stood, which were laid waste by the Indians about September of the year 1655; we made a fire there with the help of burning fuses which we had with us. We found in the shallow water on the strand some oysters which we fried and ate. While thus occupied, a fine herd of cattle came right by us feeding along the beach; there were about sixteen cows both old and young, and five to six horses.*

Eleven years later, in 1664, the Halletts increased their holdings and bought additional acreage from Sachems Shawestcont and Erramorhar, land that contained a creek called "Sunswick" or "Sint Sinck." They further added to their claim with land purchased from Chief Mattano, a most active Indian realtor. Through a series of purchases, Elizabeth and William eventually consolidated a Long Island plantation that consisted of 2,200 acres, extending from Bowery Bay to Sunswick Creek and including all of modern-day Astoria and Steinway.[155] There they raised tons of tobacco, flax, corn, and a wide variety of vegetables, which they sold to New Amsterdam and other local towns.

The Hallett farm on western Long Island was one of the most productive Dutch plantations, worked in part with enslaved African labor, and was operated by William and Elizabeth's descendants well into the mid 1800s.

Since besting English authorities at many of their legal games, William Hallett, now a profitable planter, became unafraid of dealing with the highest Dutch governmental authorities and often brought suit over many property disputes within New Netherland's courts, many concerning neighboring farmers who disputed property boundaries, and the ownership of islands within the East River. In 1655, the same year the Hallett's house was burned down by Indians in the Esopus conflict, one neighbor, Hendrick the Swede, demanded 177 florins from the Halletts to pay for damage their cattle had done to his turnips, tobacco, pumpkins, and maize. [156]

William and Toby Feake continued their legal battles with each other over property and inheritance issues concerning the Greenwich property for many years while they both lived near each other on Long Island. Toby brought one well-known suit against William Hallett, who had become a respected sheriff within New Netherland, claiming that since William had assumed Robert Feake's position as acting head of household in Greenwich, he had also assumed the legal guardianship of Toby Feake. Therefore, William Hallett was liable to pay an outstanding debt of Robert Feake's instead of Toby himself. The man who sought repayment asserted that Toby, as Robert's heir and ward, should pay it back. Toby insisted that William Hallett, as Robert's replacement, should pay it, a position not upheld by the Dutch council, even after Toby's repeated appeals.

Toby never did inherit any of the Feake-Patrick property in Greenwich, property he had some legitimate claim to through his marriage to Anneken Patrick and through being Robert Feake's legal ward. Ironically, his sister Judith came to own most of it instead. Judith Feake, Robert's other ward and niece, had not moved to Greenwich from Watertown with the family for she had married a Massachusetts man named William Palmer who had arrived in Plymouth as a boy, and they raised their family in Yarmouth, Massachusetts. When William Palmer died, she moved to

Stamford and married Jeffrey Ferris as his third wife, bringing many of her Palmer children along with her to Greenwich. Jeffrey had purchased all remaining Feake-Patrick land from William Hallett when the Halletts moved to Long Island for safety. Judith and her Palmer children inherited all this property upon the death of Jeffrey Ferris, and many of her Palmer and Ferris descendants populate the town of Greenwich to this day.

After Anneken Patrick died in 1656 in Vlissingen at the age of forty-two, Toby married again, to a woman named Mary Patrick. Her relationship, if any, to the Patrick family is not certain, and they may have had a child together named Elizabeth Feake. (It's also possible that this Elizabeth may have been Mary's child from a previous marriage.) On June 24, 1662, Tobias travelled to Holland to collect an inheritance that belonged to his first wife, Anneken, which Adrien van der Donck, acting as his new world attorney, had previously arranged. Instead of returning to America with the money, however, he remained in England, and this embittered man deserted his entire American family by Anneken Patrick; his Patrick stepchildren; his natural son James Feake, whom he had by Anneken Patrick; and his second wife, Mary Patrick, and her daughter Elizabeth. In his will,[157] made on July 7, 1669, at Wapping, County Middlesex, England, Tobias Feake "of Wapping, Middlesex, mariner," mentioned no wife or children but stated he was indebted instead to the widow Anne Garaway also of Wapping. He left her "a good & valuable sum of money," and she became his sole heir and executrix.

ANNETJE PATRICK

There was an additional connection between the Feakes, the Patricks, and Fort Amsterdam. While he was head of the Patrick household, Toby contracted for Daniel and Anneken's daughter, Annetje Patrick, to work as an indentured servant for the Van Tienhoven family in March 1649, for two consecutive years, a common arrangement then and Toby received £50 for her services there.

Cornelius van Tienhoven had been Director Kieft's secretary at the fort and his signature appears on hundreds of West India Company documents. Interestingly, Van Tienhoven, William Kieft's best friend, also had a history of treating his wives and children badly. When he first sailed to Fort Amsterdam from Holland, he had married a woman on Manhattan under false pretenses, telling her he was single when, in fact, he had left a wife behind in Europe. It was to the home of this second wife, Rachel, that Annetje Patrick was sent to care for the three Van Tienhoven children.

When Stuyvesant took over from Kieft, he excluded Cornelius van Tienhoven from his administration because Cornelius and his brother, who had worked as receiver-general for the company, had been charged with fraud, not surprisingly, while serving in William Kieft's administration. Faced with the possibility of indictment for embezzlement, Cornelius proceeded to fake his own suicide[158] and then absconded from the province forever. He threw his hat and cane into the East River in 1656 and disappeared without a trace. It seems that no one was fooled by the deception, yet his name never appears in any record again.

After serving as the Van Tienhovens' nanny, Annetje Patrick married a man named Bartholomew Applegate and they had a child together. Never far removed from Indian-European violence in this era, in 1671 she and her child were captured by Indians and held for ransom. The administrators of Gravesend, New York, where she lived, ordered the payment of £10, half in coin and half in "red cloth," to obtain their release. Presumably she and her child were released, for she and Bartholomew then moved to Monmouth, New Jersey, and established the large Applegate family there.

Chapter Sixteen

Religious Evolution

On Long Island, William and Elizabeth Hallett were stunned, angry, and smarting from the treatment they had received in Connecticut at the hands of New Haven's Puritans, and they came to abandon that outlook which had proved far more punitive than personally rewarding to them. Surrounded by a greater mix of divergent views within New Netherland, they now found great favor with an emerging and exciting new faith. Like the raging Job in the Bible and John Winthrop before them, they decided to seek an entirely new kind of engagement with God rather than reject Him entirely or submit meekly to Him. This resolute couple, along with daughter Hannah and husband John Bowne, began championing a new take on faith then emerging on Long Island called "The Society of Friends."

The Quakers, like the Halletts, found that the Puritan way had not offered them a better quality of life on earth and rationalized this to be because the Puritan religion had not reformed Christianity far enough and that a new "true" church remained to be found. Excitement over new philosophies proposed by the Quakers in the early 1650s near Manhattan gave rise to the perception by the Halletts and their like-minded Friends that Christ's second coming, as prophesied by Paul, had already happened. Christ's return, as explained by Quaker leader George Fox in 1647, was not a physical phenomenon, but was an experience of inward revelation. Fox lectured to these spiritually hungry and disenfranchised English settlers that all Puritan Church rites and institutions should be

abolished since they had been designed only for the waiting or antici-
pation of Christ's second coming. Since Christ was perceived to have
already "come again," to those who had experienced "convincement,"
and because God had now established a new covenant with humanity, a
new form of worship was needed to address this change in the human
condition.

Christ's second manifestation in one's soul meant that one had experienced a direct encounter with God, and needed no sermons, priests, or
ceremonies to further communicate with him. To Quakers this meant
they could dispense with traditional church buildings, holidays, customs,
music, and outward sacrament. The Quakers of the 1640s and 1650s created a theology that was stripped down to an even purer and more abstract
essence than the Puritan's rejection of perceived Catholic excesses.

Accordingly, "Friends" met in homes, barns, meetinghouses, or the
outdoors without any seating hierarchy, for they perceived no place
more holy than any other. They conducted their meetings without any
appointed thought leaders; any man, woman, or child could stand and
speak at will when prompted by God to offer his or her "ministry" to
the gathered group. When this happened, the speaker would kneel on
the floor to speak and all others would rise and remove their hats; the
only time that they would do so. Leadership was informal and there was
no fixed reporting structure in the movement's early years. Ministry by
women made up almost half of the early Quaker movement, and this was
a welcome and radical departure from Puritan practice.

Quakers worshipped by employing a "liturgy of silence," and they
would pray or meditate in utter silence for up to three hours at a time,
rocking back and forth on their bench, or "quaking" when moved by an
inner revelation. Silence, which is both a positive and negative space, was
the medium through which God's unadulterated guidance was known.
What had previously been considered a void was now believed to be the
clearest channel for spiritual communication. Only through silence was

God's Word clearly heard, and silence was used to express ideas that they felt words, sounds, or music could not.

Applied Quaker philosophy meant that its converts stopped treating Sunday or any religious holidays as special; perceiving all days to be equally sacred, they referred to the months by number instead of name and they frequently conducted business on the weekends. They refused to pay tithes or swear oaths, as an oath implied that one was otherwise untruthful, dishonest, and lacking in integrity. They accordingly became renowned for their truth, integrity, and honesty in business and became most famous as honest bankers. They spoke clearly and straightforwardly without preambles of flowery flattery, and dressed in solemn, plain clothing. They married each other without ministers or rings and buried each other without headstones. They also rejected what they considered to be superfluous social customs, such as doffing one's hat on meeting, which they considered projected a false sense of social deference. Their many unusual customs caused some critical Puritans to refer to them as a "frequently annoying people."

Quakers believed theirs was the true church and importantly, that all people could be of "the Elect," that all could attain salvation, and that all were spiritually equal to each other. While Anne Hutchinson's best friend Mary Dyer was hanged in Boston in 1659 for her religious differences with the Puritans, and Anne Hutchinson, John Underhill, and Daniel Patrick were banished from the Bay Colony, the English Quakers joined with the Dutch in pioneering religious toleration in America.

Although he may have understood the search and desire to practice a religion that was thought to please God better, John Winthrop Sr. surely would have been sorrowed to learn that his Puritan experiment never created the kind of perfect world he dreamed of, though reverberations of its tenets became deeply etched on the earliest American psyche for many generations, but was in fact discarded by Elizabeth's branch of his own family. That John Winthrop's own ward, daughter-in-law, and niece, Elizabeth Fones Winthrop Feake Hallett, turned against the Puritan doctrine and its societal dreams spoke of the great difficulties there were in implementing its lofty ideals in the rugged frontier of early America. It also spoke to her modernity in rejecting religious tenets that hobbled her life and of embracing new ones that nourished her uniquely American experience.

The appeal of the Quaker belief to so many on western Long Island in the 1650s was its more democratic assembly and its doctrinal belief that *all* people were born with God's grace, not just a few, as the Puritans held. It also offered women a more democratic voice within the church and encouraged them to take leadership positions. The Hallett and Feake families on Long Island, however, were soon to find that becoming Quakers with Peter Stuyvesant in charge of Dutch territory was almost as difficult as being a Puritan in John Winthrop's Connecticut.

Peter Stuyvesant, son of a strict Calvinist minister, wanted only the Dutch Reformed religion to operate within New Netherland and tried to prevent the growing Quaker movement from gaining popularity, fearing the political power of its synods, or groups of church elders, that could challenge his authority. He issued an edict making his position known, a position that was not supported by the many non-Dutch settlers within Dutch territory or by West India Company directors. The company allowed religions other than that of the Reformed Dutch Church to be practiced in New Netherland, but disallowed the construction of their buildings.

When William Hallett, who came to hold the position of a certified Dutch Sheriff in Flushing, invited friend and Quaker leader William Wickendam to his and Elizabeth's temporary home in Flushing in 1656 to preach and administer Communion, the autocratic Stuyvesant became enraged. Forty-year-old William Hallett became the first recorded Quaker arrested and ordered to be banished from New Netherland by the Governor.[159] This was a calamitous outcome for William and Elizabeth, and one that would make them homeless for the third time in their lives.

William Hallett was an able, respected, and astute sheriff for the Dutch who had also recently helped acquit two people accused of witchcraft in Fort

Amsterdam's only witch trial.[160] In his New Netherland banishment decree, Peter Stuyvesant directed that William Hallett be replaced as *schout* or sheriff of Flushing, by none other than William's nemesis, Toby Feake, Stuyvesant having no idea that Toby was also a Friend, or Quaker. Always enterprising, by December 21, 1656, William successfully petitioned the Fort Amsterdam Council to repeal Stuyvesant's order,[161] and to his certain delight, they rebuked Stuyvesant for his actions. Despite his dislike of William Hallett, Toby Feake was also an ardent supporter of the Long Island Quaker movement, and was the first man to sign his name to the now-famous "Flushing Remonstrance," which objected to Stuyvesant's crackdown. This document became the first American treatise, other than Anne Hutchinson's trial record, that demanded the right to religious freedom in America.

Most of the Feake and Hallett children became committed Quakers, including the second daughter of Robert and Elizabeth Feake Hallett, Hannah Feake. Hannah and her husband, John Bowne, were enormously active in promoting the Friends on Long Island and in England. Proving stubbornly resistant to West India Company administrators who warned him off such actions, Stuyvesant also arrested, imprisoned, and successfully banished John Bowne six years later, who followed his father-in-law William Hallett's earlier lead and successfully appealed to West India Company administrators, who revoked his longer term and more difficult banishment as well. Bowne consequently helped write the first American laws protecting diversity of religious practice in 1664. The important yet deteriorating John Bowne house on Long Island survives to this day and is only occasionally open to the public for lack of adequate funding.

Hannah Feake Bowne died years later in London in 1677, after meeting with the couple's many British and Irish Friends who helped them financially support the Quaker movement in America. In his eulogy to Hannah, who died in London during a fundraising trip and was buried there, John Bowne sincerely expressed his passionate, deep, and committed love for Hannah Feake and their eight children, including a daughter poignantly named Martha Johana.

CHAPTER SEVENTEEN

Dutch and Munsee Decline

PETER STUYVESANT GOVERNED A NEW NETHERLAND THAT HAD BECOME an awkwardly functioning but fully developed community in spite of those who wanted it to remain only a small, tightly controlled trading post. He tried as well as he could to keep up a very brave front given the many limitations leveled on him by the West India Company, which had been losing money for a long time on this fractious and far-flung division. The company had turned its attentions now to Brazil and began neglecting New Netherland. As a result, by the time of Stuyvesant's tenure, Dutch financial support for their great North American endeavor had turned into a trickle.

English settlers in the Dutch territories of New York, New Jersey, Connecticut, and Long Island were increasingly insistent on representation within the Dutch Council—privileges they were used to within their own English colonies—and Stuyvesant was forced to allow them small measures of representation. The company's board of directors in Holland did little to bolster Stuyvesant's authority over the region's growing English population and encroaching English colony claims other than "utter pious wishes for its welfare," to Stuyvesant's growing dismay. Prickly, proud, and now without company support, Stuyvesant was forced to admit to his fellow Dutchmen that the colony had stalled and he had little means to protect its residents from the English, or from the Indians.

The Dutch became a conquered company psychologically, if not physically, when the English increased their protests against the autocracy of Dutch authority. Local boundary disputes within New Netherland were often reviewed by English authorities, who were perceived as stronger enforcing agents than the Dutch.[162] In 1664, when English ships appeared right off the tip of Manhattan, the company ceded control of New Netherland to the English without any armed resistance. The English promptly renamed Fort Amsterdam "Fort James" and the little village of New Amsterdam became "New York," in honor of England's Duke of York. The forty-year boom and bust of New Netherland was captured by Adrien van der Donck, who considered it mismanaged from the beginning, when he opined:[163]

We have already stated that the Liberty to trade with the Indians was the cause of the increase of the population of New Netherland. We shall now show that it is also the cause of its ruin; producing two opposite effects, and that not without reason as will appear from what follows.

This Liberty then, which in every respect was most gratefully received; which should have been used like a precious gift, was very soon perverted to a great abuse. For everyone thought that now was the acceptable time to make his fortune; withdrew himself from his fellow, as if deeming him suspected and the enemy of his desire. They sought communication with the Indians from whom it appeared his profit was to be derived, all contrary to their High Mightinesses' motto, "Union is Strength." That created first, a division of power of dangerous consequence; then produced altogether too much familiarity with the Indians, which in short time brought forth Contempt, usually the Father of Hate. For, not satisfied with merely taking them into their houses in the customary manner, they attracted them by extraordinary attention, such as admitting them to the table, laying napkins before them, presenting wine to them, and more of that kind of thing, which

they did not receive like Esop's man, but as their due and dessert, inso-
much as they were not content, but began to hate, when such civilities
were not shown to them. To this familiarity and freedom succeeded
another Evil; as the cattle usually roamed through the woods without
a herdsman, they frequently came upon the corn of the Indians, which
was unfenced on all sides, committing great damage there. This led to
frequent complaints on the part of the latter, and finally to revenge on
the cattle, without even sparing the horses, which were valuable in
the country.

Moreover, many of ours took the Indians into their employ, mak-
ing use of them in their housework, thus exposing them to our entire
circumstances. Soon becoming weary of work, the Indians took leg-
bail and stole much more than the amount of their wages. This lib-
erty caused still greater mischief. This added to the previous contempt
and greatly augmented the hatred which stimulated them to conspire
against us, beginning first with insults which they everywhere indis-
creetly uttered, calling us "Materiotty," (Matah: without, and Otee:
heart) or "Cowards." They would say we might indeed be something
on the water, but on the land we had neither a great Sachem nor
Chiefs.

New Netherland's legacy is that every aspect of the Dutch experience in America provides a useful lesson on the perils of nation-building.
When it became clear that New Amsterdam no longer functioned as a
simplistic trading outpost and that it had morphed into a full-fledged
colony in need of serious infrastructure, funding, and community controls, the West India Company could have made a more timely transition to English control, cut its losses quickly, and recalled or relocated its
many employees to more profitable and less problematic regions when
it saw no game-changing revenue support in its immediate future. That
Manhattan's decreasing profitability and increasing community problems

were reasons to simply stop further funding resulted in stagnation. The decision not to nation-build any further after a significant, yet unstable, European presence had been established left New Netherland without clear objectives and increased its corruption and instability.

The English would have absorbed New Netherland sooner than they inevitably did and this would have reshaped the Indian-European dynamic, but a fatal outcome for the Indians might only have been delayed. Thirty years after the 1644 Munsee massacre, in "King Phillip's War" of 1675, an armed conflict between English colonists and northeastern Indians near the Massachusetts area, Benjamin Church, a latter-day John Underhill, was celebrated for his repeated killing of many hundreds of Indians, thus "winning" this war for the English.

The Dutch experience is also a cautionary tale of long-distance oversight that is unable to address the dangerous actions of an errant individual who uses his authority to mutilate a corporate mission, dismiss credible complaint, and establish a pattern of autocratic action. Kieft rejected and evaded all controls meant to contain a foolish yahoo like himself and sadly, the power of one man trumped the compassionate intentions of others. When one maverick individual countermanded established organizational policies that had been carefully crafted from experience, judgment, and common sense, the disastrous result included tragic death and tarnished legacies that went far beyond those of just one individual.

The West India Company, if not William Kieft, was for its time racially and religiously tolerant as a corporation for purely pragmatic reasons. Their need to work with many races, nations, and religions drove its worldwide business in the Caribbean, Africa, East Asia, and Manhattan, although their "work" with other people extended to buying and selling them as well, for the company was an active slave trader, and the enslaved at this time were a class entirely left out of compassionate consideration. They were almost entirely negated as human beings and not granted any rights of Europeans. If one could possibly set aside this corporate abuse of the enslaved, as difficult as that is for us to do today, the company can be credited for readily soliciting sales and supply-side workers from all over the world to operate, and near New York it needed diverse Indian groups to supply its vast network. Seventeen languages were spoken in New Amsterdam and any faith was welcome. "The consciences of men ought to be free and unshackled," wrote company directors to Peter Stuyvesant when they scolded him for banishing William Hallett and his son-in-law John Bowne, "so long as they continue moderate, peaceable, inoffensive and not hostile to the government; such have been the maxims of prudence and toleration by which the magistrates of this city (Amsterdam) have been governed and the consequences have been that the oppressed and persecuted from every country have found among us an asylum from distress. Follow in the same steps and you will be blessed" (April 16, 1663).

When England assumed control over all the claims of New Netherland in 1664, the large tract of land in Greenwich that Stuyvesant had first confiscated, then purchased, and then prohibited development on, remained largely undeveloped by Europeans. Seven years later, in 1672, Greenwich and Stamford farmers divided up a large part of this tantalizing open space, which was prized for its convenient coastal aspect, abundant hay and meadowlands, and profitable proximity to the renamed town of "New York," to which they could quickly sell perishable goods such as cattle, produce, apples, and oysters. In this way, Stuyvesant's confiscation, along with the jurisdictional legal limbo that the Treaty of Hartford created, was ultimately undone.

After the fall of New Netherland, Munsees continued to live near Manhattan for over 150 years and sporadic murders, farm burnings, thefts, rapes, and other outrages between Indians and Europeans continued. Unjust land sales, disease, and the insidious introduction of European vices and societal destruction permanently handicapped Indian society, but the speed at which this damage was inflicted slowed in comparison to the many tragedies the Indian had endured during the reign of William Kieft. Remnants of groups remained in Connecticut and Westchester into the 1800s. Groups of Westchester Weichquaesgeck banded together and became known as the Highland Indians. In Connecticut, a large collected group became known as the Stamford Indians. The Weichquaesgeck and their lower Hudson River Delawaran neighbors moved north in increasing numbers during the last decades of the 1800s, and they became known as the River Indians. The Munsees along the Hudson River submitted themselves to English authority on September 24, 1664, following the fall of New Netherland to the English; descendants of these groups today live in Stockbridge, Massachusetts; Ontario, Canada; Wisconsin; and Oklahoma.

In 1686 the last recorded Indians living in Greenwich called the land west of the Mianus River "Paihomsing," which the English inelegantly rechristened "Horseneck." These Indians were Kouko, Peattun, Rumpannus, and Querrecqui, with wives Pakochero, Wettorum, and Oruns, and someone's grandmother whose name was Kowaconussa. This group's four children included three ten-year-olds, including one set of boy and girl twins, and a one-year-old baby boy. They sold their rights to seven Greenwich men but reserved thirty acres for themselves and their four "papooses" on Cos Cob Neck, the Indian Field Road area on the west side of the Mianus River, to use unmolested for the remainder of their lives.

Chapter Eighteen

Hallett Epilogue

Elizabeth Fones Winthrop Feake Hallett

Elizabeth most likely died early in the 1670s, when she was in her sixties and her last child, Samuel Hallett, was a teenager. If so, her death would have occurred after the English assumed control over all of New Netherland. True to form for a woman who charted her own course through the new world, her last written record was another personal purchase of land in Flushing from Edward Griffin, another signer of the famous Flushing Remonstrance. Her unique and turbulent time witnessed sea changes in American and English history, and within this era of enormous transition her own identity evolved as she struggled to maintain her life, her spirit, her property, and her family in a wilderness frontier that made a mockery of the established ways of her old world.

A romantic London teenager who was almost instantly widowed, she became one of America's very first colonists almost accidentally. Maturing as a wife, she dealt with mental illness in an age that offered her no answers and forced her to choose between her children and her husband. Suffering for the inadequate medical care of her day, she was severely tested when she lost newborns to early deaths, a grown daughter to lead poisoning, one husband to insanity, and another to stupidity.

Living on the cusp of New England and New Netherland, she operated fully within the parallel societies of English, Dutch, and the Munsees who, like live electrical wires, caused huge shocks whenever intersecting. Caught up in the struggle between Indian and enslaved African survival and European settlement, she celebrated their censure to ensure the safety of her own, and, she suffered retribution when they took out their revenge.

Growing ever stronger in the strength of her resolve she, like Anne Hutchinson, repeatedly confronted male authority as she fended off inter-colony Puritan political schemes and enterprising male relatives who looked to assume all her assets. Practical, pragmatic, and politically astute, she used Winthrop family weight to leave her own society for a safer life among Dutch strangers. As committed to the protection of her soul as her uncle ever was, she rejected his religion and its political metastasis which threatened her life and tried to fracture her young family. A true pioneer, she was among the first to embrace this Quaker Way, a new, even more anti-authoritarian religion that valued her femaleness and better reconciled her faith to the realities of life within her century.

Her daughters' choices of husbands reflected the old and new dimensions of her life when one married the security and safety her family found with John Underhill, the old Puritan warrior and mercenary, and another ignited a large religious movement with John Bowne that led the country in an entirely new direction. Elizabeth and her family were one of the very first to substitute the patriarchal authority of the Puritans for the authority of the individual, but not without a price when her third husband, William Hallett, was the first recorded Quaker banished by Stuyvesant in 1656, preceding her son-in-law, John Bowne, by six unsettling years.

Elizabeth tested this young country's strengths and suffered for its weaknesses, and while the modern age indicts her society for Indian massacre and slavery, our feelings toward Elizabeth herself, a most resilient and resolute woman, must engender our respect, for one can only hope to survive life's harsh surprises with the courage and conviction that she did.

ROBERT FEAKE

By 1660, Robert Feake's mental illness had progressed so far that Watertown, Massachusetts, officials spent £90 of the town's own money toward his care. They did this compassionately for they feared that if the formerly wealthy Robert realized he lived in poverty, it would further destabilize and depress him. In 1663, Robert Feake, former town freeman and scion of a prestigious English merchant family, died right next door to his original Watertown land grants, which he had farmed in 1630,[164] in pitiful circumstances at the home of his caretaker, the deacon Samuel Thatcher.

WILLIAM HALLETT MARRIES AGAIN

It is thought that Elizabeth died in the early 1670s, for William Hallett married a Flushing widow named Susannah Booth Thorne in 1674 when he was fifty-eight. He did not have a relationship with her like the one he shared with Elizabeth, for he divorced her rather quickly. Records show he disputed a bill he had received for 3,333 pounds of tobacco, forty beavers, and an order of silver, and the payment was to be made out in blankets. When a Dutch court found the invoice to be valid, William resisted paying it for some reason, but his new wife Susannah paid this bill "in the absence of her husband." Upon returning home William was outraged at Susannah's action and he sued for the return of his funds, charging that the payment was unjust.[165] The court's decision is unknown, but William and Susannah's divorce occurred soon thereafter. Her grown children, including John Thorne, another signer of the Flushing Remonstrance, brought a suit against William, charging him with failure to provide proper child support of the Thorne children. How William settled this dispute is unknown, but he clearly was a man who most often had his way.

Still seeking affection, companionship, and household help, William married a third time to a widow named Rebecca Bayles. Rebecca presumably paid no bills of William's, for they remained married until he died at the age of eighty-nine.

Used to matching wits with wily politicians and winning, William Hallett became a patriarch of a very large family when his sons William Jr. and Samuel by Elizabeth had many children and came to own a great deal of desirable western Long Island real estate, became somewhat cranky as he neared his ninetieth birthday and used his will, which is privately held by a Hallett family descendant today,[166] to chide Elizabeth Jackson, one of his many married granddaughters. (Elizabeth Hallett Jackson and her husband were the original owners of nearby Jackson Heights.) His wry bequest to her was a generous "one pewter dish and a pewter candlestick purchased with the money her husband owes me." He also penalized his son, William Hallett Jr., who now had ten children of his own, for "undutyfullness to me" in his failure to supply the bricks to build a Quaker meetinghouse. (William Jr. was the boy born while his mother fled from New Haven authorities to New London, and whom the English considered illegitimate.)

Also mentioned in his will is the name of his sole surviving sister, one "Hannah Bird," for whom he provides generously. The 1694 will of one John Buckout of Mespath was witnessed simultaneously by an Andrew Bird and William Hallett, and this Mr. Bird was perhaps her husband. Concerning his other sisters, Susannah Hallett married a man name Walter Hide, Elizabeth Hallett became a Mrs. Welch, and Alice Hallett first married Mordecai or Mordecay Nichols and then later married Thomas Clark, a Plymouth minister in Boston, in 1664. The original William Hallett homestead and William Jr.'s fieldstone home stood near the intersection of 30th Avenue and 8th Street on Hallett's Point, now Astoria, but then called Hellgate Neck, near the present site of Two Coves Community Gardens, named for Pot Cove and Hallett's Cove on either side of Hallett's Point.

WILLIAM HALLETT III

Turmoil in Elizabeth's family continued into the third generation when a great tragedy befell her grandson, William Hallett III, son of William Jr., and two of the enslaved people he had either purchased or inherited. By 1707, he was a grown man of thirty-seven who lived in Newtown on Long Island with his pregnant wife and their five children. On one evening, this entire family was murdered by the family's enslaved Indian man named Sam and their enslaved African woman.[167]

It was reported in the *Boston News Letter* that the African "bonds-woman" had convinced Sam to murder the entire family in order to seize the Hallett property, instigated by a grievance that the Halletts had not allowed them a day off on a Sunday. These two, and several other enslaved Africans, were said to have allegedly conspired together to commit the murders, and supposedly there was evidence of a larger plot in which several other slave-owning families were targeted.

Both Hallett perpetrators were viciously executed within two weeks of the crime. The woman was burned at the stake, and the man hung in gibbets and placed astride a shar iron, and, "in a state of delirium which ensued, believing himself to be on horseback, would urge forward his animal, while the blood oozing from his lacerated flesh, streamed to the ground."

The English government's reaction to these acts of rebellion and insurrection was immediate. An "Act for Preventing the Conspiracy of Slaves" was passed by the Colonial Assembly in 1708 and this law, the first of its kind in America, was a direct reaction to the circumstances surrounding the murders of William Hallett III's family.[168] The act newly leveled the death sentence for any slave who murdered or attempted to murder their master. Now, as America's next generation looked toward the 1700s, its suspicions and fears turned from fear of Indian attack to fears of those they had continued to enslave.

An Act for Preventing the Conspiracy of Slaves
   Passed October, 1708
      Be it enacted by the Governour Council and Assembly and it is hereby enacted by the authority of the same that all and every Negro

Indian or other slave or slaves within this colony who at any time after the execrable and barbarous murder committed on the person and family of William Hallett Junior late of New Town in Queens County gentleman deceased have has or shall murder or otherwise kill unless by misadventure or in execution of justice or conspire or attempt the death of his her or their Master or any other of her Majesty's liege people not being Negroes Mulattos or slaves within this Colony and shall thereof be lawfully convicted before three or more of her Majesty's Justices of the Peace one whereof to be of the quorum who are hereby authorized and empowered to hear and determine the same and put their judgments in execution according to this Act or before and Court of Oyer and Terminer or General Goal Delivery he she or they so offending shall suffer the pains of death in such manner and with such circumstances as the aggravation and enormity of their crime in the judgment of the justices aforesaid of those courts shall merit and require AND be it further enacted by the authority aforesaid that the owner or owners of such Negro or Indian slaves or slaves to be executed by virtue of this Act shall be paid for the same in the like manner and under the same regulations as is declared in and by an Act of the General Assembly of this Colony made in the fourth year of her Majesty's Reign, entitled an Act to Prevent the running away of Negro Slaves out of the City and County of Albany to the French at Canada provided the value of such slaves shall not exceed the price of twenty-five pounds lawful money of the Colony, nor the charges of prosecution above five pounds.—Colonial Laws of New York, Vol. 1 p. 631. (New York Ecclesiastical Records Vol. 1:1710).

William Jr. had the extremely sad task of serving as administrator to his son William Hallett III's estate just one year after his father William Hallett Senior's death, and no information is known about the sorrows endured by the enslaved and alleged perpetrators' families. In the Surrogates Records in the State Archives in Albany, one finds an extensive inventory of William Hallett III's early colonial farm holdings, tallied on June 1, 1708 and it included:

2 Horses: 10£
2 Mares: 5£
2 colts, 3£
7 cows: 19.5 shillings
29 sheep: 8.15£
1 silver tankard: 7£
7 spoons: 16£ 6s.
57½ bushels of wheat: 11£ 4s.

William Hallett III's homestead, west of the present-day intersection of 31st Avenue and Newtown Road near 44th Street, was referred to as a haunted house for years afterward.

The murdered William III's portion of the original family farm passed on to his brother, Joseph Hallett. Through the inheritance of this land and the use of slave labor, Joseph became one of the most prominent and wealthy shipping merchants of Manhattan in the 1700s by trading tobacco produced on Hallett's Point with Great Britain and the Caribbean. At one point in time he also held the monopoly on linseed oil—the result of crushed flaxseed heads—which he sold to Ireland. In addition to his summer home on Hallett's Point, he had a home on Pearl Street in Manhattan (which bounded the island's original shoreline), and owned numerous stores and wharves there, as well as large amounts of land in other states. After succumbing to smallpox in 1731, a year that saw three other Hallett family members also die of this disease, Joseph and his wife were interred in the Hallett vault of the First Presbyterian Church in Manhattan, now located at Fifth and Twelfth Streets.

Joseph Hallett WILLIAM SMITH PELLETREAU, *HISTORIC HOMES AND INSTITUTIONS,* (NEW YORK AND CHICAGO: LEWIS PUBLISHING, 1907), 213

ROBERT FEKE (JR.), COLONIAL PORTRAIT PAINTER

A startling story about one of Elizabeth's great-grandsons concerns Robert Feke, the respected early colonial portrait painter. He is credited in the modern world with being "the best native-born portrait painter working in the American colonies before Copley," and was said by *New York Times* art critic John Canaday in 1966 to have painted with "extraordinary natural talent." Robert (Jr.) was descended from Elizabeth's son John Feakes, also spelled Feke, who had married Elisabeth Prior, and they, like the rest of the Feake, Hallett, Bowne, and Underhill families, were prominent Quakers. John Feake and Elizabeth Prior had a son named Robert (Sr.) and this Robert "Feaks," married Clemence Ludlam and became a well known and very strict Quaker leader on Long Island. Their son, Robert Feke (Jr.), was the talented painter.

Carrying on his family's longstanding tradition of readily adopting new takes on faith that fit one better personally rather than communally, the budding artist denied his father's Quaker faith—which undoubtedly embarrassed his stern minister father—and became a committed Baptist. Incensed over this perceived ecclesiastical treason, the Quaker leader disinherited his son, who clearly felt strongly about his new religious conviction, also a longstanding Feake family trait. As a teenager, the rebellious son abandoned his large and extended Feake/Underhill/Cox/Cocks family in Oyster Bay, Long Island, and sailed to England to live his Baptist life alone.

Robert served as an English sailor for several years, but was captured during a military dispute and was held prisoner for some time in a Spanish jail. There he created sketches and drawings that he sold to buy his way to freedom. Once released, he returned to America and settled in the far more cosmopolitan Newport, Rhode Island, where he married a Quakeress named Eleanor Cozzens on September 26, 1742, in the First Baptist Church in Newport. (He may have known her from his early life as her family was from Oyster Bay.) Robert and Eleanor had three sons and

Robert Feke, American, about 1707–1751, self portrait about 1741 PHOTOGRAPH

two daughters. Their eldest son, John, was a ship captain who drowned on the *Peggy* with all on board off Portland, Maine in 1767. Their second son, Charles Feke, became a well-known pharmacist in Newport, which echoes Thomas Fones, but he died without issue, and is buried in the Underhill Family Burial Ground. Their third son, Horatio, died very early and also without issue. As a result, all of Robert Feke's descendants are traced back to his daughters: Philadelphia, who married John Townsend, the famous Newport cabinetmaker and Sarah, who married John Thurston.

Over a period of twenty years in Newport, with the exception of occasional trips to Philadelphia, Robert Feke painted about sixty portraits of individuals in the top level of colonial society in the Northeast. Working largely without instruction, he was well known for his naturally skillful portraits such as that of James Bowdoin, and he also painted many Feake/Feke family members, which, tragically, were destroyed in a Feake family fire in the eighteenth century.

In Newport he continued to practice his Baptist faith, dropping his wife off at the Friends Meeting House each Sunday while he worshipped elsewhere. As his health declined, he moved to Bermuda, where he died and was buried at the age of forty-five.[169] An exhibition of thirty Feke canvases was showcased by the Whitney Museum in Manhattan in 1946.

HALLETT'S POINT

Peace was a long time coming to Elizabeth and William and to their final resting place. Their family graveyard on Hallett's Point experienced upheaval in 1852 and again in the 1930s as Hallett descendants sold portions of their very large ancestral estate to developers and Hallett's Point became largely known as Astoria as a political gesture to John Jacob Astor, who never set foot there. When the industrial revolution encroached far too closely on the Hallett's private burial ground, the family transferred its ancestors to the more bucolic and nearby Mount Olivet Cemetery, in

Hallett family plot in Mt. Olivet Cemetery, Maspeth, New York PHOTO BY AUTHOR

Maspeth, Queens, New York, which was part of William's original holdings. Elizabeth and William's graves and many of their family, including all of William III's murdered family, are located on a rise from which the eastern skyline of Manhattan may be seen. As was the custom with Quakers at the time, their graves were never marked.

Chapter Nineteen

Feake-Patrick-Hallett Disputes Resolved

By 1685, THE TOWN OF GREENWICH FOUND IT NECESSARY TO RESOLVE any remaining question about the ownership of the Feake-Patrick land so they asked an agreeable Daniel Patrick Jr. and John Feake to sign quit claim deeds that renounced their rights to claim any further ownership of their parents' former Greenwich property. Daniel Patrick Jr. renounced his right for £50, plus a horse saddle, bridle, and halter, in addition to the "3 horses, wheat, peas, pork and color corn" Greenwich townsmen had given him previously in 1671.[170]

Elizabeth's sons by Robert Feake knew they would never inherit any of William Hallett's extensive Long Island property; that would go only to Hallett's own sons, William and Samuel. The Feake/Feke/Feeks boys moved east of Hallett's Point to live near their sister, Elizabeth, who had married Captain John Underhill and was raising her large Feake-Underhill family in Oyster Bay. These "Feeks" sons and the son of Daniel Patrick bought farms that adjoined John Underhill's property, which was named "Killingworth" in Matinecock, a section of Oyster Bay, almost directly south across Long Island Sound from Greenwich, Connecticut. There, the captain became an acting father to almost all of Robert Feake's children, presumably with Elizabeth's blessing. An extensive, well-documented survey of this site may be found in an Underhill Family publication called *The Underhill Burial Ground*, published in 1926. Today one finds this ground containing many Fekes and

Marker in Underhill family burial ground for Elizabeth Feake Underhill, a granddaughter of Elizabeth Fones Winthrop Feake Hallett. The location of her mother, Elizabeth Feake's daughter, is unknown, but likely near John Underhill, her husband. PHOTO BY AUTHOR

Underhills near "Feeks Lane" in a beautiful residential neighborhood. Next to the Underhills, the Feeks, or Fekes, are the largest family group residing there. Somewhere here, though unmarked, are the remains of Elizabeth's daughter, Elizabeth, who married John Underhill as his second wife. There is visible a rough field stone engraved with the initials "E.U" for the elder Elizabeth's seventeen-year-old granddaughter also named Elizabeth. Resting here too is Robert Feke, the Quaker minister (son of John Feke and Elizabeth Prier/Pryor/Prior) who banished his son, Robert Feke the painter. Elizabeth's grandson Charles Feke— the Newport apothecarist who took after her father, Thomas Fones—is found on these grounds as well.

John Underhill's monument plaque PHOTO BY AUTHOR

JOHN UNDERHILL

In 1908, the extended descendants of John Underhill erected a monument over his grave in the grounds described above, and in the act of reburying his body they found that he had had red hair. Buoyed by generations of gratitude and reverence to the man, including John Greenleaf Whittier's ode to his many exploits, the family invited President Theodore Roosevelt and the editor of the Brooklyn *Daily Times* to speak at the large granite monument's unveiling ceremonies. The newspaper editor, to his credit, felt somewhat squeamish at extolling the virtues of a man who had slain close to a thousand Indians personally, noted that Underhill, "judged by today, would have been called a butcher." He also appropriately reminded his audience to "judge him as of his own time, and not as our time, to which he did not belong." It is undeniable, however, that the man had a mental construct that allowed him to kill hundreds of men, women, and children when others of his day would not.

Thomas Lyon's Heirs Continue the Quest for
Martha Johana Winthrop's Inheritance

Martha Johana Lyon, Elizabeth's first child by the tragically drowned Henry Winthrop, married Stamford's Thomas Lyon, who seemed most interested in accessing her inheritance. After Martha Johana's early death from lead poisoning, Thomas Lyon moved to Fairfield with his daughter Mary (Lyon) whom he had by Martha Johana. In Fairfield, Thomas Lyon took Mary Hoyt to be his second wife and he too became an ardent Quaker against the will of the Fairfield's Puritan fathers who still were not open to allowing another religion to operate within New England. His new religious affiliation brought penalties and fines upon his Fairfield family. Mary Hoyt Lyon wrote to John Winthrop Jr., the ever-effective Winthrop family problem-solver, for help solving her family's difficulties created, yet again, by Thomas Lyon:[171]

> Fairfield June the 22, 1668
>> Honored Sir,
>> My husband being from home, I am bold to present you with my grievance. We have seven children, four of them small. Last year they took away an ox for half a year. Since they fined us six pound more, and for that have sold the greater part of our home lot. Now, honored Sir, I have no man but yourself, whom God hath empowered to redress this great oppression. My husband cannot act against his conscience. They are resolved in their way. Thus hoping you will consider my distress, I rest.
>> Your poor servant to command,
>> Mary Lion [sic]

A few weeks later, John Winthrop Jr., now the governor of the Connecticut Colony, must have sent for Mary, his niece. When she arrived at John Jr.'s home, he and his wife, Elizabeth, were shocked by her unkempt, poverty-stricken appearance. In his anger, John Winthrop Jr. and his wife spread word of Lyon's neglect, a story that, unfortunately, was an old one to them.

Thomas Lyon addressed the Winthrops' outrage over Mary's poor care, and tried to deflect their criticism by upbraiding them for writing to his wife Mary Hoyt to complain to instead of to himself. Using a classic diversionary ploy, Lyon attempted to shift the blame onto the Winthrops, arguing that they should feel guilty for causing his wife shame. He also refused to accept any responsibility for his daughter's poor condition.[172]

Thomas Lyon moved back to Greenwich in or before 1672 from Fairfield for suddenly, this heretofore impoverished farmer owned three hundred acres of land in Byram, then called Rye, near the current Connecticut state line abutting Port Chester, New York. William Coddington, the governor of Rhode Island and John Winthrop Jr. wrote each other about him. Coddington, who knew the family from having dated Elizabeth, Lyon's mother-in-law, observed that "some of our friends [Quakers] about Rye or Greenage have had some of their goods taken away ... Thomas Lyon being one, with some others."[173] Thomas Lyon Sr., or perhaps his son Thomas, were to find that, like the Halletts and Bownes on Long Island, being a Quaker in Greenwich carried the same penalties as being a Quaker in Fairfield, for Puritan administrators of both towns continued to prohibit religious plurality. Documents from the Bowne House in Flushing, the home of Elizabeth Feake Hallett's daughter Hannah, show that in 1672, Greenwich townsmen accused and punished Thomas Lyon, Gersham Lockwood, Thomas Young, and John Marshall for being Quakers and issued arrest warrants for the latter two. Because these documents were in Hannah Feake Bowne's hands, it appears that Feake and Bowne family members were still keeping an eye on the activities of Thomas Lyon.

Mary, his only and poorly attired child by Martha Johana Winthrop, who probably still lived a life of grinding deprivation, claimed his 300 acres of Byram land was given to him free by the town and denied it was

Thomas Lyon house, Greenwich, Connecticut, 2011 PHOTO BY AUTHOR

given in exchange for him dropping an ongoing claim against her mother's 300-acre inheritance—part of the original Feake-Patrick purchase. Mary now claimed this right to her mother's inheritance. In 1698, she wrote a letter to Fitz-John Winthrop, John Jr.'s son, concerning this matter[174] and said her father let others purchase her land unfairly, and that he had withheld the deed for it from her. Winthrop noted at the bottom of this letter that the persons holding Mary Lyon Wilson's claimed land were John Mead, Robert Husted, and James Ferris. Greenwich townsmen likely did give her father the Byram land as a compromise to recompense him for his unjust loss of inheritance—and to end his constant complaining.

She lost her case twice in the Connecticut courts and appealed to the General Assembly of Connecticut. They awarded her £50 damages in consideration, finally bringing closure to part of Greenwich's first, but not last, great real estate debate.

Thomas Lyon left a portion of the Byram land, bordered by the Byram River, to his son Thomas, who constructed a house there and ran a farm that was managed in part by two slaves. This homestead was occupied by many generations of the large Lyon family until it was given to the town of Greenwich to manage in the early 1920s. Moved to a nearby site then to allow for the widening of the Post Road into Port Chester, New York, this house was referred to in 2012 as "the oldest unaltered house in Greenwich," and today funds are sought to save and maintain this rare and importance piece of the town's colonial heritage.

Lyon died in Byram on November 4, 1691, and in his will he mentioned his wife Mary, his sons John, Thomas, Samuel, and Joseph, his first daughter Mary, along with her Lyon stepsisters: Abigail, Elizabeth, Sarah, and Deborah.

Mary married twice: first to Joseph Stedwell of Rye, and then to John Wilson of Bedford, later of Rye. Her son Samuel Wilson married Susannah Ogden and they began lines of family descent claimed by Greenwich citizens today.

The Munsee Massacre Site

While a few contemporary scholars report Kieft's War in detail, some of the most popular New Netherland authors summarize it briefly or do not discuss the largest genocide of Kieft's War at all. Perhaps one of the reasons that this grotesque event, where possibly more people perished than at the Mystic Massacre of 1637, remains obscure is that its location, unlike that of Mystic, has never been verified by professional archaeologists. (Amateur archaeologists, please take note that if you consider potential new sites, it is against federal laws to disturb the remains of America's native people.) Four widely dispersed locations north and northwest of Tomac Cove in Old Greenwich have been proposed as the location of the Munsees massacre over the last 150 years and they are: Cos Cob, Connecticut; Bedford, New York; Poundridge, New York; and Cross River, New York.

When the Dutch launched a number of forays against the Wiechquaesgeck in the winter of 1644, their actions were dutifully transcribed by Fort Amsterdam officials and sent to West India Company administrators in Holland. From this bureaucratic record keeping we learn of Underhill's greatest massacre and several specific location descriptors:

a. Three yachts, landed at Greenwich, where they were obliged to pass the night by reason of the great snow and storm. In

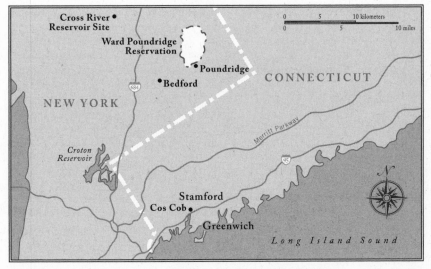

The four historically proposed Kieft's War massacre site locations

the morning they marched northwest up over stony hills, over which some were obliged to creep.

b. In the evening, about eight o'clock, they came within a league of the Indians, and inasmuch as they should have arrived too early and had to cross two rivers, one of two hundred feet wide and three feet deep, and that the men could not afterwards rest in consequence of the cold, it was determined to remain there until about ten o'clock.

c. [The Indian village was] in a low recess of a mountain, affording complete shelter from the northwest wind.

d. On the next day, the party set out much refreshed in good order, so as to arrive at Stamford in the evening. They marched with great courage over that wearisome mountain . . .

e. . . . and came in the afternoon to Stamford after a march of two days and one night, with little rest.

STICLINS PLAIN IN COS COB, CONNECTICUT:
FIRST CITED AS LARGEST MASSACRE LOCATION

One of the first attempts to report earliest American history was undertaken by the Reverend Thomas Prince in the 1700s, a well-respected minister of the Old South Meetinghouse in Boston. He collected local histories from regional northeastern ministers, but died before he could complete his great work. Benjamin Trumbull completed the task in 1736, entitling Prince's work *A Chronological History of New England.* The information Dr. Prince received about Greenwich was from a minister named Stephen Monson or Munson from the First Congregational Church at Horseneck, which was the English name for land on the west side of the Mianus River. In 1728 Munson reported to Prince[175] that by 1665, the year the English claimed all of New Netherland, Greenwich was inhabited by only eight families on the east side of the Mianus river, but, "About the year 1680, the oldest part of the town being very much increased, many of the inhabitants moved across the river called the Mianus and settled the village commonly called Horseneck but by the Indians called Paihomsing." He continued that, "There was in this part of the town called Horseneck a very bloody battle fought between the Dutch and Indians on a plain called and known by the name of Sticlins Plain in the year 1646, where the Dutch with much difficulty obtained the victory. Great numbers were slain and their graves remain unto this day appearing like many small hills."

Munson supplied Prince with an incorrect battle date of 1646, an error that subsequent historians perpetuated for decades, and his letter began the long history of placing the largest massacre on Strickland Plain in modern day Cos Cob, Connecticut.[176]

When New York Secretary John Brodhead finally brought the trove of missing Dutch documentation back to America in the late 1840s and published its translation called "Holland Documents" in 1854, a surge of regional historians wrote new American histories based on this exciting Dutch archival information. Rampant speculations about the great massacre location were based on mixes of urban legend, civic self-importance, and Dutch documentation.

Brodhead referenced Munson's assertion that the massacre location was in Cos Cob when *Holland Documents* was first published, but by a latter revision, he questioned how Sticlin's Plain, now Strickland Plain, could be the largest genocide's location due to incompatible site description, as does this author.

BEDFORD, NEW YORK

Bedford, New York, specifically the base of Indian Hill in Bedford, was the second site proposed for the location of the great massacre. This conjecture was made after Brodhead published *Holland Documents* and a full two hundred years after the actual event. Citing a secondhand witness, and without archaeological evidence, in 1848 historian Robert Bolton placed the event at Bedford, New York, based on the eighty-three-year-old memories of "an aged Mrs. Holmes."[177]

> *The summit of the high mountain ridge east of Bedford continues to be called the "Indian Farm." There is a tradition current in the neighborhood, that the south side of this mountain, sometimes denominated as Stony hill, was the scene of a bloody fight between the early settlers and the aborigines. Mrs. Martha Holmes, an aged inhabitant of Bedford (still living) remembers in 1765 to have seen several Indian mounds at the foot of this hill (a little south of the old school house), which were pointed out to her as the graves of those who fell in the conflict. This may have been the battle fought between the Dutch and the Indians in February 1644, an account of which is recorded in the journal of New Netherlands.*

Satisfied with such evidence, a number of historians[178] perpetuated the placement of the massacre in Bedford, New York, after Bolton's report.

Ten years later, in 1857, Daniel M. Mead sought to restore Cos Cob, Connecticut, as the massacre's true location and he wrote a history of Greenwich using Brodhead's information as well.[179] Mead blended this information with a fanciful bolstering of Cos Cob as the massacre location by challenging Bolton's "aged Mrs. Holmes" with Cos Cob's "aged Mrs. Howe" who had "died 40 years since." He had his deceased source, Mrs. Howe, fingering these mounds quite specifically, "five of them between the present (1846) houses of J.K. Stearns, Esq., and Mrs. Hitchcock, and twenty were scattered about just across the lane southeast of the present residence of William White, Esq., on the land of Edward Mead." (The Hitchcock farming family burial ground, often but erroneously believed to be an Indian burial ground, is near the intersection of the haplessly misspelled Sinawoy Road and the Boston Post Road, across from the drive that leads to the Cos Cob Library.)

In his account, Daniel Mead rightfully railed against Cos Cob residents who, some fifty years before he took pen to paper, purportedly abused Indian gravesites through heartless planting and construction.

"Their old burial place as yet is not all extinct," Mead fumed, "what remains is but a monument of the carelessness of the people of the neighborhood. Not only is the place long neglected, but absolutely is being demolished by the penny grinders who want dirt to fill in the docks, or for some other purpose. It should have been fenced long ago and protected from men who will take dirt from dead men's bones." He notes additionally that "Bushels of flint arrowheads have been plowed up by the owners of land on all parts of Strickland's plain. Some of them are beautifully cut from the finest white flint; but the greater part of them are rougher hewn, from blue flint." In the collection of the National Museum of the American Indian in Washington, D.C., the sole arrowhead from Greenwich, Connecticut, is fashioned from gleaming white quartz.

Daniel S. Mead FREDERICK A. HUBBARD, *OTHER DAYS IN GREENWICH* (NEW YORK: J.F. TAPLEY CO., 1913)

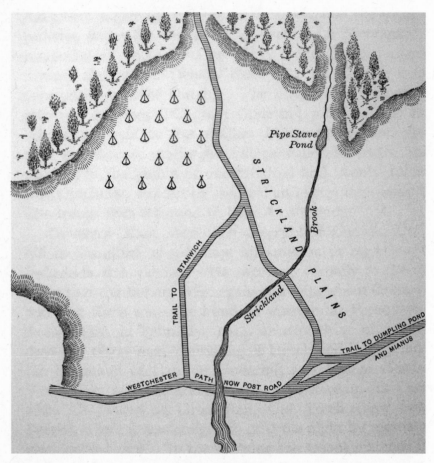

Spencer Mead's map of a Cos Cob Indian village location SPENCER MEAD, *YE HISTORIE OF YE TOWN OF GREENWICH* (THE KNICKERBOCKER PRESS, 1863, 1911, REPRINTED HARBOR HILL BOOKS, HARRISON, NY, 1979)

If truly a Wiechquaesgeck village site, Strickland Plain, on the west bank of the Mianus River, is not the great massacre site but the site of the prior foray that was close to Tomac Cove. Here, according to Brodhead's *Holland Documents*, soldiers embarked from Tomac Cove and reached a site "immediately," killing eighteen to twenty and taking an older man hostage who would serve as the guide that would "lead them to the Weichquaesgeck." By boat from Tomac Cove, it would take a very short time to reach Strickland Plain. The area is west, not northwest of the foray's launch point; it never would have taken a full day's march to reach; and it lacks the geological features of two closely spaced rivers, "one two hundred feet wide and three feet deep," "stony hills over which some were obliged to creep," or the description of having a recess in a "mountain."

Nevertheless, six years after Daniels's history was published, his cousin Spencer Mead continued the family tradition of writing Greenwich histories and in 1863 he drew an actual map of an Indian village in Cos Cob.[180] His graphic depiction more clearly denotes where Indian remains might have been found, and unlike his irascible cousin, didn't upset specific neighbors.

A modern-day USGS topographic map that shows Spencer Mead's village location depicts a very small northwest-running ridgeline along Valleywood Road in Cos Cob; but it reveals no prominence that would constitute any "mountain" exhibiting a "low recess."

POUNDRIDGE, NEW YORK

The location of Poundridge, New York, was first proposed in 1960 by Allen Trelease in his wonderful book, *Indian Affairs in Colonial New York*.[181] His account provides excellent detail of the Dutch forays, but does not supply rationale for citing Poundridge as the great genocide's location. As the marchers' destination, Poundridge is also at variance with the primary source document description that soldiers marched in a northwest direction, and that they had to cross two closely spaced rivers near the Indian village. Poundridge is due north of the launch point and does not feature the river geography. Nevertheless, many authors followed Trelease's lead in proposing Poundridge as the great genocide site.[182]

215

CROSS RIVER, NEW YORK

In 1945, Thatcher T. P. Luquer proposed a fourth possibility for the massacre site as[183] twenty-four miles north of the Tomac Cove, near the intersection of where the Croton River met the Cross River before the creation of the Croton River Reservoir in 1892. Luquer acknowledged Bedford legends, but speculated, without supporting evidence, that the event may have occurred ten miles even further north. Luquer's proposed site is on or near Pepsico's World Headquarters in Somers, New York, and his hypothesis requires the 130 Dutch soldiers or hired mercenaries to have marched twenty-four miles, in deep snow, in one day, and then successfully battled hundreds of Indians. Few agree with Luquer's proposal.

NORTHWEST OF TOMAC COVE

This author believes the event to have occurred legitimately northwest of Tomac Cove and that the site may well be nearby or drowned by the Kensico Reservoir. Many of the reservoir's coves uniquely conform to Dutch site descriptors of the village being located within a low recess of a mountain that is within a northwest running ridgeline. The area is also within reasonable marching distance for 130 foot troops marching a full twelve-hour day, in very cold conditions with deep snow, in a northwest direction from Tomac Cove. A possible Kensico Reservoir area location accommodates the text that the troops scaled the very stony hills of northwest Greenwich, and crossed two closely spaced rivers, which may have been either the "Aquehung," which is now known as the Bronx River, the Mamaroneck River, then known as the "Armenperai," or the Sprain River, then known as the "Neperhan," before reaching the tragically doomed Indian village within the mountain notch.

APPENDIX II

Greenwich Place Names

MANY INDIAN NAMES WERE LEARNED FROM MISSIONARIES WHO SOUGHT to convert the Indians by teaching them the Bible, which they then translated into Indian languages, fashioning the first Indian-to-English dictionaries. Some Indians themselves were educated in the English manner and they created additional dictionaries. Old deeds are another source that provide Indian-to-English equivalents. James Hammond Trumbull studied John Eliot's *Indian Bible*, and in 1881 he published *Indian Names of Places In & On the Border of Connecticut* and later, *The Natick Dictionary*. Brodhead relied on J. H. Trumbull's work in translating the many Dutch documents he had found in Europe.

It is important to consider that there were many Indian groups with regional dialects, many quite distinctive, so complete consistency in translation is rarely possible. The Greenwich area is also on the edge of what is believed to be the Unami-speaking Lenape and the Munsee-speaking people, so dialects and languages describing things and places could have had great variation. Many places near Fort Amsterdam, including the Greenwich area, have had three and four names over time, and were variously referred to by their Indian, Dutch, and English names. These naming variations, coupled with the fact that European spellers were hugely inconsistent, cause some degree of inconsistency as to the meaning and spelling of words of this era and this area.

THE BYRAM RIVER

Trumbull, Mead, and many Indian linguists agree that "Armonk" was the Munsee name of the Byram River[184] from the word "amaug," meaning "a fishing place." The Indian name for Byram was "Sasomuck."

THE ASAMUCK AND THE PATOUMUCK CREEKS

The Asamuck is the creek that runs through Binney Park in Old Greenwich and enters Greenwich Cove. The Patoumuck, also written as the Tatoumuck, is the small stream, mostly piped over, which runs generally along the Greenwich and Stamford border, and empties into Tomac Cove. The Asamuck was renamed "Long Meadow Creek" soon after European presence was established. The local sachems with jurisdiction over the Asamuck or Binney Park area were Amogerone and Owenoke. Those with jurisdiction over the Patoumuck were Ramathone and Nawhorone.

HASSEKY AND MIOSSEHASAKY MEADOWS

In 1848, Robert Bolton reported that the meadows bordering the Armonck River aka the Byram River were called "haseco" and "miossehasaky," meaning that these extensive meadows were wet and marshy.[185] There was another large, wet meadow in eastern Greenwich along Long Meadow Creek north of the Post Road. Hassake Road, according to Joe Zeranski, former Greenwich Wetlands and Conservation Department member, is a remnant of a path that went north from Sound Beach Avenue through this wetland. A Providence, Rhode Island, word, "moshassuck," denotes a "great fresh meadow" or marshy land. The nineteenth-century linguist Edward Manning Ruttenber says the word miossehassaky means "a bog." A contemporary of his, named William M. Beauchamp, wrote in *Aboriginal Place Names of New York* that the root "Miosse" means a marshy meadow that is larger than usual.

Spencer Mead misinterpreted the meaning of the word "miossehasky" from being a marshy meadow to the name of an Indian group, which is clearly an error. The English settlers may have maintained the use of this word as it was similar in sound to hassock-filled meadows, or "those with grass tufts throughout." Both meadows, at either end of town, are cited early and often in early land records.

Cos Cob

There is no primary source documentation that tells us what the words "Cos Cob" mean. Trumbull writes that the word Cassacubque means "a great ledge of rocks," and notes its additional use describing such a site in Colchester, Connecticut.[186] He cites: "Kussukôbse = Mass. Kussuh-koe-ompsk 'high rock.'" He feels that the Greenwich word "Cos Cob" was comparable to "Cassacubque." This author rejects the proposal that Cos Cob is named after the early Coe family, as in "Coe's Cob." In this usage, a "cob" would refer either to a type of harbor or a type of wattle-and-daub building construction. Early Greenwich records clearly show the family name "Coe" most often spelled with an "e," whereas 1600s Greenwich residents almost always spelled Coscob as a single word without an "e."

Strickland

Strickland Road and Strickland Brook are visible today near the Cos Cob Library and Firehouse properties. These names are corruptions of "Sticlins Plains" and "Sticklins Brook," frequently cited in early Greenwich deeds, and named for the early settler Edmond Sticklin. He may have been a relative of Watertown settler John Stickland, whose name is found in Watertown, Massachusetts, records as a landowner there, with property abutting that of Daniel Patrick and Robert Feake. Sticklin Plain and Sticklin Brook are mentioned often in Greenwich's earliest deeds.

The "plain" of "Strickland Plain" is the relatively flat land that the Post Road bisects in Cos Cob on the western side of the Mianus River between Indian Field Road and the rocky rise known as Diamond Hill.

Another large cleared meadow cited early and often in 1640s Town of Greenwich records was "Coscob fielde." While its exact location is unknown, it is speculated to have been on the west bank of the Mianus River, south of I-95. It probably included the flatlands of Stricklands plains west to Brother's Brook.

PEMBERWICK

The name of the western Greenwich community called Pemberwick is an English variant of the Munsee word "Pempewock," "Pimpewog," or "Pemperwog."

CHICKAHOMINY

This name is thought to have been employed for a western region of Greenwich in reference to a Civil War battle fought in Chickahominy, Virginia.

LADDINS ROCK

The "legend" of Laddins Rock, first published in an 1800s newspaper, is a tale wherein a Dutch farmer leaps off this Old Greenwich rocky cliff now next to present-day I-95 to escape the lethal pursuit of local Indians. The story is not supported in primary source documents. Labeled on an early Greenwich map as "Lattin's Rock," "Laddin" is likely a corruption of early Stamford settler Richard Lattin's name, a man who moved from Wethersfield to Stamford and then on to Hempstead on western Long Island.

Source Notes

Abbreviations

IACNY   Indian Affairs in Colonial New York

DRCHSNY   Documents Relative to the Colonial History of the State
of New York

DWS   Divided We Stand, Watertown, Massachusetts 1630–1680

WP   The Winthrop Papers

1.   Teunis B. Bergen, *Early Settlers of King's County, Long Island, N.Y.* (New York: S. W. Green's Son, 1881), 14. Bartholomew of Gravesend, m. Oct., 1650, at Gravesend, Hannah Patricke. Aug. 10, 1667, from Nathan Whitman he bought plantation lot N° 12, in Gravesend. From a town record entry on the Gravesend record of Nov. 6, 1671: "whereas the Governor was pleased to order Wm. Wilkins to pay ten pounds towards the release of Hanna Apelgate and her child, this sheweth that Thos Whitlock received of Mr. Delavall five pounds of the aforesaid somme, of the which the said Thomas delivered five pounds to the constable and overseers of Gravesend in red cloth," etc. Possibly she was in the hands of Indians, and the money and red cloth were used for her ransom.

2.   Mccurdyfamilylineage.Com/Ancestry/P242.2010. Daniel Patrick lineage. Accessed 7/22/2010.

3.   Worthington C. Ford, ed., *The Winthrop Papers (1498–1628)*, 6 vols. (Boston: Massachusetts Historical Society, 1929).1:356–357 (hereafter cited as *WP*). Henry Winthrop to Emmanuel Downing, 22 August 1627. Henry to go to Barbados to gain experience in maritime affairs.

4.   *WP,* 1:403–404. Henry Winthrop granted credit by John Winthrop and Emmanuel Downing.

5.   *WP,* 2:66–69. John Winthrop to Henry Winthrop, 30 January 1628/9. Reprimand letter.

6.   *WP,* 2:78–79. Thomas Fones complains to John Winthrop.

7.   Philip J. Greven Jr., *Four Generations: Population, Land and Family in Colonial Andover, Massachusetts.* (Ithaca, NY and London: Cornell University Press, 1970), 31–37, 117–122, 206–210. Also, Daniel Scott Smith, "The Demographic History of Colonial New England," (*Journal of Economic History,* XXXII, 1972), 165–183.

8.   *WP,* 2:84–85. John Winthrop to Margaret Winthrop, 28 April 1629: "keep my son at home as much as thou can, especially from Hadleigh."

9.   Francis J. Bremer, *The Puritan Experiment: New England Society from Bradford to Edwards* (Hanover, NJ: University Press of New England, 1995), 41–46. Great Migration rationale. Also, Roger Thompson, *Divided We Stand: Watertown, Massachusetts 1630–1680* (Amherst: University of Massachusetts Press, 2001), 164–175.

10.   Caleb Snow, *A History of Boston: The Metropolis of Massachusetts, From Its Origin to the Present Period With Some Account of the Environs* (Boston: Abel Owen, 1828), 2:32–33. Boston's native name.

11.   Richard S. Dunn, *Puritans and Yankees, the Winthrop Dynasty of New England, 1630–1717* (Princeton, NJ: Princeton University Press, 1962), 27. Coy relations between Winthrop and Charles I.

12.   nationalhumanitiescenter.org/tserve/eighteen/ekeyinfo/puritan.htm. Reasons for social rankings. Accessed 6/11/2008.

13.   Roger Thompson, *Divided We Stand Watertown, Massachusetts, 1630–1680* (Amherst: Sheridan Books, Inc., 2001), 145, 246 note #9. (Hereafter cited as DWS). Indian disease epidemics.

14.   Henry Bond, *Family Memorials: Genealogies of the Families and Descendants of the Early Settlers of Watertown, Massachusetts, Including Waltham and Weston; to Which Is Appended the Early History of the Town* (Boston: Little, Brown and Company, 1855), 2:1055. Nathaniel Shurtleff, ed., *Records of the Governor and Company of Massachusetts Bay* (Boston: William White Publishing, 1853), 1:79, 91, 96. Patrick and Underhill assignments in Watertown.

15.   *WP,* 2:301–302. Henry Winthrop drowns July 16, 1630.

16.   *WP,* 2:301–302. John Winthrop to wife Margaret Tyndal concerning Henry's death.

17.   *New York Genealogical and Biographical Record* (New York: The NYGBR Society, 1880), 11:14. William Coddington.

18.   *WP,* 3:28–29. Elizabeth very much employed in her surgery.

19.   *WP,* 2:304–306. John Winthrop to care for Elizabeth Fones Winthrop as if she were his own.

20.   J. Franklin Jameson and James Kendall Hosmer, eds., *Winthrop's Journal "History of New England 1630–1649"* (New York: Charles Scribners' Sons, 1908), 80. The *Lyon's* arrival in Boston.

21.   *WP,* 3:23. Martha's letters to John Winthrop Jr.

22.   *DWS,* 187. Robert Feake's lineage.

23.   Laurel Thatcher Ulrich, *Good Wives: Image and Reality in the Lives of Women in Northern New England 1650–1750* (New York: Vintage Books, 1982), 8. Social orders.

24.   Ibid., 6–7. Wife and woman.

25.   Henry Bond, *Family Memorials: Genealogies of the Families and Descendants of the Early Settlers of Watertown, Massachusetts, Including Waltham and Weston; to Which Is Appended the Early History of the Town* (Boston: Little, Brown and Company, 1855), 1:1031. Mount Feake.

26.   Robert Charles Anderson, ed., *The Great Migration Begins: Immigrants to New England 1620–1633* (Boston: New England Historic and Genealogical Society, 1995), 3:1405–1406. Daniel Patrick, Anna van Beyeren, and their children.
27.   Laurel Thatcher Ulrich, *A Midwife's Tale: The Life of Martha Ballard, Based on Her Diary, 1785–1812* (New York: Vintage Books, 1990), 40. Midwife roles.
28.   Ibid., 128. Betony used for childbirth pains.
29.   Ibid., 131. Childbirth imagery of redemption.
30.   Ibid., 135. Breast infection treatment; Edward Holyoke et al, *The Holyoke Diaries 1709–1856* (Salem, MA, The Essex Institute, 1911), 88.
31.   Laurel Thatcher Ulrich, *A Midwife's Tale: The Life of Martha Ballard, Based on Her Diary, 1785–1812* (New York: Vintage Books, 1990), 170–175, 186–187. Infant mortality rates.
32.   Laurel Thatcher Ulrich, *Good Wives: Image and Reality in the Lives of Women in Northern New England 1650–1750* (New York: Vintage Books, 1982), 23. Womens' value.
33.   *DWS*, 85, 225n9. Farm animal value.
34.   Warren Billings, John Selby, and Thad Tate, *Colonial Virginia: A History* (Millwood, NY: KTO, 1986), 44. Virginia settlement death count: 347, one third of its population.
35.   Philip Vincent, *A True Relation of the Late Battell Fought in New England*, (1638) Theatrum Orbis Terrarum, 1974. Repeated in Charles Orr, *History of the Pequot War: The Contemporary Accounts of Mason, Underhill, Vincent and Gardener* (Cleveland, OH: The Helman-Taylor Company, 1897), 103. Steven Katz, "The Pequot War Reconsidered" (*The New England Quarterly*, June 1991), 64, no. 2: 206–224.
36.   Adriaen van der Donck, *A Description of New Netherland*, Charles T Gehring, William A Starna, and D. W.Goedhuys, eds., (Lincoln: University of Nebraska Press, 2008), 59–84. Fortified village description.
37.   John Underhill, *Newes From America*, 1638. Underhill explaining his actions reprinted in Charles Orr, *History of the Pequot War* (Cleveland, OH: The Helman-Taylor Company, 1897), 47, 81.
38.   Nathaniel Morton, *New England's Memorial* (Boston: Congregational Board of Publication, 1855), 33. Indian deaths approved by the Puritans: "It pleased the Lord to vanquish their enemies."
39.   Francis J. Bremer, *The Puritan Experiment: New England Society from Bradford to Edwards* (Hanover, NJ: University Press of New England, 1995), 263. "The English, including Winthrop, neither sought nor found any merit in native customs and values."
40.   J. Franklin Jameson and James Kendall Hosmer, eds., *Winthrop's Journal "History of New England 1630–1649"* (New York: Charles Scribners' Sons, 1908), 1:273–277. Underhill adultery in Boston. *Records of the First Church of Boston, 1630–1868* (Boston: The Colonial Society of Massachusetts, 1961), 28. Underhill denunciation in Boston.
41.   Ibid., Vol. 7, Issue 1:329. Winthrop comments on Underhill's conversion.
42.   *WP*, 4:300–301. Sturgis testimony against Daniel Patrick.
43.   Henry Bond, *Family Memorials: Genealogies of the Families and Descendants of the Early Settlers of Watertown, Massachusetts, Including Waltham and Weston; to Which Is Appended the Early History of the Town* (Boston: Little, Brown and Company, 1855), 1:127. Harsh disciplinarians.

44. *WP*, 3:287–288. Elizabeth Feake desires to move near JWJ.

45. *WP*, 3:287. Robert Feake to JWJ: Unsettled about move away from Watertown.

46. Eve LaPlante, *American Jezebel, The Uncommon Life of Anne Hutchinson, the Woman Who Defied the Puritans* (San Francisco: Harper Collins, 2004), 132.

47. *DWS*, 171–172. Puritan arguments.

48. Ibid., 64. Early Puritan religious concerns.

49. Eve LaPlante, *American Jezebel, The Uncommon Life of Anne Hutchinson, the Woman Who Defied the Puritans* (San Francisco: Harper Collins, 2004), 54. Earthly striving will not attain God's grace.

50. Ibid., 55. Anne Hutchinson as a prophetess.

51. Francis J. Bremer, *John Winthrop America's Forgotten Founding Father* (New York: Oxford University Press, Inc., 2003), 95. Antinomianism: that the moral law does not bind those predestined to salvation. Familism: that man can achieve perfection in life.

52. Robert Bolton, *A History of the County of Westchester* (New York: A. S. Gould, 1898), 6. Stamford purchase deed for New Haven Colony. The Stamford purchase deed reads: The first of July 1640 Bought of Ponus Sagamore of Toquams and of Wascussue Sagamore of Shippan by me Nathanael Turner of Quinipeac all the ground that belongs to both the above said Sagamores except a piece of ground which the above said Sagamores reserved for his the rest of the said Indians to plant on all which ground being expressed by meadows upland grass with the rivers and trees and in consideration hereof I the said Nathanael Turner am to give and bring or send to the abovesaid Sagamores within the space of one month twelve coats, twelve hoes, twelve hatchets, twelve glasses, twelve knives, two kettles, four fathoms of white wampum, all which land both we the said Sagamores do promise faithfully to perform both for ourselves, heirs, executors or assigns to the abovesaid Nathanael Turner of Quinipiacke to his heirs, executors or assigns and hereunto we have set our marks in the presence of many of the said Indians they fully consenting hereuntoWitnessed by us;William Wilkes, James, Mark of Ponus Sagamore, Mark of Wascassue Sagamore, Witnessed by two Indians, The mark of Owenoke Sagamore Ponus's Son.

Toquams is now known as Shippan Point, a part of greater Stamford. Steven Grumet, *The Munsee Indians, A History* (Norman, OK: University of Oklahoma Press, 2009), 318n2: Ponus signed the April 20, 1640, device as "Pomenate," as "Ponus" on the July 1, 1640, deed, and as the witness "Pauonohas" on a July 18, 1640, document. "Owenoke" is identified as Ponus's eldest son in the August 15, 1655, confirmation of the July 1, 1640, deed.

53. *DWS*, 57. The Feakes richly endowed with meadows and plowland in Watertowne.

54. Henry Fitz-Gilbert, ed., *"The New England Historical and Genealogical Register,"* (Boston, New England Historic Genealogical Society, 1880), 47:517. A will made by Robert and Christopher Feake's grandmother Mary (married to William) details the family connections. Also: familysearch.org/search/records#count=20&query=%2Bgive nname%3Achristopher~%20%2Bsurname%3Afeake~%20%2Bany_place%3Aengland~, George McCracken's genealogy of the Feake family at longislandsurnames.com/ genealogy/showsource.php?sourceID=S2 748&tree=Dodge, and freepages.genealogy .rootsweb.ancestry.com/~dav4is/ODTs/FEAKE.shtml#~FEAKE.

55. *DWS*, 78n50. Feake's book found in George Phillips's bookshelf, *"One Hundred Sermons on the Apocalypse"* inscribed, "This is Mr. Feake, his book, 1634." *Publications of the Colonial Society of Massachusetts* (Boston: The Society, 1932), 27:193.

56. O'Callaghan, E. B. and Berthold Fernow, trans., *Documents Relative to the Colonial History of the State of New York* (Albany: Weed, Parsons and Company, 1856), 1:545. Petuckquapoch is Greenwich. (Hereafter cited as *DRCHSNY*). Spencer Percival Mead, *Ye Historie of Ye Town of Greenwich, County of Fairfield and State of Connecticut, with Genealogical Notes* (Harrison, NY, Harbor Hill Books, 1863), 5–6. Feake-Patrick purchase of Greenwich July 18, 1640. Town of Greenwich Land Records, Book One.

57. Charles J. Hoadley, *Records of the Colony and Plantation of New Haven, from 1638 to 1649* (Hartford, CT: Case, Tiffany and Co., 1857), 199.

58. *DRCHSNY*, (1856), 1:366. Greenwich attractiveness.

59. *DWS*, 130. Women's land purchase.

60. J. Franklin Jameson, ed., *Narratives of New Netherland 1609–1664* (Charles Scribners's Sons, Elibron Classics, Adamant Media Corporation, 2005), 8:205. (Hereafter cited as *NNN*). DeVries sights Feake and Patrick homesteads from Long Island Sound.

61. olivetreegenealogy.com/nn/church/rdcbapt.shtml. Dutch Reformed Church baptism records of Feake and Patrick children.

62. *NNN*, 305. Travel from Stamford to the Hudson River and back by foot possible in one day "if one knows the Indian paths."

63. J. Franklin Jameson and James Kendall Hosmer, eds., *Winthrop's Journal "History of New England 1630–1649"* (New York: Charles Scribners' Sons, 1908), 2:193–194. Busheag's attack.

64. *DRCHSNY*, 2:142. William Kieft demands Greenwich sovereignty.

65. E. B. O'Callaghan, trans., *History of New Netherland or New York Under the Dutch* (New York: D. Appleton, 1845), 1:252. Feake and Patrick submit to Dutch sovereignty.

66. A. J. F. Van Laer, trans., eds., *Council Minutes 1638–1649* (Baltimore: Genealogical Publishing Co., Inc., 1974), 487, Doc.# 305. Greenwich is Groenwits. Also, personal communication with Dr. Charles Gehring 11/1/09, that Groenwits is the Dutch approximation of Greenwich.

67. Laurel Thatcher Ulrich, *Good Wives: Image and Reality in the Lives of Women in Northern New England 1650–1750* (New York: Vintage Books, 1982), 35–50. Deputy husbands.

68. *DRCHSNY*, 1:11–12. Dutch boundaries.

69. Nathaniel Morton, *New England's Memorial* (Boston: Congregational Board of Publication, 1855), 22. Pilgrims intentionally put off course by the Dutch.

70. *NNN*, 311. "Knocking on a deaf man's door."

71. Allen W. Trelease, *Indian Affairs in Colonial New York The Seventeenth Century* (Ithaca, NY: Cornell University Press, Bison Books, 1997), 43. Pelt prices. (Hereafter cited as *IACNY*).

72. J. Thomas Scharf, *History of Westchester County, New York Including Morrisania, Kings Bridge, and West Farms, Which Have Been Annexed to New York City.* (Philadelphia: L. E. Preston & Co., 1886), 1:13. Pelts traded.

73. Robert Steven Grumet, *The Munsee Indians, A History* (Norman: University of Oklahoma Press, 2009), 330–331n15. Siwanoy word placement on Long Island.

74. Ibid., 158.

75. Ibid., 33. Tankiteke means Little River and location.

76. *IACNY*, 2. A significant feature of Algonkian organization was its fragmentation.

77. Robert Steven Grumet, *The Munsee Indians, A History*. (Norman: University of Oklahoma Press, 2009), 32. Delawarean origins.

78. Edward Manning Ruttenber, *History of the Indian Tribes of Hudson's River* (Albany, NY: J. Munsell, 1872), 366. Robert Bolton, *History of the County of Westchester* (New York: A. S. Gould, 1898), 1:182. Defined Wiechquaesgeck place of the bark kettles.

79. Reginald Pelham Bolton, *New York City in Indian Possession*, within Foster Saville, *A Montauk Cemetery at East Hampton, Long Island* (New York: Museum of the American Indian, Heye Foundation, 1922), 3. Wiechquaesgeck are subservient to the enforced dominations of the Mohawk Iroquois, who compelled them . . . to pay tribute to their military superiority.

80. *IACNY*, 56. The Dutch decide to open trade.

81. Ibid., 43. Freedoms and Exemptions Act, June 7, 1629.

82. *DRCHSNY*, 1:332, 338. Kieft taxes Indians, company disavows responsibility. Also in *NNN*, 332, 334 and in *IACNY*, 65.

83. *DRCHSNY*, 1:150, 13:7. Sachem's brother tortured with split stick of wood by Van Tienhoven's soldiers; *NNN*, 208–211, IACNY, 66.

84. Swits murder; *NNN*, 213, 274–275. Berthold Fernow and Waleyn Van der Veen, trans., *The Minutes of the Orphanmasters of New Amsterdam 1655 to 1663* (New York: F. P. Harper, 1902), 5, 24–25. Claes Swits's family kidnapped. Claes's head found ten years later: *DRCHSNY*, 1:150.

85. *DRCHSNY*, 1:183. "Sorry twenty Christians not murdered," references Daniel Patrick's April letter regarding this.

86. *DRCHSNY*, 1:415. Council of Twelve Men convened.

87. J. Franklin Jameson, *NNN*, 227–228. DeVries on Pavonia.

88. *DRCHSNY*, (Charles van Benthuysen, 1851), 4:99–112. Breeden Raedt, Underhill, fort atrocities.

89. *DRCHSNY*, 13:12–14. Kieft assassination attempt.

90. *IACNY*, 77. Estimated force of 50–60 soldiers, 250 colonists. Dutch against 1,500 Indians.

91. *Winthrop's Journal*, 57.

92. *DRCHSNY*, 13:14. Dutch-Indian peace treaty: "All injuries done by the tribes to the Dutch or by the Dutch to the Indians shall henceforth be forever forgotten and forgiven."

93. J. Thomas Scharf, *History of Westchester County, New York Including Morrisania, Kings Bridge, and West Farms, Which Have Been Annexed to New York City* (Philadelphia: L. E. Preston & Co., 1886), 1:19. Eve LaPlante, *American Jezebel, The Uncommon Life of Anne Hutchinson, the Woman Who Defied the Puritans* (San Francisco: Harper Collins, 2004), 121, 237. Lemuel A. Welles. "The Site of Anne Hutchinson's Massacre," *New York Genealogical and Biographical Record*. New York, April 1929, vol. 60, no. 2:120–123.

94. *DRCHSNY,* 13:18. Autumn Leaf: Susan Hutchinson.
95. Eve LaPlante, *American Jezebel, The Uncommon Life of Anne Hutchinson, the Woman Who Defied the Puritans* (San Francisco: Harper Collins, 2004), 239.
96. *DRCHSNY,* 13:139. Settlers appeal to Holland for protection.
97. J. Franklin Jameson, ed., *Narratives of New Netherland 1609–1664* (Charles Scribners's Sons, Elibron Classics, Adamant Media Corporation, 2005), 260. French Father Jorges notes two score Dutch deaths in 1643. "That the natives . . . while I was there . . . actually killed some two score Hollanders, and burnt many houses and barns full of wheat."
98. *DRCHSNY,*1:186–188. Dutch massacre document.
99. J. Franklin Jameson, and Wendell Hosmer, eds., *Winthrop's Journal 1630–1649* (New York: Charles Scribner's Sons, 1908), 153–154. Daniel Patrick's murder. Author's note: Daniel Patrick and the infant Sarah Feake may be the first burials in Old Greenwich's Tomac Cemetery, interred when it was joint Feake/Patrick property. Tomac wasn't recognized as a church cemetery until 1667, twenty-three years after Patrick's murder. Alternatively, Patrick possibly could have been buried in Stamford, as he was assassinated in Stamford in Captain Underhill's house. The first Stamford burial ground was where Stamford's Columbus Park now stands. Early graves from this area were moved to Stamford's Old Northfield Cemetery to make way for the route of Stamford's current Main Street. (Personal communication with Stamford Historical Society director Ron Marcus, 6/17/10.)
100 Mike Dash, *Batavia's Graveyard* (New York: Three Rivers Press, 2002), 162.
101. *DRCHSNY,* 1:186.
102. *WP,* 4:188–189. John Winthrop considers Kieft's request a Dutch plot to involve the English against the Indians.
103. Paul Andrew Otto, *The Dutch-Munsee Encounter in America, The Struggle for Sovereignty in the Hudson Valley* (New York: Berghahn Books, 2006), 125. The conflict between Dutch and Munsee.
104. *DRCHSNY,* 1:187.
105. A. J. F. Van Laer, trans., Kenneth Scott and Ken Stryker-Rodda, eds., *Register of the Provincial Secretary, 1638–1660* (Baltimore: Genealogical Publishing Company, Inc., 1974), 2:100. A gravely wounded Dutch participant named Jan Mange sent for his wife to come to Stamford on March 11, 1644, where he dictated his will to her before dying.
106. Ibid., 2:205, Doc. #101b. Underhill's tavern rampage.
107. Jeanne Magdalany and Edith Wicks, *The Early Settlement of Stamford, Connecticut 1641–1700* (Bowie, MD: Heritage Books, Inc., 1990), 14. Map of Stamford. Note that a significant Stamford population moved to western Long Island in the spring of 1644.
108. *DRCHSNY,* 13:48. Underhill signs peace agreement in Stamford with Indians after massacre. "April 16, 1644. Of the arrival at Stamford of Mamarunock, Wapgaurin, chiefs of the Kitchawank, Mongochkonnone, Pappenoharrow, of Wiechquaesgeck and Nohcpeem, together with the Wappings, have come to Stamford to solicit Captain Underhill to apply to the Governor of New Netherland for peace, and have promised now and forever not to do any harm to either people, cattle, houses, or anything else

within the territory of New Netherland, also that they will not come upon Manhatans Island, as long as we Dutch are at war with other heathens, unless in one canoe as far as Fort Amsterdam, and whereas they likewise promise to do their best in looking up Pacham. Therefore, we promise not to molest them, if the aforesaid chiefs and the people with them observe the forgoing they may cultivate their lands in peace, as far as we are concerned. In confirmation hereof, some of their prisoners are returned to them. [This may have included the Hutchinson child.] Done at Ft. Amsterdam the sixth of April, 1644."

109. Cornelus Melyn, *Extracts from a work called Breeden raedt aen de Vereenighde Nederlandsche* (Amsterdam, Fr. Muller, 1850).

110. *DRCHSNY,* 1:213. Massacre aftermath.

111. *DRCHSNY,* (1856), 13:23–24. Lenient Indian policy.

112. *WP,* 2:214 footnote. Editor describes Hallett as an agent of Robert Feake, but support for this is not found.

113. *DWS,* 132. No divorce on grounds of insanity.

114. *DWS,* 32 and 243n33. Puritan divorce rationale.

115. *Winthrop's Journal,* 50. Winthrop argues to judge each adultery case individually.

116. Laurel Thatcher Ulrich, *Good Wives: Image and Reality in the Lives of Women in Northern New England 1650–1750.* (New York: Vintage Books, 1982), 94. Adultery charges usually reduced.

117. *WP,* 4:444–445. Lucy Downing to John Winthrop, "Patrick is cut," Feb. 24, 1643/44; "she lives where all good means is wanting."

118. *DRCHSNY,* 14:116. Purchasers of Feake-Patrick land write Stuyvesant to guarantee their titles.

119. *New York Genealogical and Biographical Record,* (1880), 11:16. Robert Feake sanity testimony.

120. *WP,* 5:179–180. Thomas Lyon's first letter to John Winthrop 25 August 1647. Elizabeth W. Feake may not be married yet. "To the Right Worshipful Governor Mr. Winthrop at Boston this delivered. From Stamford, ye 25 August, 1647. Kind and Loving Grandfather, My humble duty remembered unto you and hearty thanks unto you for all your kindness shown both to me and my wife. I am sorrowful to hear of that sad news of the loss of my Grandmother*, but the Lord knows best what to do. The occasion of my writing is seeing the Lord hath brought me into this condition as for to marry one of your grandchildren, my desire is for to seek both for her soul's good and her body's. Therefore, seeing my time is in the Lord's hands (how soon I may be taken from her I know not), I would provide as comfortably as I could. For her to go to her mother [Elizabeth Feake], if the Lord should take me away, is not my desire, considering her condition, for I have known enough. Therefore, I hearing by some since I married her that there was something both given her and appointed to be given her, caused me to write you entreating you to send me word how it is. If there be anything, it is better she have her right to do her good another day than those that be as strangers or have no right at all. And as for her Mother, I think if she could marry here (as yet she may not be suffered) she will go somewhere else with the fellow, if he be as willing, so that my

wife has not nor is like to have little or no comfort or help of her Mother. So if there be anything by right for my wife, I would pray you to consider of her and send word . . . Your dutiful and obedient Grandson, Thomas Lyon" *The 'governor's second wife, Margaret Tyndal Winthrop, had died two months before.

121. *WP,* 5:213–216. Thomas Lyon's second letter to John Winthrop; April 14, 1648; "The fellow she now has to be her husband," "She confessed she is married to him and is with child by him." The Dutch have the Greenwich property.

122. *WP,* 5:237–239. John Haynes to JWJ, July 21, 1648. Hallett to use English courts.

123. David Pulsifer, ed., *Records of the Colony of New Plymouth, in New England* (Boston, William White, 1859), 1:149. John Whitmore's death.

124. *WP,* 5:299–300. Theo. Eaton 2nd letter to JWJ.

125. *WP,* 5:363.

126. *WP,* 5:362 Martha Johana letter.

127. *WP,* 6:95 second Martha Johana letter.

128. *WP,* 6:95. "My mother is removing farther off from me."

129. *WP,* 5:322–323. Mr. Hallett was to prove what part of the estate belonged to him . . . I shall pass by her injurious writing to myself . . . her departure was without allowance . . . she stole away.

130. *WP,* 5: 237–239. Eaton to JWJ. Wm. Hallett are come to your plantation at Naumeag, their grievous miscarriage hath certainly given great offence to many.

131. *WP,* 5:345–346. John Haynes to JWJ. Cognizance taken by our court . . .

132. *WP,* 5:322–333. Her many injurious writings.

133. A. J. F. Van Laer, trans., ed., *Council Minutes 1638–1649 (*Baltimore: Genealogical Publishing Co., Inc., 1974), 48, Doc. #305. Elizabeth Feake.

134. Allyn Bailey Forbes, ed. *The Winthrop Papers.* Boston: Massachusetts Historical Society, 1992. 5:298–299. JWJ to Stuyvesant questioning jurisdiction and requesting the Halletts be allowed to return to Greenwich. Jan. 1649/19. If Stuyvesant considers Greenwich under English jurisdiction, "I will take the best care that I can that it shall be justly disposed of by the direction of my father, and the English magistrates, according to the English laws in that behalf." Elizabeth apparently divorced in New Netherland by Kieft. English separation terms listed.

135. *DRCHSNY,* 13:24. Deed to Westchester County, Eastern Half: "Indian Deed for Westchester County, Eastern Half This day, date as below, appeared before the Hon. Director-General and Council. Megteckickhama, Oteyyockque and Wegtakachkey, lawful owners of the lands lying on the east side of the North River [Hudson River] of New Netherland, called Wiequaeskeck stretching in breadth through a wood to a kil [a waterway] called Seweyruc, dividing it at the East River [Long Island Sound] by a North and South Line at Greenwich on a kil called Kechkawes. This land between the two kils [the Patomuck area] runs to the middle of the woods between the North [Hudson] and East Rivers [Long Island Sound] through the center of the wood, so that the westerly half remains to the above said proprietors and the other easterly half is divided from it by a line drawn North and South through the center of the Wood. The aforesaid owners acknowledge in the presence of the chief Seyseychhimus and

all their other friends and blood relations to have sold the said parcel; to the Noble Petrus Stuyvesant, Director-General of New Netherland, in consideration of a certain lot of merchandise which they acknowledge to have received and accepted before the passing of this act, namely, six fathoms of duffels [canvas cloth], 6 strings of wampum, 6 kettles, 6 axes, addices [adzes], 10 knives, some iron, corals, one gun, 2 staves of lead, 2 lbs of [gun] powder, 1 coat of duffels." Stephen Grumet, *The Munsee Indians A History*, 296:n16, notes that Seyseychimmus was originally from Long Island and that he moved to Wiechquaesgeck and later Wappinger territories after selling his lands in Brooklyn. William Martin Beauchamp, *Aboriginal Place Names of New York* (Albany, NY: New York State Education Department, New York State Museum Bulletin 108, Archeology 12, 1907), 242–245. Kechkawes is Maharnes/Mianus, meaning a chief or principal stream. Meharnes is Mianus is the Kechkawes, p. 247. Kechkawes is the Mianus River in *Proceedings of the New York State Historical Association*, (1906), 6:35. Also in Foster Harmon Saville, *Within A Montauk Cemetery at Easthampton, Long Island*, vol. 2, Issues 1–7. In Reginald Pelham Bolton's, *New York City in Indian Possession*, (New York: Heye Foundation, 1920), Section III, "The Mahikan of the Mainland," 263. The Kechkawes is the Mianus River.

136. *DRCHSNY*, 1:360. Samuel Hazard et al., *Pennsylvania Archives* (Harrisburg, Lane S. Hart, 1877), 5:173–174. Van Tienhoven's explanation of Stuyvesant's purchase of Greenwich to block English expansion.

137. *WP*, 5:185, 298. JWJ to Stuyvesant. Robert Feake approves of Hallett, allow return to Greenwich.

138. Susan Hardman Moore, *New World Settlers & the Call of Home* (New York and London, Yale University Press, 2007).

139. A. J. F. Van Laer, trans. ed., *Council Minutes 1638–1649* (Baltimore: Genealogical Publishing Co., Inc., 1974), 4:510, Doc. #379. James Hallett theft from Greenwich.

140. Charles T. Gehring, ed., *Council Minutes 1655–1656* (New York: The Holland Society, 1995), 286.

141. Frances Manwaring Caulkins, *History of New London, Connecticut from the First Survey of the Coast in 1612, to 1852* (Hartford, CT: Tiffany and Company, 1852), 60. Hallett home lot in New London sold to JWJ.

142. *WP*, 5:348. Elizabeth Hallett to JWJ June 1649: "we left the rack in the yard."

143. *WP*, 6: 17–18. We are in health and peace at Greenwich.

144. *DRCHSNY*, 1:457–461. Adrien Van der Donck's scathing yet erroneous criticism that Treaty of Hartford terms include that Greenwich was given over to the English. Van der Donck had third-hand knowledge of the treaty's terms, and was attempting to incite company anger over Stuyvesant's negotiations.

145. *WP*, 6:68–69. Wm. Hallett to JWJ; New Haven Colony wanting Greenwich under them. The Halletts plans to move: Greenwich, this ? of October, 1650 Worshipful Sir, I received a letter by you from Goodman Gallope, wherein I find a further manifest of your love and care of us in inquiring after our condition. Through the mercy of God we are yet in health and peace. We hear that New Haven have propounded to our Governor to have Greenwich under them. We know not what is done as yet. I have sold my house

and land and intend in the spring to remove nearer to Manhattan. I received also the things you write of for the sale of our house, which I did not desire, that and much more being due to you from us. I shall take it as a token of your love a free gift, and acknowledge myself further obliged to you, and do heartily desire it may lie in my power to express my love to you again by doing service to you or yours. I am sorry you spoke not to our Governor because he doth so much desire to see you. My wife and my self desire to remember our love to yourself, as also to Mistress Winthrop, Mistress Lake, and your children and remain yours to my utmost ability, William Hallett.

146. Ebenezer Hazard, *Historical Collections: Consisting of State Papers, and Other Authentic Documents, Intended As Materials for an History of the United States of America.* (Philadelpha: T. Dobson, 1794), 2:178. Stuyvesant grievances, Greenwich residents treated as jurisdictional neutrals.

147. *WP,* 6:239–240.Wm. Hallett to JWJ; Hellgate purchase through Stuyvesant, "every plantation willing to receive us" after Indian threats.

148. Elias Atwater, *History of the Colony of New Haven to Its Absorption Into Connecticut* (Meriden, CT, Journal Publishing Co., 1902), 413. The wantonness of Greenwich.

149. Greenwich was not founded by the New Haven Colony. Greenwich only informally requested protection via Robert Feake, re: *Records of the Colony or Jurisdiction of New Haven from May 1653 to the Union, together with the Code of 1656,* Charles Hoadly, ed., (Hartford, CT: Case, Lockwood and Company, 1858), 144: "The Court considered [in 1655, 15 years after the Dutch defended Greenwich as their own], of the several particulars and remembered how Greenwich at first was by Mr. Robert Feake, the first purchaser of the said lands, freely put under this jurisdiction, though after Captain Patrick did injuriously put himself and it under the Dutch, yet after, it was by agreement at Hartford with the Dutch Governor, 1650 to be resigned to New Haven jurisdiction again . . ."

150. With this statement, New Haven Colony changes the facts of the 1650 Treaty of Hartford terms. Treaty terms stated that Greenwich was to remain under Dutch jurisdiction. Feake's verbal request did not make Greenwich become confederated under New Haven Colony in 1640. 1650 Treaty of Hartford terms in Ebenezer Hazard, *Historical Collections* (1724) and E. B. O'Callaghan, *Laws and Ordinances of New Netherland* (Albany, Weed, Parsons and Company, 1868), 215–217, state that both the Dutch and English agreed that Greenwich was to remain a Dutch territory. Treaty of Hartford terms: "Articles of Agreement made and conclude at Hartford September 19, 1650: The bounds begin upon the main to begin at the west side of Greenwich Bay being about four miles from Stamford, and so to run a northerly line twenty miles up into the country, and after it shall be agreed by the two governments of the Dutch and of New Haven provided the said line come not within ten miles of Hudson's River. And it is agreed that the Dutch shall not at any time hereafter build any house or habitation within six miles of the said line. The inhabitants of Greenwich to remain till further consideration thereof be had under the government of the Dutch." Benjamin Trumbull, in *A Complete History of Connecticut* (New Haven: Maltby, Goldsmith and Company, 1818), 1:193, contradicts this text. In Ibid., 1:36, 118 he writes, "The Dutch were always

mere intruders. They had no right to any part of this country. The English ever denied their right." Unfortunately his view has perpetuated the erroneous belief that Greenwich was founded under the auspices of the New Haven Colony to the present day.

151. *WP,* 5:355. Wm. Hallett urges JWJ to settle in New Netherland 16 July 1649.

152. *The Works of Washington Irving: Part Fourth, Tales of A Traveler* (Philadelphia: Lea and Blanchard, 1840), 1:149–151. Hellgate description.

153. Benjamin F. Thompson, *The History of Long Island from Its Discovery and Settlement.* (New York: Gould, Banks & Co., 1843), 2:50. Hellgate area beauty.

154. Charles Gehring, trans., *Correspondence 1654–1658* (Syracuse, NY: Syracuse University Press, 2003), 113. Stuyvesant on the 'Halletts' Long Island home burning in 1655.

155. Vincent F. Seyfried, *300 Years of Long Island City, 1630–1930* (Garden City, NY: Greater Astoria Historical Society, 1984). Hallett genealogy (that is not entirely accurate), and holdings. (Genealogies supplied by this author are based on actual wills of William, Samuel Jr., and Jacob Hallett held by the Hallett family.) Deed to William Hallett: "Beginning at the first Crick, called Sunswick, westward below Hellgate upon Long Island, and from the mouth of said Crick, south to a marked tree fast by a great Rock, and from the said tree southward 15 score rods, to another marked tree, which stands from another rock, a little westward, and from the marked tree right to the Point, upon an Island, which belongs to the Poor's Bowery (the poor Farm on Ward's Island today) and so round by the River through Hellgate to the foresaid Creek westward, where it began, and which the said Hallett did formerly live upon, to have and to hold & c. unto the foresaid William Hallett, his heirs, Executors administrators and assigns forever Sealed &c. John Coe Shawetsout, Z His mark Erromohar, X His mark.

When the English took over New Netherland in 1664, Hallett had to prove the validity of his Long Island purchases to English Governor Nicolls by presenting the actual Indian sellers to him. On April 8, 1668, Hallett received his patent of confirmation for what the English called the Hell Gate Neck tract. During the next six years, he and his family restored the farm buildings at Astoria. Their Jamaica farm was sold to John Baylis in 1676. In 1670, he bought 100 acres from Burger Jorisen along the ridge, the line of Ridge Street or 33rd Avenue extending from the river to 29th Street. He bought a narrow holding of Abraham Lubbertson's to the east of his own property extending from the Dutch Kills headwaters north to about Astoria Boulevard. His last purchase was land north and east of Lubbertson's land east of Steinway Street, from Thomas Sherman. By 1678, the Halletts had forty-eight acres under cultivation at Hallett's Cove and owned two yoke of oxen, seven horses and colts, twenty-three cattle, and thirty-four sheep. On the shore south of Astoria Boulevard, they built a home for their son William Hallett Jr. Between their homes ran Welling Street. At the east end of Welling Street began the path that is today's Newtown Avenue. At its west end and upon the shore there was a dock the Halletts used to take goods and produce to Manhattan. The meadows were divided for drainage by a main ditch probably along the present 21st Street. To keep salt water out at high tide, Hallett built a dam in 1679 across the mouth of Sunswick Creek, which was maintained for two hundred years. Everything north of Welling Street and Astoria Boulevard he retained for himself and Samuel. This included much cleared land, the homestead, and an extensive orchard on the north side of Main Street. In 1679 he deeded about 280 acres of the southern portion to William Jr.; possibly in 1688 he gave him another large tract. The final division line between the two brothers' lands was run southeasterly along Newtown Avenue, the west division line being the current Grand or 30th Avenue. William Hallett III's homestead was in Astoria west of 31st Avenue and Newtown Road near 44th Street. The extensive Hallett holdings were rapidly broken up among fourth-generation descendants. In 1752, Samuel Hallett II, grandson of the original William, and owner of the northern half of the original patent, deeded his land to his three sons, John, James, and Samuel III. By the year 1800, the Halletts retained only the area of old Astoria village, all the land to the north and east having been sold off to the Lawrences, Rapalyes, Penfolds, Polhemuses, and Luysters. The south Hallett farm, which William II gave to his second eldest son Joseph and he to his son Robert, had been established at Ridge Road (33rd Avenue) and 33rd Street before 1738. Robert owned the farm through the American Revolution and died there in 1792. West of the farmhouse and along the line of the ridge road were clay pits and a lime yard where several eighteenth-century Halletts manufactured bricks. At the west end of the Ridge Road and near Sunswick Creek, John Buckhout and John McDonough established farms on former Hallett property by marrying into the family. At the junction of Broadway and Steinway Street for the space of four blocks east and west lay the farm of Samuel Hallett II, son of Samuel Hallett I and grandson of the original William. He died there in 1756. Another great-grandson of William and Elizabeth Hallett, John Hallett, had a farmhouse generally at 30th Avenue and Steinway Street, established before 1752. Sold upon his death in 1759 to William Lawrence, it consisted of one hundred acres from 30th Avenue north to Astoria Boulevard and east to 48th Street. At the northwest corner of the present 33rd Street and 30th Avenue and facing Newtown Avenue was the house of a later Samuel Hallett, which was still standing in 1920. On the north side of Newtown Avenue, about 23rd to 27th Streets, stood the farmhouse of James Hallett, great-grandson of the original William, and son of Samuel II. The house had been built about 1750; James Hallett died in 1781 leaving his farm to his son Stephen and his wife Lydia. Stephen was still in possession of one hundred acres at his death in 1822. The Halletts gradually disappeared from the scene by 1880, when there was but one Hallett still residing in Astoria, Charles W. Hallett, an alderman in the City Council. The original family burial ground lay between Astoria Boulevard and Main Street on land probably only a few hundred feet from the original ancestral homestead, and on the line marking the division between property of the founder's two sons. This is where William II's entire family was buried together. All fifty bodies in the plot, thirty-five of them dating from 1724 to 1861, were transferred to Mount Olivet Cemetery in April 1905 and the stones were recut and re-erected over the new graves.

156. Berthold Fernow, *Records of New Amsterdam 1653–1674* (Baltimore: Genealogical Publishing Company, 1976), 7 vols., 1:293. Hendrick the Swede asks Hallett to pay for cattle damage.

157. Henry Fitz-Gilbert Waters, *The New England Historical and Genealogical Register* (New York: New England Genealogical Society, 1999), Vol. 153:476. Anne Garaway.

158. *DRCHSNY*, 8:70, 14:342, O'Callaghan, *History of New Netherland* 2:322. Van Tienhoven fakes suicide.

159. *DRCHSNY,* 14:369. Stuyvesant banishes William Hallett first for promoting the Quaker faith: SENTENCE OF WILLIAM HALLETT OF FLUSHING FOR ALLOWING BAPTIST CONVENTICLES IN HIS HOUSE AND OF WILLIAM WICKENDAM FOR OFFICIATING AS MINISTER OF THE GOSPEL AT FLUSHING. Whereas, William Hallett, born in Dorset shire, in England, about 40 years old, a resident of the village of Vlishing [Flushing], and now a prisoner, has had the audacity to call and allow to be called conventicles and gatherings at his house, and to permit there, in contemptuous disobedience of published and several times renown placates of the Director-General and Council of New Netherland, and exegesis and interpretation of God's Holy Word, as he confesses, the administration and service of the sacraments by one William Wickendam, while the latter, as he ought to have known, had neither by ecclesiastical nor secular authority been called or appointed thereto; and whereas he with several others, has been present at and listened to this exegesis and interpretation and after hearing it has with others from the hands of the said Wickendam received the bread in the form and manner, in which the sacrament of the Lord's Supper is usually celebrated and given; all of which is in direct contradiction with the general political and ecclesiastical rules of our Fatherland and especially contrary to the said placates of the Director-General and Council, which he, as Schout, in the aforesaid village was bound to uphold and strictly enforce. Which, however, he has not only failed to do, but him self has transgressed and disobeyed."

160. George Lincoln Burr, ed. *Narratives of the New England Witchcraft Cases 1648–1706.* Charles Scribner's Sons 1914, 15:44. Wm. Hallett witch trial juror in the case of Hall and Harrison, October 2, 1665.

161. *DRCHSNY,* 14:369. Wm. Hallett's banishment repeal: PETITION OF WILLIAM HALLETT FOR REMISSION OF THE SENTENCE OF BANISHMENT: The Humble petition of William Hallett, inhabitant of Vlishing unto the Hon. Governor-General and Counsel off the New Netherlands. Right Honorable, your poor petitioner having Received the Sentence of Banishment and being thereby much disenabled from making the best advantage off that little estate I have left and being bound in Conscience to look unto the maintenance off my family which might Suffer much, if my sudden departure should be exacted, for these Reasons Right honorable I am bold to Solicit your Lordships that you would be pleased to remit pass by and take off my banishment, which request if your honor Please to grant, your humble petitioner shall ever Remain thankful and Serviceable unto his Power. From Flishinge this 26th 9th 1656 William Hallett After a vote had been taken, it was resolved as follows: The petitioner, William Hallett, is granted and receives permission to earn his living as a private inhabitant quietly and properly within this Province, provided that upon sight hereof he pays the fine and the missives of law, to which he was condemned. This done in Council at Fort Amsterdam, in N.N. the 21st of December 1656."

162. Herbert L. Osgood, *The American Colonies in the 17th Century* (Cranbury, NJ: P. Smith, 1957), 155. The English referred to for settling land disputes.

163. J. Franklin Jameson, ed., *Narratives of New Netherland 1609–1664* (Charles Scribners's Sons, Elibron Classics, Adamant Media Corporation, 2005), 273. The boom and bust of New Netherland.

164. *DWS*, 189, fn48. Robert Feake's last days: "By early 1660 his distress had become unmanageable. He died in 1663 next door to his original 1630 land grant. Over 13 years Watertown spent £90 on his care, not spending Feake's own money for a compassionate reason and fear that "if something had not been spared such as he might call his own, it would have been further destruction of his mind." His last posessions included "one suit and cloak and an old jacket, two old coats . . . some other old clothes, one Bible, three books . . . valued in all at 9.92d"

165. Berthold Fernow, *Records of New Amsterdam 1653–1674* (Baltimore: Genealogical Publishing Company, 1976), 7 vols, 5:285. Hallett's second wife paid the bill unjustly.

166. Will of William Hallett. Private collection of William Hallett, Sea Cliff, NY, with permission. Abridged text: In the name of God, Amen. William Hallett Senior in Queens County on Nassau Island in the province of New York. Yeoman being of weak in body but, God be praised of perfect sense and memory and not knowing the certainty of death nor how or when it will please God to take me out of this inseparable [?] and being willing to settle all things here as far as it is The End. I hide no disputes or controversies or insights after my decease arise doth make these presents to routinize my last will and testament in manner and form following (that is to say) First I begin with my soul to God that gave it and my body to the earth from whence it came to be decently buried at the direction of my [?] executor [?]. Hereafter is [illegible] through the will of my blessed Savior and Redeemer in this Parish that I shall enjoy everlasting peace within this heavenly Kingdom and as [?] the worldly estate which it hath pleased the Almighty to bestow on me after my just debts and funeral charges are paid and satisfied. I give and bequeath as followeth—I do give and bequeath to my son William Hallett and Joseph Hallett his son and to their heirs forever all that piece of land containing twenty five morgen [?] to the west to the land of Adrian Derkson extending in the breadth north west and east southeast fifty eight rod and so running into the wood in length on earth [?] three hundred rod as by a certain [illegible] from under my house and here and before [illegible]. I give and bequeath unto my said son William Hallett (& the Cause is why I don't give him more) it is because of his undutyfulness toward me. I give and bequeath unto William Hallett, son of William Hallett aforesaid, twenty shillings. Sarah Phillips, fourty shillings Rebecca Jackson, twenty shillings Moses Hallett one [?] with two plates, two porringers, and one pewter tankard Charity Moore, twenty shillings Joseph Hallett, one iron pot and four sheep George Hallett, one cow, one horse and four sheep Richard Hallett, one cow, one horse and four sheep Mary Hallett, one three year old horse and four sheep Elizabeth Hallett, one three year old horse and four sheep To my son Samuel and to his heirs forever all the land whereupon I now live as deed of [?] relation thereunto being had made more plainly and at large [illegible]. Item. I give and bequeath unto Samuel Hallett, son to [?] and Samuel Hallett the great copper anchor kettle, one bed and furnishings, furniture, two cows, five sheep, the crop of wheat which shall be on the land at my decease, our chest and all my wearing apparel and one warming pan. Elizabeth Jackson, one pewter dish and pewter

candlestick with the money her husband owes me. Sarah Cornwall, twenty shillings, Hannah Washburn, twenty shillings, Margaret Hallett, one pewter dish, two plates, two porringers, Grace Hallett, one bed with furnishings, two pewter dishes, two plates, two porringers, one cow and four sheep. Martha Hallett, one cow, four sheep, one small brass kettle, Mawsie Hallett, one pewter dish, one pewter sauce pan, one basin, one bed pan, one looking glass. My sister Hannah Bird twenty pounds to be paid twenty pounds yearly, until the full sum of twenty pounds is satisfied provided she lives but in case she dies before and any payments remaining behind they fall to my son Samuel Hallett and it's further my will that most of my legacy is or shall be paid until the expiration of one full year after my decease and not before. And lastly I [?] bequeath unto my son Samuel all the remainder of my estate both [?] and performance not yet disposed of be it in Negroes, money, plate or household stuffs. And I do constitute and appoint my said son Samuel Hallett and Samuel Hallett his son my whole and sole [?] of this my last will and testament revoking all others heretofore by me and this alone in force and no others. In testimony whereof I have here unto set my hand and fixed my seal to this my will contained in two sheets of writing paper. This seventeenth day of April in the fifth year of the reign of our sovereign lady Queen Anne by the grace of God of England, Scotland, France and Ireland. Signed, sealed published and [?] by the said William Hallett Sr. to be his last will and testament in the presence of us: Thomas Cardale, Samuel Rusco, J.W. Basford.

The will of William Jr., written after the murder of his son, William III and his family, highlights early colonial assets of the day. After a review of his property boundaries, he bequeaths to his son Joseph "my eldest son now living, all my houses, lands, tenements, and meadows situated at Hellgate Neck." After a review of his property's boundaries he notes that Joseph is to share the lane between various Hallett properties with his uncle Samuel, William Jr.'s brother, and reiterates previous deeds to Joseph's sons Moses, George and Richard. He continues: "I also leave to my son Joseph a negro man and a negro wench, and a waggon, plough, and my great riding horse and a cupboard and the Great Table and great chest, and my silver tankard. I leave to my [grand]sons George and Richard and to my grandsons Joseph Hallett and to my [grand]daughters Sarah Phillips, Rebecca Jackson, Sarah Blackwell and Charity Moore, certain negroes. I leave to my true and loving wife one third of the remainder of all my moveable estate and the priviledge of a chamber in the stone house during her widowhood. My son Joseph is to furnish her sufficient support and firewood. I leave two thirds of my moveables to my five daughters Sarah Phillips, Rebecca Jackson, Charity Moore, Mary Blackwell and Elizabeth Fish. And my son Joseph is to keep for his mother, four head of cattle, winter and summer. I leave to my son Joseph and [grand]son George all my apparel. I make my wife Mary and my sons and James Jackson and Samuel Moore executors. Dated September 16, 1727. Witnesses Samuel Hallett, Samuel Hallett Jr., Samuel Richards William Smith Pelletreau, *Abstracts of the wills on file in the Surrogates Office, City of New York* (New York: Collections of the New York Historical Society, 1903), 35:154–156.

167. Carolee R. Inskeep, *The Graveyard Shift, A Family Historian's Guide to New York City Cemeteries* (Orem, Utah: Ancestry, 2000), 81. Wm. Hallett III family deaths described in *Boston News Letter.*

168. L. Lloyd Stewart, *A Far Cry From Freedom 1799–1827 New York State's Crime Against Humanity* (Bloomington, IN: Authorhouse, 2005), 48. Wm. Hallett III murders cause first slave conspiracy statute.

169. *Newport Daily News*, Nov. 15, 1859. Robert Feke's life as reported by his grandson.

170. *Town of Greenwich Land Records*, Book #1. Quit claim deeds by Feake and Patrick sons.

171. *WP*, 6:11. Mary Lyon to JWJ.

172. *WP*, 6:95. Thomas Lyon to JWJ re: daughter Mary Lyon's poor care.

173. *Proceedings of the Massachusetts Historical Society*. Published by the Society, Boston, 1890–91, series 2, vol. 6:18.

174. In October of the same year Mary wrote Fitz-John Winthrop again saying that she had hired an attorney, a Major Jonathan Selleck, to plead her case in court. Major Selleck had determined that she had a legal claim, but could probably not pay his fees. Litigation was pending over Elizabeth's Greenwich land once again in 1701. There was some squabble between Mary and one of her attorney's relatives who was offended at something Mary Lyon had done to disrespect her, and was spreading malicious gossip about her. Mary assured the Major that the woman had been well treated, that she had even given her a cow. Mary Lyon Wilson's claim was based upon the original Feake/Patrick purchase deed from the Indians, and the letter noting that Martha Johana was to receive three hundred acres.

175. Connecticut Historical Society Collections, *"Extracts of Letters to Rev. Thomas Prince,"* (Hartford, Connecticut Historical Society, 1895). 3:312. Stephen Munson letter to Rev. Prince. The Society states that this letter is no longer in existence.

176. Benjamin Trumbull, *A Complete History of Connecticut, Civil and Ecclesiastical from the Emigration of Its First Planters from England, in MDCXXX, to MDCCXXIII* (Hartford, CT: Hudson & Goodwin, 1797), 161. Massacre first placed on Strickland Plain. John Warner Barber, Historical Collections of the State of New York (New York: S. Tuttle, 1842), 18. Strickland Plain cited. E.B. O'Callaghan, *History of New Netherland or New York Under the Dutch* (New York: D. Appleton, 1845), 297. Strickland Plain cited. John Romeyn Brodhead, *History of the State of New York* (New York: Harper & Brothers, 1853), 319. By 1853, Brodhead doubts the Strickland Plain location for the largest episode, as placed by Trumbull. Daniel Mead, *A History of the Town of Greenwich, Fairfield County, Conn. With Many Important Statistics* (New York: Baker & Godwin, 1857), 18–52. Strickland Plain cited. Spencer Percival Mead, *Ye Historie of Ye Town of Greenwich, County of Fairfield and State of Connecticut, With Genealogical Notes*, (Harrison, NY: Harbor Hill Books, 1863, 1979), 18. Silas Wood and A.J. Spooner, *A Sketch of the First Settlement of the Several Towns on Long Island with Their Political Condition, to the End of the American Revolution* (Brooklyn, NY: The Furmant Club, 1865), 76. Massacre placed on Strickland Plain; references Trumbull directly. "The great battle of Strickland Plains" placed in Cos Cob. Mary Louise Booth, *History of the City of New York* (New York: W. R. C. Clark, 1867), 121. Strickland Plain. Martha Lamb, *History of the City of New York: Its Origin, Rise and Progress* (New York: Banes and Company, 1877). Strickland Plain, full event description. Edward Manning Ruttenber, *Footprints*

of the Red Men: Indian Geographical Names in the Valley of Hudson's River, The Valley of the Mohawk, and on the Delaware: Their Location and the Probable Meaning of Some of Them (Newburgh, NY: Newburgh Journal Print, 1906), 86. Mariana Van Rensselaer, *History of the City of New York in the Seventeenth Century* (New York: The Macmillan Company, 1909), 231–232. Strickland Plain, "not far from Bedford." The two towns are fifteen miles apart. Lydia Holland and Margaret Leaf, *Greenwich Old & New A History* (Greenwich, CT: Greenwich Press, 1935), 4. Massacre referenced as a large battle in Cos Cob. Florence Crofut and S. Marcy, *Guide to the History and the Historic Sites of Connecticut*, Tercentenary Commission of the State of Connecticut, Connecticut Daughters of the American Revolution (New Haven, CT: Yale University Press, 1937), 114. Massacre placed in Cos Cob; references two Mead histories. David Knapp, *Muskets & Mansions: The Greenwich Story* (Greenwich, CT: Fairview Printers, 1966). Massacre placed near the Mianus River. Robert W. Carder, *Captain John Underhill in Connecticut, 1642–1644*, (Bulletin of the Underhill Society of America, 1967). Multiple locations discussed. Elizabeth W. Clarke, *Before and After 1776; A Chronology of Greenwich, Connecticut* (Greenwich, CT: Young Offset Company, 1976), 4. Strickland Plain. Michael Bellesiles, *Lethal Imagination: Violence and Brutality in American History* (New York and London: New York University Press, 1999), 32. Massacre placed "near Stamford." Donna Merwick, *The Shame And The Sorrow Dutch-Amerindian Encounters in New Netherland* (Philadelphia: University of Pennsylvania Press, 2006), 147, 285n31. Massacre placed on Strickland Plain. Booth cited.

177. Robert Bolton, *History of the County of Westchester* (Philadelphia: L. E. Preston & Company, 1886), 1:19. Mrs. Holmes.

178. J. Thomas Scharf, *History of Westchester County, New York including Morrisania, Kings Bridge, and West Farms, Which Have Been Annexed to New York City* (Philadelphia: L. E. Preston & Co., 1886), 19. Chapter by James Woods reprinted later freestanding as *The History of the Town of Bedford to 1917*. Massacre placed in Bedford, NY. *New York State Museum Bulletin* (Albany: The University of the State of New York, July-August, 1920), nos. 235, 236. Massacre placed in Bedford. *A Tour of Some Historical Points of Interest in the Town of Bedford* (Bedford Historical Society, 1930). Massacre placed at Indian Hill; references Bolton's placement at Naniechiestawack. Frederick Shonnard and Walter Spooner, *History of Westchester County, New York, From Its Earliest Settlement to the Year 1900* (Harrison, NY: Harbor Hill Books, 1974), 101. Massacre at Bedford; references Robert Bolton. Robert S. Grumet, *Native American Place Names in New York City, New York* (Museum of the City of New York, 1981), 61. Massacre placed in Bedford. Alvah French, *History of Westchester County* (New York: Lewis Historical Publishing Company, 2010), 25. Massacre placed "in a village near Bedford"; summary description.

179. Daniel Mead, *A History of the Town of Greenwich, Fairfield County* (New York: Baker & Godwin, 1857), 51–53.

180. Spencer Percival Mead, *Ye Historie of Ye Town of Greenwich, County of Fairfield and State of Connecticut, With Genealogical Notes* (Harrison, NY: Harbor Hill Books, 1863, 1979), 18. Map of "Indian village of Petuckquapaen." Map shows an area in Cos Cob on

west side of the Mianus River. "Petuckquapoch: was native name of area on east side of Mianus River near Tomac Cove in modern day Old Greenwich."
181. *IACNY*, 60–84. Kieft's war fully described. Poundridge, NY cited as location.
182. F. H. Saville, *A Montauk Cemetery at Easthampton, Long Island* (New York: Museum of the American Indian, Heye Foundation, 1920). This book inserts Reginald Bolton's previously published, *Indian Notes and Monographs*, wherein he states the word "Naniechiestawack," found on the Janssen-Visscher map, as being the largest massacre's village site and places the event in Poundridge, NY. Jay Harris, *God's Country, A History of Poundridge* (New York: Pequot Press, 1971), 15. Massacre placed specifically off Old Poundridge Road. Edwin Burrows and Mike Wallace, *Gotham: A History of New York City to 1898* (London: Oxford Press, 2000), 39. Massacre located "near Poundridge."
183. Thatcher T. P. Luquer, *The Indian Village of 1643* (The Quarterly Bulletin of the Westchester County Historical Society, 1945), Nos. 2 & 3:21–24.
184. J. Hammond Trumbull, *Indian Names of Places, Etc., In and On the Borders of Connecticut With Interpretations of Some of Them.* (Hartford, CT: Lockwood & Brainard Co., 1881), Armonck, Asamuck: 5; Cassacubque, 8; Cos Cob, 12; Miossehasaky, 30. Benjamin Trumbull incorrectly quotes *DRCHSNY*, 1:545, and says Greenwich is Petuckquapaen. It is correctly Petuckquapoch. "Armonck" is the Byram River according to James Hammond Trumbull, *Indian Names of Places . . . in and on the Borders of Connecticut* (Hartford, CT, Case, Lockwood & Brainard, 1881), ix, and in Reginald Bolton's *History of the County of Westchester*, 2. William Martin Beauchamp, *Indian Names of Places* (New York: H. C. Beauchamp, 1893), 89, says the word "Amaug" meant "beaver." Wm. Wallace Tooker, *Some Fishing Stations in Long Island*, 15, 1901, says "amaug" means "a fishing place." Trumbull was not sure about which creek was the Asamuck of Greenwich's first deed, and incorrectly speculated that it was "Brothers' Brook," also known as "Greenwich Creek." Thirty years later, in 1909, R. A. Douglas-Lithgow repeated Trumbull's incorrect speculation that the Asamuck "is the area west of the Mianus that incorporates Greenwich Creek as its fresh waterway."
185. Edward Manning Rutteber, *History of the Indian Tribes of Hudson's River* (Albany, NY: J. Munsell, 1872), 367. The meadows bordering the Byram River are the Haseco and the Miossehassaky. William Martin Beauchamp, *Aboriginal Place Names of New York* (Albany: New York State Museum, 1907), 245. Miossehassaky is a bog, marsh, or fresh meadow.
186. James Hammond Trumbull, *Indian Names of Places . . . in and on the Borders of Connecticut* (Hartford, CT: Case, Lockwood & Brainard, 1881), 8. *Cassacubque*: "a great ledge of rocks."

Bibliography

Manuscripts

Bowne House, Flushing, NY: Greenwich, CT's accusations and punishments of Thomas Lyons, Gersham Lockwood, Thomas Young and John Marshall. Warrant issued by Greenwich for arrest of John Marshall and Thomas Young, Quakers.

Bowne House, Flushing, NY: Deed from Edward Griffin to Elizabeth Hallett.

Greenwich, CT Town Hall: Greenwich Common Place Book.

Greenwich, CT Town Hall: Greenwich Land Records, Book One.

Private collection of William Hallett, Seacliff, NY, 2011: Last will and testament of Jacob Hallett, son of Samuel Sr.

Private collection of William Hallett, Seacliff, NY, 2011: Last will and testament of William Hallett Sr.

Microfilm

Queens County Records Microfilm.

A:114–115. English confirmation of lands purchased from Indians.

A:1 Mary Feke wills property to James Feke 2nd wife and son of Tobias Feke witnessed by Daniel K. Patrick.

Winthrop, John Jr. *Medical Journal 1657–1669*. The Massachusetts Historical Society. Microfilm Reel #38, vol. 28 a-b.

Electronic Citations

Atkins, Scott Eric. *The American Sense of Puritan*. xroads.virginia.edu/~cap/puritan/purmain.html. A work completed for the Capitol Project, from the American Studies group at the University of Virginia.

Colonial Connecticut Records April 1636–April 1665: colonialct.uconn.edu/.

Daniel Patrick family genealogy:
mccurdyfamilylineage.com/ancestry/p242.

Feake family genealogy:
familysearch.org
freepages.genealogy.rootsweb.ancestry.com
LDS.org
longislandsurnames.com/genealogy

Heyman, C. L. *Puritanism and Predestination Divining America.* nationalhumanities
center.org/tserve/eighteen/ekeyinfo/puritan.htm.
Reformed Dutch Church Baptisms 1639–1801: olivetreegenealogy.com/nn/church/
rdcbapt.shtml.
Sheib, Brooke. *Revising Anne: A Critical Look at the Histories of Hutchinson and the
Antinomians.* smu.edu/ecenter/discourse/Schieb.htm.
US Army Corps of Engineers: Hellgate destruction. nan.usace.army.mil/whoweare/
hellgate.pdf.

NEWSPAPERS
Newport Daily News, Nov. 15, 1859. "Robert Feke, the Artist." Nov. 15, 1859.
Newport Mercury News, July 23, 1904. Re: John Fones "servant to Wm. Coddington."
Descendants. newspaperarchive.com/FlashViewer/Viewer.aspx?img=55509758&fir
stvisit=true&src=search&currentResult=0&currentPage=0&fpo=False.
Newport Mercury News, Aug. 9, 1919. "The Doctor Johnson Window." Re: Charles Feke,
apothecarist.
New York Times. Sept. 18, 1966. John Canaday. "With Special Reference to Robert
Feke." ProQuest Historical Newspapers: *The New York Times* 1851–2007, 145.
New York Times, Oct. 8, 1946. Edward Alden Jewell. "30 Feke Canvases Shown at
Museum," ProQuest Historical Newspapers: *The New York Times* 1851–2007, 21.

PERSONAL COMMUNICATIONS
Personal Communication with Dr. Charles Gehring, Director New Netherland Projects
that "Groenwits" is the Dutch equivalent of "Greenwich," Oct. 2, 2009.

PUBLICATIONS
Adair, James. *The History of the American Indians.* London: Edward and Charles Dilly,
1775.
Adams, Charles Francis. *Three Episodes of Massachusetts History.* Boston: Houghton,
Mifflin and Company, 1892.
Anderson, Robert Charles. *The Great Migration Begins: Immigrants to New England,
1620–1633.* Boston: New England Historic Genealogical Society, 1995.
Atwater, Howard E. *History of the Colony of New Haven to Its Absorption Into Connecticut.*
Meriden, CT: Journal Publishing Co., 1902.
Bannerman, Bruce, ed. *The Visitations of the County of Surrey.* London, 1899, 789–791.
Barber, John W. *Historical Collections of the State of New York.* New York: S. Tuttle, 1842.
Barrett, R. T., *Town of Bedford, A Commemorative History.* Bedford, NY: Town of
Bedford, 1955.
Bartlett, Gardner. *Robert Coe, Puritan: His Ancestors and Descendants.* Boston, 1911.
Bassett, Benjamin. "Fabulous Traditions and Customs of the Indians, and Historical
Collections of the Indians of New England," in *Collections of the Massachusetts*

BIBLIOGRAPHY

Historical Society for the Year 1792. Boston: Monroe and Francis, vol. 1. Reprinted 1806.

Beauchamp, William. *Aboriginal Place Names of New York.* New York State Education Dept., 1907.

———. *Horn and Bone Implements of the New York Indians.* Albany: University of the State of New York, 1902.

———. *Indian Names of New York.* Fayetteville, NY: H. C. Beauchamp, Recorder Office, 1893.

Bedford Historical Society. *A Tour of Some Historical Points of Interest in the Town of Bedford.* Published for the Society, 1930.

Bergen, Teunis. *Early Settlers of King's County, Long Island, N.Y.* New York: S. W. Green's Son, 1881.

Billings, W. *Colonial Virginia: A History.* Millwood, NY: KTO2 Press, 1986.

Bingham, H. J. *History of Connecticut.* New York and Florida: Lewis Historical Publishing, 1962.

Bolton, Reginald Pelham. *Indian Life of Long Ago in the City of New York.* New York: J. Graham, 1934.

———. *New York City in Indian Possession.* New York: Museum of the American Indian, Heye Foundation, 1922.

Bond, Henry. *Family Memorials: Genealogies of the Families and Descendants of the Early Settlers of Watertown, Massachusetts, Including Waltham and Weston.* Boston: Little, Brown and Company, 1855.

Booth, Mary Louise. *History of the City of New York.* New York: W. R. C. Clark, 1867.

Bragdon, Kathleen J. *Native People of Southern New England, 1500–1650.* Norman: University of Oklahoma Press, 1996.

Bremer, Francis J. *John Winthrop: America's Forgotten Founding Father.* New York: Oxford University Press, Inc., 2003.

———. *The Puritan Experiment: New England Society from Bradford to Edwards.* Hanover, NJ: University Press of New England, 1995.

Brodhead, John Romeyn. *The History of the State of New York 1609–1691.* New York: Harper & Brothers, 1853–1871, 2 vols.

Buckland John A. "Governor Kieft's War Against the Wiechquaeskecks 1643–44," in *The Role of Native Americans in Military Engagements from the 17th to the 19th Centuries.* Bowie, MD: Heritage Books, Inc., 2008.

———. *The Wiechquaeskeck Indians of Southwestern Connecticut in the Seventeenth Century.* Bowie, MD: Heritage Books, 2002.

Bunker, Mary Powell. *Long Island Genealogies.* Albany, NY: Joel Munsell's Sons, 1895.

Burpee, C. W. *The Story of Connecticut.* New York: American Historical Society, 1939.

Burr, George Lincoln, ed. *Narratives of the Witchcraft Cases 1648–1706.* New York, Charles Scribner's Sons, 1914.

Burrows, Edwin G., and Mike Wallace. *Gotham: A History of New York City to 1898.* London: Oxford Press, 2000.

242

Canfield, Amos. *"Abstracts of Early Wills of Queens County, New York, Recorded in Libers A and C of Deeds, Now in the Registers Office at Jamaica, New York." New York Genealogical and Biographical Record.* New York: Apr. 1934, vol. 65, no. 2:120. Andrew Bird with William Hallett.

Cantwell, Anne-Marie, and Diana Wall. *Unearthing Gotham: The Archaeology of New York City.* New Haven, CT: Yale University Press, 2001.

Carder, Robert W. "Captain John Underhill in Connecticut 1642–1644." *Bulletin of the Underhill Society of America,* 1967.

Caulkins, Frances M. *History of New London, Connecticut: From the First Survey of the Coast in 1612, to 1852.* New London: Case, Tiffany and Co., 1852.

Cave, Alfred. *The Pequot War.* Amherst: University of Massachusetts Press, 1996.

Clark, G. L. *A History of Connecticut, Its People and Institutions.* New York and London: The Knickerbocker Press, 1914.

Clarke, Elizabeth W. *Before and After 1776: A Chronology of Greenwich, Connecticut.* Greenwich, CT: Young Offset Company, 1976.

Collections for the Year 1902. New York Historical Society, New York, 35:40. Will of Samuel Hallett. Will of William Hallett Jr., 35:156.

Collections for the Year 1893. Murder of William Hallett III, 25:332.

Collections of the Connecticut Historical Society. Hartford: Connecticut Historical Society, 1895, 3:313. Munson letter to Prince.

Corwin, E. T. *Ecclesiastical Records of the State of New York.* New York: J. B. Lyon, 1901–1916, vols. 1, 2.

Cox, George William. *History and Genealogy of the Cock, Cocks, Cox Family.* New York: Privately printed, 1914.

Cox, Henry Miller. *The Cox Family in America.* New York: The Unionist-Gazette Association, 1912.

Cox, John, and George William Cox. *Oyster Bay Town Records.* New York: Tobias Wright, 1916, vol. 1.

Crofut, Florence Marcy. Tercentenary Commission of the State of Connecticut, and Connecticut Daughters of the American Revolution. *Guide to the History and the Historic Sites of Connecticut.* New Haven, CT: Yale University Press, 1937, 2 vols.

Cummings, Abbott Lowell. *The Framed Houses of Massachusetts Bay, 1625–1725.* Cambridge, MA: Harvard University Press, 1979.

Dash, Mike. *Batavia's Graveyard: The True Story of the Mad Heretic Who Led History's Bloodiest Mutiny.* New York: Three Rivers Press, Random House Digital, 2002.

De Forest, John W. *History of the Indians of Connecticut From the Earliest Known Period to 1850.* Hartford: W. J. Hamersley, 1852.

Denton, Daniel. *A Brief Description of New York Formerly Called New Netherlands.* Gabriel Furman, ed. New York: 1845.

DeVries, David Pietersz, H. C. Murphy, trans. *Voyages from Holland to America, A.D. 1632 to 1644.* New York: Billin and Brothers, 1853.

Dexter, Franklin Bowditch, ed. *Ancient Town Records 1649–1662.* New Haven, CT: New Haven Historical Society, 1917.

Dickinson, Thorn. "Early History of the Thorne Family of Long Island." *The New York Genealogical and Biographical Record.* New York: Jan. 1962, vol. 93, no. 1, 29–35, 92–93.

DiLorenzo, Thomas. *How Capitalism Saved America: The Untold History of Our Country from the Pilgrims to the Present.* New York: Crown Forum, 2004.

Douglas-Lithgow, R. A. *Native American Place Names of Connecticut.* Bedford, MA: Applewood Books, 1909.

Drake, Francis Samuel. *Dictionary of American Biography.* New York: Charles Scribner's Sons, 1936.

Drake, Samuel Gardner. *The Old Indian Chronicle: Being a Collection of Exceeding Rare Tracts.* Boston: Antiquarian Institute, 1836.

Dunn, Richard S. *Puritans and Yankees: The Winthrop Dynasty of New England, 1630–1717.* Princeton, NJ: Princeton University Press, 1962.

Dunscombe, Frances Riker. *Katonah, The History of a New York Village and Its People.* New York: Katonah Village Improvement Society, 1961.

Durston, Christopher, and Jacqueline Eales. *The Culture of English Puritanism 1650–1700.* New York: St. Martin's Press, 2004.

Dwight, Benjamin. "Last Additions to the History of the Woolsey Family." *The New York Genealogical and Biographical Record.* New York, Jan. 1875, vol. 6, no.1, 28.

Dwight, Theodore. *The History of Connecticut.* New York: Harper and Brothers, 1841.

Eaton, Arthur W. H. "William Thorne of Flushing, Long Island, and his Wife Susannah." *The New York Genealogical and Biographical Record.* New York, Jan. 1922, vol. 53, no. 1, 18.

Fernow, Berthold, trans. and ed. *Minutes of the Orphanmasters of New Amsterdam, 1655 to 1663.* New York: Francis P. Harper, 1902–1907, 2 vols.

———. *Records of New Amsterdam 1653–1674.* New York: The Knickerbocker Press, 1897, 7 vols. Reprint, Baltimore: Genealogical Publishing Co., Inc., 1976.

Fernow, Berthold, and Arnold J. F. Van Laer. "Calendar of Council Minutes, 1668–1783." *New York Museum Bulletin,* vol. 58. Albany: University of the State of New York, 1902.

Finch, Paul R. *Stamford Town Records, Volume 1, 1641–1725.* Boston: New England Historic and Genealogical Society, 2011.

Foote, Henry Wilder. *Robert Feke, Colonial Portrait Painter.* New York: Kennedy Galleries, Inc. Da Capo Press, 1930.

Gehring, Charles T., trans. and ed. *Land Papers, 1630–1664.* Baltimore: Genealogical Publishing Co., Inc., 1980.

———. *Correspondence, 1647–1653.* New Netherland Document Series. Syracuse, NY: Syracuse University Press, 2000.

———. *Correspondence, 1654–1658.* New Netherland Document Series. Syracuse, NY: Syracuse University Press, 2003.

———. *Council Minutes, 1652–1654.* New York Historical Manuscript Series. Baltimore: Genealogical Publishing Co. Inc., 1983.

———. *Council Minutes, 1655–1656.* New Netherland Document Series. Syracuse, NY: Syracuse University Press, 1995.

———. *Laws of Writs and Appeals, 1647–1663.* New Netherland Document Series. Syracuse, NY: Syracuse University Press, 1991.

Glover, Lorrie, and Daniel Smith. *The Shipwreck That Saved Jamestown.* New York: Henry Holt and Company, 2008.

Gookin, Daniel. *Historical Collections of the Indians in New England.* Boston: Belknap and Hall, 1792.

Greven, P. J. Jr. *Four Generations: Population, Land and Family in Colonial Andover, Massachusetts.* Ithaca, NY and London: Cornell University Press, 1970.

Griffin, Ernest F. *Westchester County and Its People.* New York: Lewis Historical Publishing, 1948.

Grumet, Robert S. *Historic Contact, Indian People and Colonists in Today's Northeastern United States in the Sixteenth Through Eighteenth Centuries.* Norman: University of Oklahoma Press, 1995.

———. *The Munsee Indians, A History.* Norman: University of Oklahoma Press, 2009.

———. *Native American Place Names in New York City.* New York: Museum of the City of New York, 1981.

———. *Northeastern Indian Lives 1632–1816.* Amherst, MA: The University of Massachusetts Press, 1996.

Haefeli, Evan. "America Discovers English Puritanism." *Reviews in American History,* 2003, 31.1: 24–31.

———. "Conscience and Community: Revisiting Toleration and Religious Dissent in Early Modern England and America." *The William and Mary Quarterly,* 2003, 59. 2: 515+.

———. "Kieft's War and the Cultures of Violence in Colonial America," in *Lethal Imagination: Violence and Brutality in American History,* 17–42. New York: New York University Press, 1999, Michael A. Bellesile, ed.

Hall, David D. *The Antinomian Controversy 1636–1638: A Documentary History.* Middletown, CT: Wesleyan Press, 1968.

Hall, Edwin. *The Ancient Historical Records of Norwalk, Conn. With a Plan of the Ancient Settlement, and of the Town in 1847.* Norwalk, CT: J. Mallory, 1847.

Harris, Jay. *God's Country, A History of Poundridge, New York.* Pequot Press, 1971.

Haslam, Patricia. "The Wife of Cornelius Arent of Flushing, Long Island, Identified. *The New York Genealogical and Biographical Record.* New York: July 1982, vol. 113, no. 3, 150–152.

Hazard, Ebenezer. *Collections of the New York Historical Society for the Year 1809.* New York: I. Riley, 1811, vol. 1.

———. *Historical Collections Consisting of State Papers and Other Authentic Documents.* New York: T. Dobson, 1794.

Hazard, Samuel. *Pennsylvania Archives.* Harrisburg, PA: Lane S. Hart, 1877.

Heimert, Alan, and Andrew Delblanco, eds. *The Puritans in America: A Narrative Anthology.* Cambridge, MA: Harvard University Press, 1985.

Hoadly, Charles J. *Records of the Colony and Plantation of New Haven, From 1638 to 1649.* Hartford, CT: Case, Tiffany and Co., 1857.

———. *Records of the Colony or Jurisdiction of New Haven.* Hartford, CT: Case, Lockwood and Co., 1858.

Hoff, Henry Bainbridge. "The Ancestry of Anna van Beyeren Who Married First Daniel Patrick and Second Tobias Feake," *Genealogies of Long Island Families from the New York Genealogical & Biographical Record.* New York: NYGBR, vol. 2.

———. Long Island Source Records. *New York Genealogical and Biographical Record.* Baltimore, MD, 1987: 133. Andrew Bird and William Hallett.

———. "A New Look at the Newtown Presbyterian Church Records." *The New York Researcher. The New York Genealogical and Biographical Record.* New York, Winter 2010, vol. 21, no. 4:62.

Holland, Lydia L., and Margaret Leaf. *Greenwich Old & New, A History.* Greenwich, CT: Greenwich Press, 1935.

Hollister, Gideon H. *History of Connecticut.* New Haven: Dhurrie and Peck, 1855.

Holyoke, Rev. E. et al. *The Holyoke Diaries, 1709–1856.* Salem, MA: The Essex Institute, 1911.

Hooker, Thomas. Extracts of Letter to Rev. Thomas Prince. *Connecticut Historical Society Collections,* Hartford: Connecticut Historical Society, 1895, vol. 3.

Hubbard, Rev. William. *A General History of New England from the Discovery to MDCLXXX.* Cambridge, MA: Hillard & Metcalf, 1815.

Hubbard, W., and Cecilia Tichi, eds. *The Present State of New England Being a Narrative of the Troubles with the Indians.* Bainbridge, NY: York-Mail Print, Inc., 1972.

Huden, John C. *Indian Place Names of New England.* New York: Museum of the American Indian, Heye Foundation, 1962.

Hughes, Arthur, and Morse Allen. *Connecticut Place Names.* Hartford: Connecticut Historical Society, 1976.

Huntington, Elijah Baldwin. *History of Stamford.* Stamford, CT: Pub. by author, 1868.

———. *History of Stamford, Connecticut, From Its Settlement in 1641, to the Present Time.* Stamford, CT: Published by author, 1865.

Hurd, D. H. *History of Fairfield County, Connecticut.* Philadelphia: J. W. Lewis & Co., 1881.

Inskeep, Carol. *The Graveyard Shift, A Family Historian's Guide to New York City Cemeteries.* Orem, Utah: Ancestry Publishing, Myfamily.com Inc., 2000.

Irving, Washington. *The Complete Works of Washington Irving in One Volume, with a Memoir of the Author.* Paris: Paul Renouard, 1843.

———. *The Works of Washington Irving: Part Fourth, Tales of a Traveler.* Philadelphia: Lea and Blanchard, 1840, 149–151.

Jacobs, Jaap. *The Colony of New Netherland, A Dutch Settlement in the Seventeenth Century.* Ithaca, NY and London: Cornell University Press, 2009.

Jacobus, Donald Lines. "That Winthrop Woman Again!" *The New York Genealogical and Biographical Record.* New York: July 1966, vol. 97, no. 3, 131–134.

Jameson, J. Franklin, ed. *Narratives of New Netherland 1609–1664*. New York: Charles Scribner's Sons, 1909. Reprint, New York: Barnes and Noble, 1937.

Katz, Steven T. "The Pequot War Reconsidered." *The New England Quarterly* 64 (1991): 206–224.

Keller, A. *Life Along the Hudson*. Bronx: Fordham University Press, 1997.

Kelley, Frank Bergen, and The City History Club of New York. *Historical Guide to the City of New York, New York,* 1909. Early Hallett's Point.

Kelly, J. F. *Early Domestic Architecture of Connecticut*. New Haven, CT: The Tercentenary Commission of the State of Connecticut, and Committee on Historical Publications Tercentenary Commission, Yale University Press, 1933.

Knapp, David. *Muskets & Mansions: The Greenwich Story*. Greenwich, CT: Fairview Printers, 1966.

Kraft, Herbert C. *The Lenape Archeology, History and Ethnography*. Newark, New Jersey Historical Society, 1986.

Kross, Jessica. *The Evolution of an American Town: Newtown, New York 1642–1745*. Philadelphia: Temple University Press, 1983.

Lamb, Margaret. *History of the City of New York: Its Origin, Rise and Progress*. New York: Banes and Company, 1877.

Lambrechtsen, N. C., and F. A. Van der Kemp. *A History of the New Netherlands*. New York: Cornell University Library, 1841.

LaPlante, Eve. *American Jezebel, The Uncommon Life of Anne Hutchinson the Woman Who Defied the Puritans*. San Francisco: Harper Collins, 2004.

Latting, John J. Genealogical Fragments. *The New York Genealogical and Biographical Record*. New York, October 1880, vol. 11, no. 4, 168–170.

Luquer, Thatcher T. "The Indian Village of 1643." *The Quarterly Bulletin of the Westchester County Historical Society,* Apr.–July, 1945, vol. 21, nos 2, 3, 21–24.

Majdalany, Jeanne, and Edith Wicks. *The Early Settlement of Stamford, Connecticut 1641–1700*. Bowie, MD: Heritage Books, Inc., 1990.

Malone, Dumas, ed. *Dictionary of American Biography*. New York: Charles Scribner's Sons, 1936, vol. 20. Winthrop biographies.

McCracken, George E. "The Feake Family of Norfolk, London and Colonial America." *The New York Genealogical and Biographical Record*. New York, 1955–56, 136: 303–304, 137:307.

Mead, Daniel M. *A History of the Town of Greenwich, Fairfield County, Conn. with Many Important Statistics*. New York: Baker & Godwin, 1857.

Mead, Spencer Percival. *Ye Historie of Ye Town of Greenwich, County of Fairfield and State of Connecticut, With Genealogical Notes*. New York: Knickerbocker Press, 1863, 1911. Reprinted, Harrison, NY: Harbor Hill Books, 1979.

Megapolensis, Johannes. *A Short Account of the Maquaas Indians, in New-Netherland*. Philadelphia, 1792.

Melyn, Cornelis. Melyn Papers, 1640–1699. *Collections of the New-York Historical Society for the Year 1913*. New York, 1914.

Melyn, Cornelis and Henry Cruse Murphy, ed. *Broad Advice to the United Netherland Provinces*. Amsterdam, 1649. Reprinted, Bibliobazaar, 2009.

Merwick, Donna. *The Shame and the Sorrow: Dutch-Amerindian Encounters in New Netherland*. Philadelphia: University of Pennsylvania Press, 2006.

Montanus, Arnoldus. *Description of New Netherland*. Amsterdam, 1671. Reprinted, Bibliobazaar, 2010.

Moore, John. *Rev. John Moore of Newtown, Long Island, and Some of His Descendants*. Easton, PA: Chemical Pub. Co., 1844–1909. Hallett genealogy.

Moore, Susan Hardman. *Pilgrims, New World Settlers and the Call of Home*. New Haven, CT and London: Yale University Press, 2010.

Morton, Nathaniel. *New England's Memorial*. Boston: Congregational Board of Publication, 1855.

Muskett, Joseph James, and R. C. Winthrop. *Evidences of the Winthrops of Groton*. Privately printed, 1894. Fones, Downing, Winthrop genealogies.

Newtown, Queens County, NY. *Town Minutes of Newtown 1653–1734*. Historical Records Survey, 1941.

New York Genealogical and Biographical Record. New York: Published for the Society, 1880, vols. 11–13.

New York Genealogical and Biographical Society, *The New York Genealogical and Biographical Record*. New York: New York Genealogical and Biographical Society.

New York State Museum, Albany, 1889. Bulletin of the New York State Museum, *"Aboriginal Occupation of New York,"* William Beauchamp, Feb. 1900, no. 32, vol. 7, 159–160.

———. *"The Archeological History of New York,"* Arthur C. Parker, July-August, 1920, nos. 235, 336.

O'Callaghan, E. B., trans, *Calendar of Historical Manuscripts in the Office of the Secretary of State, Albany, NY*, 2 vols. Vol. I. *Dutch Manuscripts, 1630–1664*. Vol. II. *English Manuscripts, 1664–1776*. Albany, NY: Weed, Parsons and Company, 1865, 1866.

———. *The Documentary History of the State of New York*. Albany, NY: Weed, Parsons and Company, 1819, 4 vols.

———. *History of New Netherland or New York Under the Dutch*. New York: D. Appleton, 1845, 2 vols.

———. *Laws and Ordinances of New Netherland 1638–1674*. Albany, NY: Weed, Parsons and Company, 1868.

———. *The Register of New Netherland, 1626 to 1674*. Albany, NY: J. Munsell, 1865.

O'Callaghan, E. B., and Berthold Fernow, trans. *Documents Relative to the Colonial History of the State of New York*. Albany: Weed, Parsons and Company, 1856–1887, 15 vols.

Onderdonck, Henry. *Queens County in Olden Times*. Jamaica, NY: Chas. Welling, 1865.

Orr, Charles. *History of the Pequot War, the Contemporary Accounts of Mason, Underhill, Vincent and Gardener*. Cleveland, OH: The Helman-Taylor Co., 1897.

Osgood, Herbert L. *The American Colonies in the Seventeenth Century*. Cranbury, NJ: P. Smith, 1957, vol. 2.

Osterweis, R. G. *Three Centuries of New Haven, 1638–1938.* New Haven: Yale University Press, 1953.

Otto, Paul. *The Dutch-Munsee Encounter in America: The Struggle for Sovereignty in the Hudson Valley.* New York: Berghahn Books, 2006.

Palfrey, J. G., and F. W. Palfrey. *History of New England.* Boston: Little, Brown and Co., 1859.

Panetta, Roger G. *Dutch New York: The Roots of Hudson Valley Culture.* Bronx, NY: Hudson River Museum, Fordham University Press, 2009.

Pelletreau, W. S. *Abstracts of the Wills on File in the Surrogates Office, City of New York.* New York: Collections of the New York Historical Society, 1903.

Philbrick, Nathaniel. *Mayflower: A Story of Courage, Community, and War.* New York: Viking, 2006.

Pierce, Richard Donald. *Records of the First Church in Boston 1630–1868.* Boston: The Colonial Society of Massachusetts, 1961, vol. 40:18, 21. Underhill excommunication.

Piling, James C. *Bibliographic Notes on Eliot's Indian Bible and on His Other Translations and Works in the Indian Language of Massachusetts.* Washington: Government Printing Office, 1890.

Place, F., and J. H. French. *Index of Names in J.H. French's Gazetteer of the State of New York 1860.* Cortland, NY: Cortland County Historical Society, 1983.

Poland, William Carey. *Robert Feke, the Early Newport Portrait Painter.* Providence: Rhode Island Historical Society, 1907.

Prince, Rev. Thomas. *A Chronological History of New-England in the Form of Annals.* Boston: Privately printed, 1736, 5 vols. Reprinted, Edinburgh: Kneeland & Greene for S. Gerrish, 1887.

Proceedings of the Massachusetts Historical Society. Boston: Massachusetts Historical Society, 1879, second series vol. 6, 1890–1891.

Proceedings of the New York State Historical Association. New York: Published for the Association, 1902, 1906, 1907.

Purple, Samuel, S., ed. "Marriages from 1639–1801 in the Reformed Dutch Church of New York." *The New York Genealogical and Biographical Record.* New York: 1890, Collection, vol. 1.

Reynolds, Cuyler. *Genealogical and Family History of Southern New York and the Hudson River Valley.* New York: Lewis Historical Publishing, 1914, vol. 3. Blackwell-Hallett genealogy.

Riker, James. *The Annals of Newtown in Queens County, NY.* New York: D. Fanshaw, 1852.

Rink, Oliver A. *Holland on the Hudson: An Economic and Social History of Dutch New York.* Ithaca, NY: Cornell University Press, 1986.

Ruttenber, Edward Manning. *Footprints of the Red Men. Indian Geographical Names in the Valley of Hudson's River, the Valley of the Mohawk, and on the Delaware.* New York State Historical Association.

———. *History of the Indian Tribes of Hudson's River.* Albany, NY: J. Munsell, 1872.

————. *Indian Geographical Names*. New York State Historical Association, 1906.

Saville, Foster. *A Montauk Cemetery at East Hampton, Long Island*. New York: Museum of the American Indian, Heye Foundation, 1922, vol. 2, 7 issues.

Scharf, J. Thomas. *A History of the County of Westchester from Its First Settlement to the Present Time*. New York: A. S. Gould, 1848.

————. *History of Westchester County, New York*. Philadelphia: L.E. Preston & Co., 1886.

Schmidt, Benjamin. *Innocence Abroad: The Dutch Imagination and The New World, 1570–1670*. London: Cambridge University Press, 2004.

Schoolcraft, Henry Rowe. *Historical and Statistical Information Respecting the History, Condition and Prospects of the Indian Tribes of the United States*. Philadelphia: J. B. Lippincott, 1857.

Selleck, Charles Melbourne. *Norwalk*. Norwalk, CT: Henry M. Gardner, 1985.

Selyns, H. and F. Sypher. *Liber A: 1628–1700 of the Collegiate Churches of New York*. New York: William B. Erdmans Pub., 2009.

Seton, Anya. *The Winthrop Woman*. Boston: Houghton Mifflin, 1958.

Seyfried, Vincent F. *300 Years of Long Island City, 1630–1930*. Garden City, NY: Greater Astoria Historical Society, 1984.

Shahan, Rev. Thomas J. *The Catholic Historical Review*. Washington: The Catholic University of America, 1915.

Shannon, T. J., and New York State Historical Association. *Indians and Colonists at the Crossroads of Empire the Albany Congress of 1754*. Ithaca, NY: Cornell University Press, 2000.

Shonnard, Frederick, and W. W. Spooner. *History of Westchester County, New York, From Its Earliest Settlement to the Year 1900*. Harrison, NY: Harbor Hill Books, 1974.

Shorto, Russell. *The Island at the Center of the World: The Epic Story of Dutch Manhattan and the Forgotten Colony That Shaped America*. New York: Doubleday, 2004.

Shotwell, Ambrose M. *Annals of Our Colonial Ancestors and Their Descendants*. Lansing, MI: Robert Smith & Co., 1895–1897. Hallett genealogy.

Shurtleff, Nathaniel, ed. *Records of the Governor and Company of Massachusetts Bay*. Boston: William White Publishing, 1853.

Skinner, Alanson. *Archeological Investigations on Manhattan Island, New York City*. New York: Museum of the American Indian, Heye Foundation, 1920.

————. *Exploration of Aboriginal Sites at Throgs Neck and Clasons Point, New York City*. New York: Museum of the American Indian, Heye Foundation, 1919.

————. *The Indians of Manhattan Island and Vicinity: A Guide to the Special Exhibition at the American Museum of Natural History*. New York: The Museum, 1909.

————. *Notes on Iroquois Archeology*. New York: Museum of the American Indian, Heye Foundation, 1921.

Smith, D. S. "The Demographic History of Colonial New England." *Journal of Economic History*, 1972, 32: 165–183.

Snow, Caleb Hopkins. *A History of Boston: The Metropolis of Massachusetts, from Its Origin to the Present Period; with Some Account of the Environs*. Boston: Abel Bowen, 1828.

Squier, Ephraim G. *Historical and Mythological Traditions of the Algonquins with a Translation of the "Walum-olum," or Bark Record of the Linni-lenape*, 918.

Steele, Ian Kenneth. *Warpaths, Invasions of North America.* New York: Oxford University Press, 1994.

Stewart, L. Lloyd. *A Far Cry From Freedom: Gradual Abolition (1799–1827): New York State's Crime Against Humanity.* Bloomington, IN: Authorhouse, 2005.

Stokes, I. N. P., ed. *Iconography of Manhattan Island, 1498–1909.* New York: Robert H. Dodd, 1915–1928, 6 vols.

Sturtevant, W. C. and Smithsonian Institution. *Handbook of North American Indians.* Washington: Smithsonian Institution, 1978.

Thompson, Benjamin F. *The History of Long Island from Its Discovery and Settlement.* New York: Gould, Banks & Co., 1843.

Thompson, Roger. *Divided We Stand: Watertown, Mass. 1630–1680.* Amherst, MA: University of Massachusetts Press, 2001.

Titus, Elroy Wilson. *A History of the Titus and Related Families.* Madison, WI: University of Wisconsin, 1984.

Tooker, William Wallace, and A. F. Chamberlain. *The Indian Place-Names on Long Island and Islands Adjacent, with Their Probable Significations.* New York: G.P. Putnam's Sons, 1911.

———. *Some Indian Fishing Stations Upon Long Island with Historical and Ethnological Notes.* New York: Francis P. Harper, 1901.

Torrey, Clarence Almon, and Elizabeth Petty Bentley. *New England Marriages Prior to 1700.* Baltimore, MD: Genealogical Publishing Company, 1985.

Trelease, Allen. *Indian Affairs in Colonial New York: The Seventeenth Century.* Ithaca, NY: Cornell University Press, 1960. Reprint with an Introduction by William A. Starna. Lincoln: Nebraska University Press, 1997.

Trumbull, Benjamin. *A Complete History of Connecticut, Civil and Ecclesiastical from the Emigration of Its First Planters from England.* Hartford, CT: Hudson & Goodwin, 1797.

Trumbull, James Hammond. *Indian Names of Places, etc., In and On the Borders of Connecticut With Interpretations of Some of Them.* Hartford, CT: Lockwood & Brainard Co., 1881.

———. *Natick Dictionary: A New England Indian Lexicon.* Washington: Smithsonian Institution, 1903. Reprinted, Lincoln: University of Nebraska Press, 2009.

Trumbull, James Hammond, and C. F. Jewet. *The Memorial History of Hartford County, Connecticut, 1633–1884.* Boston: E. L. Osgood, 1886.

Ulrich, Laurel Thatcher. *Good Wives: Image and Reality in the Lives of Women in Northern New England 1650–1750.* New York: Vintage Books, 1982.

———. *John Winthrop's City of Women,* Massachusetts Historical Review, 2001, vol. 3.

———. *A Midwife's Tale: The Life of Martha Ballard, Based on Her Diary, 1785–1812.* New York: Vintage Books, 1990.

Underhill, David Harris. *The Underhill Burial Ground.* New York: The Hine Publishing Co. reprinted by Higginson Book Company, Salem, MA, 1926.

Underhill, John. *Newes From America.* Amsterdam: Theatrum Orbis, 1638.

Van der Donck, Adriaen. *A Description of New Netherland.* Charles T. Gehring and William A. Starna, eds., Diederik Willem Goedhuys, trans. Lincoln: University of Nebraska Press, 2008.

Van Laer, A. J. F., trans. *Council Minutes 1638–1649.* New York Historical Manuscript Series. Baltimore: Genealogical Publishing Co., Inc., 1974.

Van Laer, A. J. F., trans., and Kenneth Scott and Kenn Stryker-Rodda, eds. *Register of the Provincial Secretary, 1638–1660.* New York Historical Manuscript Series. Baltimore: Genealogical Publishing Co., Inc., 1974, 3 vols.

Van Rensselaer, Marianna. *History of the City of New York in the Seventeenth Century.* New York: The Macmillan Company, 1909.

Venema, Janny. *Beverwijck: A Dutch Village on the American Frontier, 1652–1664.* Hilversum, the Netherlands: Verloren, 2003.

Vincent, Phillip. *A True Relation of the Late Battell Fought in New England.* Theatrum Orbis Terrarum, 1974.

Von Skal, Georg. *Illustrated History of the Borough of Queens, New York City.* New York: Flushing Journal, 1908.

Water, Henry Fitz-Gilbert, ed. *New England Historical and Genealogical Register.* 47:517. Boston: printed for the Society. Mary Feake's will.

Watertown Historical Society. *Watertown Records: The First and Second Books of Town Proceedings, with the Land Grants and Possessions, and the First Book and Supplement of Births, Deaths and Marriages.* Watertown, MA: Fred G. Barker, 1894. Map inside back cover.

Welles, Lemuel A. "The Site of Anne Hutchinson's Massacre." *New York Genealogical and Biographical Record.* New York, Apr. 1929. Vol. 60, No. 2:120.

Westchester County Historical Society. *The Quarterly Bulletin of the Westchester County Historical Society and the Westchester County Historical Bulletin Author and Subject Index to Articles and Illustrations: Volumes 19–28, 1943–1952.* Westchester County Historical Society, 1953.

Whitaker, Katie. *A Royal Passion: The Turbulent Marriage of King Charles I of England and Henrietta Maria of France.* New York and London: W.W. Norton & Co, 2010.

Whittier, John Greenleaf. *The Poetical Works of John Greenleaf Whittier.* Boston and New York: Houghton, Mifflin and Company, 1848.

Wilson, A.N. *The Elizabethans.* New York: Farrar, Straus and Giroux, 2011.

Winthrop, John. *The Journal of John Winthrop.* Richard S. Dunn, James Savage and Laetitia Yeandle, eds. Cambridge, MA and London: Belknap Press of Harvard University Press, 1996.

———. *The Winthrop Papers.* Boston: Massachusetts Historical Society, 1931, 6 vols.

Winthrop, John Sr., James Kendall Hosmer, ed. *Winthrop's Journal History of New England 1630–1649.* New York: Charles Scribner's Sons, 1908.

Wood, James. *The History of the Town of Bedford to 1917. Reprinted from his chapter in The History of Westchester County, New York, from Its Earliest Settlement to the Year 1900.* New York: The New York History Company, 1925.

Wood, Silas. *A Sketch of the First Settlement of the Several Towns on Long Island with Their Political Condition, to the End of the American Revolution.* Brooklyn, NY: Alden Spooner, 1828.

Woodward, Walter. *Prospero's America: John Winthrop, Jr., Alchemy, and the Creation of New England Culture, 1606–1676.* Published for the Omohundro Institute of Early American History and Culture in Williamsburg, VA, by the University of North Carolina Press, Chapel Hill, NC., 2010.

Year Book of the Holland Society of New-York. New York: Holland Society of New York, 1886.

Zwierlein, Frederick J. *Religion in New Netherland: A History of the Development of the Religious Conditions in the Province of New Netherland, 1623–1664.* Rochester, NY: J. P. Smith, 1910.

INDEX

ABOUT THE AUTHOR

Historian Missy Wolfe has always loved histories and biographies that allow her to travel through time to meet unusual people and experience dramatic events. Growing up, she was particularly transported by the works of Lady Antonia Fraser, Alison Weir, and Barbara Tuchman. Impressed by their research and writing, Wolfe began investigating the earliest history of her home town, Greenwich, Connecticut. For this she was also inspired by Nathaniel Philbrick's *Mayflower* and Russell Shorto's *Island at the Center of the World*.

After receiving an MBA from Columbia University and an early career in advertising, Wolfe pursued her interests in design and its history with an associate's degree from the New York School of Interior Design and an internship at Keno Auctions. She is also a graduate of New York University's program for Appraisal Studies for Fine and Decorative Arts. She remains fascinated by the past and its appreciation by the modern world.